The Art of Successful Security Management

The Art of Successful Security Management

Dennis R. Dalton

Butterworth–Heinemann
Boston   Oxford   Johannesburg   Melbourne   New Delhi   Singapore

Library of Congress Cataloging-in-Publication Data
Dalton, Dennis R.
    The art of successful security management / Dennis R. Dalton.
      p.   cm.
    Includes bibliographical references and index.
    ISBN 0-7506-9729-6 (alk. paper)
    1. Private security services—Management.   2. Industries—Security measures—Management.   3. Corporations—Security measures—Management.   I. Title.
HV8290.D33   1997
363.28'9'068—dc21   97-5440
                                                       CIP

British Library Cataloguing-in-Publication Data
A catalogue record for this book is available from the British Library.

The publisher offers special discounts on bulk orders of this book.
For information, please contact:
Manager of Special Sales
Butterworth–Heinemann
225 Wildwood Avenue
Woburn, MA 01801-2041
Tel: 617-928-2500
Fax: 617-928-2620

For information on all our security publications,
contact our World Wide Web home page at: http://www.bh.com

10 9 8 7 6 5 4 3 2 1

Printed in the United States of America

This book is dedicated to my daughter, Kirsten. Researching and writing a book, as we have both learned, takes a lot of time and sometimes competes with other things. Thanks for your patience, understanding, support, and—most of all, your love.

Contents

Foreword
Preface: Setting the Stage for a New Perspective
Acknowledgments

PART I
BEGINNING THE JOURNEY TO SUCCESSFUL MANAGEMENT

Chapter 1: Security Management and the Art of Fly-Fishing
Murphy's Maxims
Know Your Customers ◆ Develop a Reputation for Being Proactive ◆ Seize the Moment ◆ Keep It Simple
Establish Your Credibility Early On ◆ Respect the Individual ◆ Honor Thy Sponsor
Write Only What You Would Want to Read in The Berkeley Barb ◆ Assume No Responsibility Unless You Run It
Have a Person on the Way ◆ Empower Your People

Empowerment

Security Management and the Art of Fly-Fishing
Finding the Right Spot—The Art ◆ Working The River—The Science

Value-Added Opportunities
Ten Ways to Demonstrate Added Value for External Providers
Twenty Ways to Demonstrate Added Value for Resident Security Departments

Summary

Chapter 2: In Pursuit of Quality
How Deming Views the Pursuit of Quality
Develop a Strategy for Constant Improvement ◆ Adopt a New Paradigm
Replace Mass Inspection with Employee Troubleshooting
End the Practice of Awarding Contracts on Price Alone ◆ Promote Leadership and Institute Training
Eliminate Hype and Quotas ◆ Remove Barriers and Promote Continuous Quality Improvement
The Seven Deadly Sins ◆ Obstacles to Quality

The Other Experts' Point of View

Best Practices—An Avenue to Quality
Are You Getting the Job Done? ◆ Is the Service Being Delivered Effectively?
Is the Service Being Delivered Efficiently? ◆ Insider Tips for Pursuing Best Practices
Security Applications in Best Practices

Other Techniques for Thriving

Going the Extra Mile ◆ *The Three- or Four-Word Motto* ◆ *Employee and Business Enhancement Programs*

When Pursuing Quality Misses the Mark

Company 1: A Major Manufacturer ◆ *Company 2: A High-Tech Company*

Summary

Chapter 3: Moving Beyond Customer Satisfaction

The Value Matrix

Defining Your Customers

Developing a Rapid Response Strategy

Pursuing Customer Satisfaction

Developing Strategies for Cultivating Customer Loyalty

The Customer-Supplier Gap

Service Excellence Strategies

Managing a Customer Relationship ◆ *Managing the Transaction*

A Customer-Driven Approach to Quality Assurance

Seven Critical Mistakes

Summary

Part One Summary

PART II
TODAY'S SECURITY MANAGER—A NEW APPROACH

Chapter 4: The Eclectic Manager

The Emerging New Role for Security Managers

Making the Transition from the Public Sector

The New Perspective

Changing Roles in Service Markets

Models of Security Management

The Resident Manager ◆ *The Contract Provider as Security Manager* ◆ *The Nonsecurity Security Manager*

Summary

Chapter 5: Busting the Commodity Syndrome

The Commodity Syndrome

Demand-Side/Supply-Side Cost Control

The Demand Side ◆ *The Supply Side*

Strategies for Commodity Busting

Being Willing to Say No and Walk Away ◆ *Developing Your Unique Selling Proposition*
Developing Your Strength and Continuously Playing to It ◆ *Basch's Hierarchy of Horrors*
Developing Vertical Markets ◆ *Managing Programs for Added Value*

Summary

Chapter 6: Establishing Your Collateral Value

Defining Your Collateral Value

Protecting Proprietary Property and Confidential Information
Managing the Alliance ◆ *Operationalizing Proprietary Information*

Assessing and Countering Threats to Proprietary Information
Threat Analysis ◆ *Primary Motivations for Stealing Critical Assets*

Defensive Strategies—Demonstrating Your Collateral Value
Trade Secret First Aid ◆ *Identifying Potentials for Loss* ◆ *Convincing Management to Keep a Secret*
Creating a Cost-Benefit Ratio ◆ *Focusing on the Basics* ◆ *Managing the Panic*

Supplemental Value Contributions
Corporate Secretary ◆ *Facilities Management* ◆ *Other Supplemental Opportunities*

Summary

Chapter 7: Competitive Intelligence — The Overlooked Collateral Value

Exploring Competitive Intelligence
Myths About Competitive Intelligence

Competitive Intelligence Defined
Why Your Company Needs Competitive Intelligence ◆ *Gathering Intelligence*

The Security Specialist in Competitive Intelligence
Competitive Intelligence and the Security Investigator: Comparable Characteristics
Convincing Management to Adopt Competitive Intelligence ◆ *Identifying Bad Data*

Summary

Part Two Summary

PART III
THE COLLABORATIVE APPROACH

Chapter 8: Pursuing Envisioned Leadership

Leadership Development and the Art of Distance Running

What Is an Envisioned Leader?
Coyotes Are Procedural; Roadrunners Are Experimental ◆ *Coyotes Are Earnest; Roadrunners Are Passionate*
Coyotes Are Resilient; Roadrunners Are Resourceful ◆ *Coyotes Are Smart; Roadrunners Are Wise*
Coyotes Look Back; Roadrunners Look Ahead
Coyotes Operate from What They Want; Roadrunners Operate from Who They Are

Legendary Leadership

The Five Stages of Corporate Moral Development

Mentoring—Still Alive and Still Critical for Success

The Support Cycle

Avoiding Leadership Pitfalls
Identifying the Wrong Problem ◆ *Judging Ideas Too Quickly* ◆ *Stopping with the First Good Idea*
Failing to "Get the Bandits on the Train" ◆ *Obeying Rules That Don't Exist*

Understanding and Implementing Employee Empowerment
Summary

Epilogue: Success in Today's Corporate World
End Notes
Bibliography
Index

Foreword

Since I am preparing to retire from the corporate world after forty-six years, I was extremely pleased when Dennis asked me if I would write the foreword to this book. What a compliment! Aside from working at the same organization for all those years, I have been fortunate to have had several different careers. As you might suspect, one of those careers spanned thirteen years as Bank Boston's corporate security manager. Yet, interestingly enough, the concepts and strategies that are detailed in this book have application in just about any facet of a company's support structure. That's because this book is all about managing for success. That it is written for security professionals is a bonus.

This is Dennis's second book on effective management strategies for security professionals. And, like his first, this book contains a number of proven concepts designed to help you succeed in the sometimes murky world of corporate management. What's exciting about *The Art of Successful Security Management* is the way in which Dennis translates solid management principles into specific applications for serious-minded security professionals. Of the literally dozens of practical ideas, there were a number that really hit home for even a veteran of more than forty-five years. For that matter, there were a couple that I believe warrant special consideration. I'd like to elaborate on them because they are timeless and have proven to be fundamental for a security manager's corporate success.

One of the critical tools Dennis details is the concept of networking. Networking within the security arena is essential, if not mandatory, for managers working corporate security. Whether you are a resident security manager or a contract manager assigned to a specific account, your network, external or internal, is an index of the degree of your personal success and that of your program. Dennis's anecdotes throughout the book testify to this. His accounts of John Cosenza and Doug Griffin and others are the result of his own networking over the years and the willingness within the security community to furnish resources and information that cannot be measured in monetary terms.

Organizations such as the International Bank Security Association and the International Security Management Association were formed for just that purpose. The fact that they, among many other organizations, are international in scope underscores the global recognition of the value of effective networking. For what it is worth, here is one man's observation after having been responsible for no less than four major corporate business units: security is the only business unit where networking was among the vital components for achieving success.

Another critical tool for organizational success is understanding that *perception is reality*. Take the case of the manager of data processing. He had an on-line system that was prone to frequent failures. One of his end users (known today as a business partner) who was dependent upon the system was quick to call the manager and complain, usually before the manager was aware that there was a problem. Trusting that the business partner might be somewhat appeased if failures were immediately acknowledged, the data processing manager had a special light installed in his office. At the first sign of trouble the computer operator would flip a switch, the light would go on, and the data processing manager would call the end user before the user had the opportunity to call and complain. He would explain or confirm the problem and assure the end user that the data processing staff was busy taking the necessary corrective action. If the call came in from the business partner before the manager was able to call, the manager was prepared to admit that he was aware of the problem and it was being addressed. Satisfied that his dilemma was of such importance to the data processing manager, the business partner stopped calling. In other words, the data processing manager understood that his business partner's perception that the problem was being addressed was just as important as was actually addressing the problem. *His perception was his reality.* This is a lesson security managers need to learn well if they are intent on providing value-added quality customer service.

Here's another critical concept that deserves special consideration. Having been involved in the outsourcing of the security workforce, mail/messenger service, transportation, and reprographics operations, I have had experience with being an administrator of a service-providing department as well as an administrator for an end-user department. Dalton cautions the readers not to consider such services as a commodity. Amen!

The *American Heritage Dictionary's* definition of *commodity* is "*something* that is useful." The definition of *something* is "an undetermined or unspecified thing." Whether it be proprietary or third party, to characterize security services as a commodity, when in reality they are a complementary augmentation to a company's overall operations, does no justice to either organization. Linking services to the concept of commodities is dangerous business at best. Commodities are largely price driven. Successful services are always value driven, and only a part of successful services is reflected in best pricing—note that I didn't say "lowest pricing."

In his discussion on third-party relationships Dennis makes another salient point when he states, *"Loyalty is built on satisfaction."* This challenge should be viewed as a two-way street. Developing the required level of satisfaction is a formidable task for the external partner. The same responsibility should pertain to the customer. It is interesting to read how employees of the provider firm can be treated in such a way that they consider themselves as all but employees of the customer and align with that organization. Having personally witnessed this phenomenon many times, I can attest that developing such a relationship is an opportunity here that should not be neglected.

Loyalty to a customer is essential for the long-term relationship. As the provider's employees become more integrated into the client's organization through strategic partnering, they need to be convinced that their contribution is seen as worthwhile and that they are valued. Moreover, ensuring that employees feel that they are valued need not involve elaborate stand-alone programs or costly awards. Something as simple as incorporating contract employees into already existing company-wide employee recognition programs demonstrates commitment. This is what building loyalty is all about.

For the provider, it is considerably more difficult to retain the allegiance of the customer. Although the provider may be acknowledged as the *strategic partner* and *sole provider,* I suspect that status will always be no stronger than fragile. Circumstances that may be incidental to the day-to-day operation could strain relations and jeopardize internal support resulting in an unexpected Request for Proposal (RFP) being prepared coincident with the time of year for contract renewal. Despite management's wavering support, acknowledged quality customer service is the only effective countermeasure for the provider!

I have spent most of my career in a management position. As I read this book, I found myself nodding my head in agreement with Dennis's observations, concepts, and applications. In one section he articulates that *the central principle of quality is caring.* Although this book is directed at people in the security profession, it would serve well anyone in a management position. You might consider doing yourself a favor and sharing it with your fellow managers—better still, your boss. Read on. The challenges that Dennis throws at you are cogent and achievable.

Joe Magennis,
Vice President,
Bank Boston

Preface: Setting the Stage for a New Perspective

Success is simply a matter of luck. Ask any failure.

...EARL WILSON

Marketing specialist and business strategist Jay Abraham often speaks of the need to establish your "unique selling proposition." Your USP, as he refers to the term, is that characteristic that sets you apart from those with whom you are competing. Paul Franklin, a consultant to entrepreneurial driven businesses, has taken this concept and expanded upon it. He notes that your USP is critical to defining your ultimate success. In the chapters that follow, I'd like to visit both of their perspectives in more detail with you.

By the time this text is introduced, my first book, *Security Management: Business Strategies for Success,* will have been out for more than two years. Since its publication I have received hundreds of calls and letters from security and nonsecurity managers letting me know how the book has helped them to work their way through the morass of organizational life. In short, I think it is a classic example of the right idea coming at the right time. But, like all initiatives, as time and events move forward, it's important to build upon past success and continue contributing. I hope you'll find this to be the case with *The Art of Successful Security Management*.

UNIQUE SELLING PROPOSITION I

There are a number of management texts on the market. So what separates this from the others? Or, to state it another way, what is its USP? As you venture into this book, you'll discover a number of important differences. First, to my knowledge, it's the only text that has been deliberately designed to address two primary audiences simultaneously: the resident corporate security manager and the third-party provider. It is critical to address both audiences because today there is a great deal of crossover between the two.

A considerable amount of competition and a number of significant misunderstandings exists between resident security managers and their so-called strategic partners, the managers whose departments rely on security. This is unfortunate because there is rarely a need for such discord. The end result for both sides is that they lose credibility with the people they purport to serve—their end users—and therefore they are unable to achieve the level of success they desire.

The issue is far more complex than simply developing a cooperative spirit between the two. The need to address the relationship is both timely and compelling. As organizations of all sizes, in all sectors, seek new ways to be competitive, the use of virtual support systems is rapidly becoming the norm. Downsizing of internal support teams is today's reality. For many, third-party providers are more than vendors; they are the de facto security department. For example, the California southern region for Kaiser Permanente, one of the country's largest health care providers, relies on a group of external security providers for more than 98 percent of its asset protection requirements. These service providers range from service companies to an independent systems engineering firm.

Likewise, Hewlett-Packard's microwave division in northern California relies on a resident security coordinator and uses a national firm for all other security services. To underscore the interrelationship, when someone calls the coordinator and receives his voice mail, the message directs the caller to the security company by name as opposed to using the generic term *security*. Similar examples abound in the financial services sector, other high-tech companies, oil and energy firms, and so forth.

What has changed? Actually it's quite simple. Service companies can no longer be viewed or view themselves as an external entity. From an operational perspective, the line separating provider from customer company has become quite fuzzy. While corporate counsels for each business entity may wage their legal battles over issues of joint employment, hold harmless and indemnification clauses, and independent contractor status, in reality, the resident security decision maker and the third-party provider need to become true partners in meeting the overall business objectives of the organization.

By introducing the concept of partnering between provider and customer, you encourage the development of a new relationship from the base up. It requires not only an understanding of the driving forces on both sides but also a tolerance for limitations on both sides. It also means an education, or learning, curve as some would describe it, on the part of both. Here's a quick example.

Today it is all too common for large organizations to assume that they can achieve lower operating costs by bundling large volumes of business together under one or two providers. The theory is that providers have lower overhead because they employ fewer support systems and services. The theory also goes on to assume that lower direct costs can be achieved by consolidating security assignments and replacing some labor-driven posts with new technology. To the uninitiated these strategies seem logical and commonsense. Sadly, though, when corporations pursue large regional or national security service contracts, they rarely achieve the anticipated savings in operating expenses. As proposal after proposal from providers comes in, procurement administrators, fee managers, and security executives become frustrated because the "numbers aren't there." Because of this unexpected bad news they may become suspicious of hidden profiteering on the part of the suppliers or accuse them of any one or more of the following: "not getting with the program," "dragging their feet," or "not understanding the concept of partnering."

In some cases those who are soliciting the proposals may have a basis for making such accusations. More often the problem is rooted in the customer's approach or his or her lack of understanding of how security companies provide and price their services. Conversely, it is not uncommon for security providers to take their traditional approach in responding to a proposal and miss altogether what the prospective customer thought was a clearly communicated intent. Regardless of the mixed signals, differing intents, and/or assumptions, the end result is an aura of discord before the relationship even begins.

The challenge, therefore, is to create a context for an open and candid discussion of the dynamics associated with each party's interests so that both will gain a clearer understanding of their respective needs, strengths and limitations, and business requirements. One of the hopes I have for this book is that it will serve as a forum for forging such a dialogue and serve as a stepping stone to a new and more beneficial relationship between resident security managers and their third-party providers.

UNIQUE SELLING PROPOSITION 2

The second factor that distinguishes this book from others is its approach to meeting the challenges of managing in today's turbulent times. Staying competitive is hard work. Managers face considerable uncertainty. For example, job security has come to mean staying employed for at least three years.

In my previous book, *Security Management: Business Strategies for Success*, we analyzed several new approaches available to security managers, ranging from quality improvement strategies to internal marketing. We also introduced a number of axioms I have accumulated over the years. Likewise, we explored concepts offered by other leading consultants, academicians, and practitioners. One of my favorites was Mary Woodell's idea about executive infighting, which she captures in the easy to remember acronym ELVIS, or Executive Level Vicious Infighting Syndrome. This concept takes several forms, including the hydra-headed ELVIS, the ELVIS A-Go-Go, and the retroactive ELVIS.

We will have the same kind of presentation of proven management techniques here. George Murphy gives us his Murphy's Maxims. Murphy, having recently retired from Mobil Oil as their worldwide corporate security director, now heads his own consulting company, Security Virtual. His company name is interesting in that it reflects both the entrepreneurial spirit that characterizes a lot of today's business community and the notion of relying on external partners.

We will also explore the contributions of recognized quality gurus and suggest ways in which their ideas can be effectively adopted by security managers. The ideas of Florence Stone and Randi Sachs, with the American Management Association, as reflected in their *The High-Value Manager* and Federal Express cofounder Mike Basch's, *Legendary Leadership* are applied within the context of asset protection. Well-recognized experts such as Warren Bennis and Tom Peters offer their insights regarding new paradigms in business and how they influence the way middle and senior managers approach their fundamental responsibility of providing leadership and guidance. Just as we did in *Business Strategies*, we will have a little fun with this discussion, while illustrating some very important points. Recently I had the opportunity to spend a week fly-fishing on the Deschutes River in Oregon. Having never done this type of fishing before, and yet having been invited by one of America's top fly-fishermen to find my Zen in management, I found the sport both exciting and inspiring—in more ways than one. Hence, the genesis for the title of the first chapter: "Security Management and the Art of Fly-Fishing."

Here we explore both the art and the science of what it means to "work an organization," to promote yourself and your program in a very positive way. This discussion sets the stage for the following chapter in which we explore what is meant by *added value* and review thirty perspectives on how to measure your added value, regardless of whether you are a resident manager or an external supplier. Based on this knowledge we go on to analyze what is meant by "Best Practices" and demonstrate how you know whether or not you are engaging in them.

UNIQUE SELLING PROPOSITION 3

As the book unfolds, I have taken the opportunity to push the concept of responsible security management to another level. In today's topsy-turvy world of management strategies, it is easy to overlook the individual's needs for self-expression and a sense of worth. Given the emphasis on "right-sizing" to maximize efficiencies and profitability, employees are commonly victimized. Many employees feel that they have become the sacrificial offering on the altar of profitability. Since my days as a teenager working for the local grocer, I have been a student of organizational behavior. It has always been a mystery to me how supposedly principled people can espouse morality and sensitivity to the human condition when outside their corporate environment, yet when they are operating within the context of their workplace, they can explain away otherwise unacceptable behavior by saying, "Well, this is the world of business."

Executives are particularly prone to falling into this trap. Caught up in the drive to demonstrate an ability to contribute to bottom-line performance or meet shareholder expectations, they can become ruthless—or uncaring at the very least. As a counter, I introduce my concept of the *Envisioned Leader*—an individual who understands that corporate profit is but one motive—that on a higher level, organizations exist to achieve profit while improving the human condition, which includes those who are directly affected, for example employees, suppliers and customers—internal and external. This sense of envisioned leadership is growing even as I write here and now. I firmly believe it needs to be drawn rapidly to the forefront. Although this management approach can be applied to all aspects of the organization, it has particular relevance to those charged with the responsibility of protecting lives and property.

Envisioned leadership and responsibility is not limited to just the managerial ranks. Extraordinary success can be achieved when employees at all levels of an organization are driven by a higher cause. Grounded in a passion to do the best job possible, these employees are in tune with delivering the best in customer service. They understand that satisfaction can only come when people feel welcomed, respected, and have a sense that their needs are being properly addressed. The real challenge, therefore, is for managers not only to develop a similar passion but also to seek those strategies that will encourage and nourish the passion in each of their employees. Further, this shared passion transcends customer satisfaction. It serves as the underpinning for such values as commitment and loyalty. It breaks apart the concept of *employee entitlement*, which has become an integral part of the psyche of the American worker. It forces workers to take personal accountability and ownership of job responsibilities. The passion involved in making a commitment of this nature can actually create a context for enhanced employee job security. This is because when the functional boundaries of line and staff are blended together, companies can develop a more cohesive team approach with a vision of customers' needs and expectations serving as the core of their relationship.

UNIQUE SELLING PROPOSITION 4

There is a fourth USP as well, focusing on the dynamic of customer service. After all, it has been said that more than 90 percent of security is customer service. Joan Fredericks and James Salter present a compelling argument that there is a level beyond customer satisfaction—what they refer to as "customer loyalty." If it is true that profitability is linked directly to customers' perceptions, then allow me to suggest that an internal support unit's success is directly related to its customers' perceptions. In other words, security's "profitability" is the measure of success the security team has with its end users.

The question is how does one measure the customers' perceptions? As Fredericks and Salter would suggest, one critical measure is the degree of customer loyalty. For the resident security manager a measure of loyalty is the volume of repeat business (for example, requests for service). For the external security provider it is both contract renewal *and* the number of requests for new services. By focusing on the issue of customer loyalty, as opposed to customer satisfaction, security can concentrate its limited resources on those variables that directly affect performance. Citing the experience of Witco Chemical Company, we point out that battles over nurturing customers who "love" you contributes little to bottom-line performance. Rather, what drives customers' loyalty is their confidence in your ability to deliver.

As we explored in *Business Strategies*, internal customers have both direct and subtle ways of sending you the message that they have lost, or are losing confidence in your ability to meet their needs. We will explore the concept of customer loyalty as it relates to the concept of what I call the *support cycle*. Briefly, this refers to security's ability to seek and maintain the necessary support from those who have the power to make critical decisions. Whether you are an external partner or an internal department, one measure of your success is the degree of support you have from those around you. By understanding the support cycle we will see the four characteristics involved in seeking the needed advocacy for programs. It gives you a tool for analyzing what happens when the person(s) being sought don't want to lend their support. This is critical because the ultimate success of a program is directly related to the degree of support provided by critical decision makers. The support cycle is also a quick way to measure the overall acceptance of the entire security department.

Over the years I have witnessed the fall of many security departments from one level within an organization to a much lower level. While it is true that the decline is generally the result of several factors, a loss of support from one or more central organizational advocates appears to be the common denominator. In some cases the decline has actually resulted in the elimination of the entire security program. Such action underscores what can happen when support erodes. Drawing particular attention to this dynamic is therefore critical to us as we identify success strategies.

UNIQUE SELLING PROPOSITION 5

Still another USP for this book has to do with the phenomenon I call "collateral capabilities." As part of senior management's efforts to flatten their organizations, department heads have been asked to assume greater responsibilities. Consequently, today it is not unusual to hear or read about a security manager assuming duties outside his or her core competency. Many security executives also wear the company hat of directing facility services, food services, parking, shipping and receiving, travel, and so on.

This broadening of managerial responsibility is truly a double-edged sword. On the one hand, security professionals are beginning to break away from being cast as specialists. Historically nonsecurity managers have narrowly defined the security executive's contribution. Security has been seen as having fairly strict limits. Therefore the management of this function has been equally limited. Today, out of necessity more often than not, senior managers are looking to security decision makers to assume greater roles. Such confidence is to be applauded. The question is whether or not security managers are up to the challenge. We'll look at the early indicators.

Conversely, by expanding a security managers' responsibilities outside of asset protection, companies are moving in the other direction from the concept of jettisoning noncore competencies. In other words, as companies attempt to focus on their core businesses, they have found it necessary to forgo the idea of doing everything themselves and are turning to external partners to meet their support needs. In short, retailers are focusing their resources on selling, banks on financing, manufacturers on production, and so forth. In doing this, they have found that they can outsource the support operations, including much of the security operation, to external providers. By having security managers stretch into areas outside of their individual competencies, the question needs to be asked: Why is it appropriate for the company at large to eliminate noncore resource allocations but require their managers to expand into areas beyond their own personal competencies? It's a contradiction that needs to be analyzed carefully since the ultimate success of both the company and individuals is at stake.

The quick answer is that with companies keeping smaller in-house staff, survivors need to assume greater roles. Further, a good general manager should be able to handle multiple tasks. Again, to the uninitiated, this idea may have a strong appeal. In reality, there are several serious traps, as some unfortunate security professionals have discovered. Is the answer, then, to simply let security managers be dismissed? And if so, is security not back to its original place of being cast as a limited contributor? The good news is a resounding no! This is where the notion of *collateral capabilities* enters.

In an era of reduced staffing, there are significant opportunities for security executives to expand into new areas without leaving the umbrella of asset protection. The net effect is twofold: first, the security managers' contributions to the company's bottom-line performance can be just as dramatic, if not more dramatic, than others' within the organization. Second, there is a greater likelihood of success if security managers take on a skill set that is within an area of demonstrated expertise. Good opportunities would include data security, trade secret protection, risk management, and intellectual property protection (IPP). Over the years traditional security managers venturing into these organizational turfs have encountered several objections, yet the new opportunities have synergies with the aims and purposes of traditional physical security, which is still the primary arena for most security executives.

We'll examine in depth the interrelationship of protecting information and other less tangible assets versus obtaining information about competitors and how both areas contribute to enhancing security's added value. As the CEO of NutraSweet Company notes, "Competitive intelligence is worth up to $50 million a year to our company. That's a combination of revenues gained and revenues not lost to competitive activity." This is a compelling value added, to say the least.

I see a time when corporate security as an entity will fade away. In the future it will probably commonly be considered a subset of the larger intellectual property protection program. After all, IPP covers the protection of machines and other closely held tangible assets as much as patents, processes, formulas, and data sets. Judicial decisions regarding matters of IPP invariably incorporate the central elements of classic physical security, for example, policies and practices, protection-oriented technologies, and security staffing. To this end, there is a need for security managers to play an active role in IPP, yet today few do. Therefore, our road to successfully managing an organization's assets will direct us through the theaters of both tangible and intangible properties.

UNIQUE SELLING PROPOSITION 6

Today new players are making up the security management ranks. Historically, security managers have either come up from within the security organization or have transferred to security from a career in law enforcement or the military. Today, however, security managers come from diverse career paths. For example, Mike Foil, the security director for Mellon Bank, came into the security profession with a background in retail banking. Today his broad-based management experience has positioned him as an effective administrator of security services. The recruitment of nonsecurity personnel can also be found within the security service provider group as well.

For example, Denis Brown, the CEO and president of America's second largest security firm, Pinkerton, assumed the helm after an extensive career in the high-tech arena. Likewise, Tom Marano, president of Argenbright, was groomed as a corporate executive in sales and marketing at Coca-Cola and Apple Computer. Both of these individuals bring new insights and perspectives to their leadership, and their respective organizations will probably experience new growth because of their diverse talents.

SUMMARY

This book is also a story of survival. Against the backdrop of downsizing, reengineering, and establishing a "lean and mean" organization, executive and middle management jobs continue to vanish on a daily basis. To survive you need to demonstrate an ability to be integrated into the corporation's mainstream business. It helps if you can change your perspective and develop a skill set commensurate with the new organizational order. More important, while it is critical to survive, your ultimate success will be defined by your ability to thrive in times of uncertainty and professional chaos. The text is designed to provide a blueprint to assist those managers who are willing to accept the challenge of operating in uncertain times. In a day when job security cannot be defined in terms greater than a handful of years, demonstrating value is particularly critical for ultimate success. Thriving means understanding and applying criteria that often transcend security responsibilities. It can mean the pursuit of complimentary collateral functions such as assisting in competitive intelligence gathering and intellectual property protection, or it can extend into unrelated activities that target reducing operating expenses or generating revenues as an offset to security operating expenses.

It is also important to be able to define asset protection in nonprevention terms. As mentioned previously, being in tune with court decisions and their impact on corporate liabilities draws today's security managers deeper into the fabric of the organization and thereby increases their value. The same can be said for having the capability to define security within the context of claim avoidance and to participate in the organization's efforts to minimize economic loss resulting from incidents that result in the loss of consumer confidence or result in unscheduled downtime and reproduction costs.

As you can see, this book breaks new ground for those charged with the responsibility of managing the security function within an organization. Whether in the hands of a resident manager or an external provider, or a combination of both, the challenge of security remains the same: specifically, to properly align the necessary resources with the overall business goals and aims of the organization.

Before beginning, one point needs to be emphasized. This book is all about the pursuit of success. For those in security that means meeting the needs and expectations of their customers—whoever they are. For resident managers the term *customer* means those internal to the organization, for example, other employees, regardless of their position in the organization. For third-party providers the term *customer* actually refers to both their clients in general and their clients' employees, because many companies have opted to have an external provider serve as the *de facto* security department. In these cases, the provider's on-site manager serves both the client and the client's employees. Consequently, throughout this book the use of the term *customer* generally refers to an organization's employee. Also, for purposes of this book, the terms *customer* and *end user* are, for the most part, interchangeable.

Acknowledgments

I have often joked that I am one of the best kept men I know. Actually, there's a great deal of truth to this. If it weren't for the support I receive from those around me, this book would still be a bunch of ideas in my head. I am deeply grateful for the hard work of my assistant, Rhonda Coatney. Thanks for the endless hours, your sense of humor, thoroughness, and patience with me.

I want to thank you especially, Linda. You are not only a beautiful wife and an excellent business partner; you are also a very good editor. My only hope is that you'll retire your red pen for a long time! Speaking of editors, I also want to thank Maggie Carr—your comments and copy editing really pulled my thoughts and research together. Finally I want to recognize the staff at Butterworth–Heinemann. Thanks Laurel DeWolf, Stephanie Aronson, and Maura Kelly for your support and encouragement.

Part I

Beginning the Journey to Successful Management

Security Management
and the Art of Fly-Fishing

Success, remember, is the reward of toil.
...SOPHOCLES

In introducing his book *The Road Ahead* (Viking, 1995), Bill Gates, president and founder of Microsoft, notes that there is never a reliable map for unexplored territory. Thus begins his journey into a discussion regarding today's information age, which he refers to as the new revolution. Similarly, I believe that the security profession is undergoing its own revolution. As today's businesses pell-mell their way toward achieving operational efficiency, the buzzword of the 1990s for corporate America appears to be *reengineering*. For many managers, the concept of reengineering is more of a euphemistic label for an entirely different concept called *downsizing*—the practice of eliminating jobs with the intent of enhancing profitability by lowering overhead costs.

As one of many corporate support functions, corporate security has experienced its share of the trimming knife. As senior managers reengineer the way in which asset protection is both defined and accomplished, it is not uncommon to find a great deal of anxiety and trepidation on the part of employees at all levels. As one cynic recently noted, "Career development means identifying ways in which you can be assured of keeping your job for the next ninety days." Despite such anxiety, it is against this backdrop of uncertainty that I believe there is an opportunity

3

for both security managers and their line staff not only to *survive* but actually to *thrive*.

At the same time it seems somewhat ironic that despite the continued decrease in the overall crime rate since 1993, today's employee is more afraid and has a heightened feeling of insecurity in the workplace. This anxiety is directly rooted in the emergence of what is commonly referred to today as "workplace violence." As workers' personal problems are brought into the job site or as feelings of disenfranchisement arise from the pressures and stresses of organizations, one would assume that companies would respond by heightening security measures and increase resources. In fact, at many companies just the opposite is occurring. Because of the need to remain competitive in today's marketplace, senior managers rarely discriminate among support units when it comes to cutting costs. The consequence for managers of security programs has been straightforward: maintain, and if possible, enhance the level of asset protection and employee safety with fewer resources. So how is this aim to be achieved? The answer, not as simple as the question, is grounded in number of organizational issues and management strategies.

Although these are certainly turbulent times, there are a number of opportunities for security professionals to achieve significant gains and become an integrated part of the overall business plan by demonstrating, in a multiplicity of ways, added value.

MURPHY'S MAXIMS

As you will see with the unfolding of this chapter, there are a number of formal and informal sources for identifying those strategies that can assist you in demonstrating your value to a company. Among the informal sources are a set of maxims that George Murphy developed before his retirement as security manager for Mobil Oil Corporation. Collectively they serve as an excellent launching pad for a detailed review of successful business management strategies.[1]

Know Your Customers

Murphy begins by asking a simple question. Do you know who your customers really are? Whether you're on the organization's staff or assigned to serve as a representative for an external provider, the question remains the same. Knowing who your customers are involves more than just recognizing names and positions within the organization. To be successful you need a much deeper and more intimate knowledge; for instance, you should understand your end users' perspective, have some familiarity with their plans for both the here and now and over the intermediate term, and be acquainted with the markets or industries the company serves and who its external providers are. When taken collectively these factors begin to define who your customers are and give you an appreciation of those influences that drive your customers' expectations and needs.

For security decision makers expectations and needs are particularly important. Your success is defined by your ability to know and be able to react to each unit head's particular requirements. Expectations are just as real as needs. Both are important in defining an interactive relationship. This is not to suggest, however, that service providers—resident or external—should roll over and assume that unchangeable forces are driving the relationship. Knowing your customers means being sensitive to their wants and accommodating them when doing so does not present a conflict or tax limited resources. Knowing your customer also means having the fortitude to challenge their demands when you, as supplier, realize that there are more effective ways of delivering a service—even if it means guiding your customer to redefine their demands.

Without overcomplicating the issue, it is also important to note that knowing your customers also entails adjusting to their particular biases and level of acceptance of security and safety. As we shall see later on in this chapter and in Chapter 6, recognizing their perception of you and knowing what contribution security makes to the overall aims of their company are two critical means of defining what it is that you can do for your customers.

Develop a Reputation for Being Proactive

Here Murphy offers two strong warnings: Do not wait to be told to do something, and do not operate solely in the proverbial professional black box. The very nature of security demands that your team be more reactive than proactive. Jim McKiernan, a thirty-year veteran of the Fremont, California, police department notes, "Over time it's easy to understand how both law enforcement and private security have come to be more reactive in nature. With continuing cutbacks, both professions have witnessed reductions in staff and other resources. This, in turn, drives the need to establish priorities. Unfortunately, the urgencies associated with unfolding events will invariably overshadow the need for proactive strategic planning. To get in front of the power curve, the concept of doing more with less should be the impetus for developing programs designed to get ahead of the potential for something happening as opposed to waiting for it to occur."

Like Murphy, McKiernan is trying to caution us that our success is rooted in developing programs and offering ideas that tackle potential losses before they become actual losses. Combining both warnings under one positive strategy, Murphy's successor, Mike Farmer, has continued his concept of proactive investigations for Mobil Oil. This program involves conducting investigations when there is no known threat or suspected loss, as a means of identifying risks and exposures before losses occur. By testing controls the security team can identify areas where vulnerabilities have cropped up in the business unit's way of doing business without management's notice. Where such openings exist opportunists can operate just below established thresholds without being detected. Through their proactive investigations, the Mobil security staff is both demonstrating an approach that is outside of the conventional security "black box" way of doing things and simultaneously positioning Mobil Oil as a corporation ahead of the loss curve.

Seize the Moment

You don't need to spend much time in security before you see that people are motivated to pay attention to security only when an event has either affected them directly or occurred very near to them. Security support escalates dramatically—and for a very defined interval of time—immediately following a crisis. Whether such a crisis is natural or man-made, such as the terrorist bombings at the World Trade Center and the Oklahoma City Federal Building, the net effect is a heightened awareness on the part of both management and line staff. Organizational theorist Abraham Maslow taught us decades ago that for an individual to achieve self-actualization, his or her most basic and fundamental needs must be adequately addressed up front. Of these needs, personal safety and security are the base-level motivators. When an event occurs that threatens the safety of an individual, it is incumbent upon the security manager to seize the opportunity not only to enhance the individual's awareness regarding security but also to develop within that individual a sense of ownership and support for reasonable security programs.

Highly successful managers understand well that there is nothing unethical about taking advantage of an opportunity when it presents itself. Regardless of whether it is generated from a crisis or not, an opportunity is an opportunity. The unsuccessful manager is reluctant to seize the moment on the mistaken premise that it is somehow inappropriate to promote a necessary or beneficial program on the heels of someone else's misfortune. The question of such behavior being unethical or immoral should surface only when such opportunism is self-serving and does not benefit others.

Keep It Simple

We commonly read about how it is important to speak the listener's language. Since most of the senior managers who are making critical decisions are not apt to be security experts, it is important that what you tell them sounds both realistic and grounded in common sense, and it is especially important when you are requesting funding for new programs. Murphy advises that the first three minutes of any presentation are the most important. Most commonly it's at the beginning of an exchange that people have your attention and are going to be responsive to what you have to say. In a world where most managers spend over 90 percent of their time in meetings, managers want to get to the point as soon as possible, and they appreciate clarity. Therefore it is important to state up front both the purpose of the meeting and what you hope to accomplish.

Take the example of the security director for a mass retailer who was interested in procuring antishoplifting equipment. For years he had watched his predecessor grow frustrated trying to convince the store's capital improvement committee of the need for more loss prevention specialists and the latest state-of-the-art devices. His predecessor would present total incidents, total losses, and provide anecdotal examples of the company's reputation for being an easy mark. Year after year the appeals fell on deaf ears. The new security director took a different approach. He began by demonstrating that the per hour cost for loss prevention specialists dedicated to preventing shoplifting on a per store basis during peak times was costing the company approximately $36 per hour. This was the cost associated with compensation, training and supervision, and associated overhead. Having completed an independent but parallel study of actual losses resulting from shoplifting activity on a per store basis, he concluded that the hourly wholesale loss rate was approximately $16 per hour. In other words, per hour, his cost of prevention was more than twice his actual loss. Drawing on the expertise of a systems engineer, he discovered that with the introduction of state-of-the-art anti-pilfering tags and the use of wireless closed-circuit television cameras, he could reduce his prevention cost to a level below the actual rate of wholesale loss.

After putting together the appropriate slides, he requested permission to give a fifteen-minute presentation to the capital budgeting committee. He then proceeded to present the associated costs and benefits. He closed by showing that his staff projected a return on investment (ROI) for the required security devices within approximately thirty-six months. This was well within the company's ROI parameters, so he requested authorization for the funds necessary to achieve his goal. This straightforward and simplistic presentation, which took less than ten minutes, was sufficient to convince the capital budget committee to grant approval for the necessary funding. Why? Because this security director was able to follow the formula of presenting the problem, offering the solution in a language that the committee members understood, and assuring them that he had data available to justify his recommendation. Because of the security director's style of presentation and his ability to lay out the objective and the resolution, approval of his proposal was swift.

Establish Your Credibility Early On

Managers who enjoy a high level of respect know well that their ultimate success is inextricably linked to the degree of credibility they have with senior management. Security, as an organizational support unit, needs to have credibility and be respected by those employed within the organization, irrespective of position or job function. People want to know that integrity and an ability to perform are highly valued objectives in their security unit. When credibility is missing, there is a general distrust and a resulting unwillingness among employees to cooperate with security. Just as people want to trust their local police and are taken aback when they hear of episodes of incompetence and/or excessive force, they also look to their security department to be above reproach and perform in a professional manner. When the reputation of security suffers, the effect can be derogatory labels such as "corporate cops," "rent-a-cop," and so forth.

Approval comes quickly to those who have an established track record for accomplishing what they say they will accomplish. Internal customers will seek security's assistance if they know their requests will be handled efficiently and with dispatch. Security should not become known as that department where people go to get a no for an answer. Occasions will arise when security will have to take a position that is contrary to the wishes of the end user. This is part of organizational life. The measure of success, however, is that employees know that security is there for them and can accomplish what it says it can—and then some. The ability to get things done, as simple as the concept may be, is a lost art with many of today's support units. People do not want to get bogged down in bureaucratic entanglements. The very nature of reengineering, after all, is to design systems that are streamlined to accommodate customer service not impede it. When roadblocks are created and people are told that these steps are being taken "for security reasons," they can become extremely agitated because they believe they have no recourse.

One of the best examples I know of how *not to succeed* was a recent encounter I had with America Online. If someone were ever to create a

Corporate Bozo Award, AOL would, without a doubt, be a prime candidate. Here's what happened. Our business received a book we did not order. Understandably, AOL charged us for the book. When we protested, they acknowledged the mistake and said that a credit would be issued. They asked us to return the book, which we did. After a short period of time, they canceled our subscription because of a computer snafu. We again protested; they acknowledged the mistake and reinstated our account. This happened two more times over the course of the next several months. Our frustration grew. A few months later, having been assured that the problem was resolved, we discovered that the account had been terminated for the fourth time. When I called this time, I was informed that the account was in my wife's name and that "for security reasons" only she could call to have it reinstated. Despite giving her our user identification code and explaining that it was a business account, the customer service supervisor said she needed to hear a female's voice to correct the problem, that this step was required as a matter of security because the account was in a female's name. When I asked the customer service representative how she was going to distinguish my wife's voice from that of any other female, she couldn't answer the question. (She had not been prepared to answer such a logical question.) Needless to say, we canceled the account. This incident brings into serious question the professional reputation and credibility of AOL's security department as a credible support unit for customer service.

Respect the Individual

To be effective, the security department also needs to be perceived as an advocate for individual employee rights. This is particularly important in an age in which issues of privacy are continuously being tested with E-mail, fax transmissions, and voice-mail systems. Respect for individual rights is especially critical in corporate investigations involving matters of dishonesty and violations of company policy. Just as there is an expectation in the broader society that police officers will respect the constitutional rights of U.S. citizens, employees expect that company officials will demonstrate a respect for those accused of wrongdoing until the facts can be clearly established to demonstrate culpability.

Unfortunately popular movies such as *The Firm* characterize corporate security as senior management's strong arm, a gang of thugs who think nothing of violating employee rights and treating people with disrespect. As a part of my business, I assist litigators in matters associated with security operations. Over the course of three years, and after more than fifty cases, I have only encountered two cases that dealt with security personnel accused of treating someone with disrespect. In reality, it has been my experience that most members of security operations go out of their way to assure that employees' civil liberties are protected and also recognize that their organizational success is closely linked to the degree of respect they show to individual staff members.

It is more common to find nonsecurity executives violating employees' rights, mostly because they are not familiar with the law and/or court decisions. In an effort to determine culpability and seek retribution in instances of wrongdoing nonsecurity managers may easily and inadvertently step across the line. This is one area where security staff can demonstrate their added value. In this respect Murphy suggests one cardinal rule to be followed by all security executives: success comes to those who adhere to the principle that the employee deserves the benefit of the doubt.

Honor Thy Sponsor

All security managers, whether internal or external to the corporation, report to someone. Regardless of the organizational hierarchy, asset protection managers need to understand that the support they give to those above them can significantly and directly enhance their own success. The effectiveness of such support is manifested in the way they communicate with their superiors and the frequency with which they do so.

In today's fast-paced organizations the principle of "no surprises" reigns supreme. Executives do not want to be caught off guard, especially with regard to something going wrong. Here we are talking about losses that should have been reported to higher-ups in a timely fashion but that were not; or complaints to upper management from internal or external customers without benefit of advance notification by or discussion with the security manager. Murphy explains that to be successful, security managers need to keep those who are critical to the decision-making process informed about relevant facts and conditions at all times.

In his text *The Handbook of Management Tactics* Richard Buskirk points out the Machiavellian principle of never wounding a king. This principle underscores what George means by honoring thy sponsor. In other words, do not hurt someone who is in a position to exact revenge. If the injured party has the means to redress his injury, the chances are that he will use it. As Buskirk points out: "Kings now take many forms. They do not all wear crowns or sit on thrones and there are many ways of wounding them. Let us restate this tactic for the modern manager. The adept executive appraises the retaliatory capabilities of an individual or firm before selecting which tactics he intends to use. Definitely kings want different tactics than peasants."[2]

Senior managers need trust, and they also want to be seen as successful in their bosses' eyes. In my previous book there is a discussion about the two spheres of organizational success. The first focuses on competence. Equally important, the second centers on trust. As organizations trim down, decision makers are relying more and more on those under their charge. If they cannot be confident in their subordinates' abilities, or if they suspect that there is a lack of respect from anyone, which includes the security manager or account representative, they will employ their royal powers.

Write Only What You Would Want to Read in The Berkeley Barb

A number of years ago, the University of California at Berkeley underground newspaper *The Berkeley Barb* published an internal memo from a large hi-tech firm. Needless to say, the memo proved to be embarrassing for the company. As a result, Murphy cautions us that regardless of the topic, any written communication should always be generated with this perspective in mind: if it were to be published, how embarrassing would it be for those involved?

In a society as litigious as ours, the written word can either be our strongest ally or our worst nightmare. Adept attorneys, like their management counterparts, can put a spin on facts that could convince even the most skeptical jurist. Therefore the written word can prove to be either a very powerful tool in counteracting such spins or the smoking gun that points to the culpable.

Assume No Responsibility Unless You Run It

You should assume accountability only when you have the ability and the power to influence the outcome. If you lack control, your chances for achieving success are random at best, and more likely the outcome will not be achieved at all. This is particularly true for third-party providers, who, more often than not, are expected to achieve results in areas where they have no control or influence. It's easy for senior management to assign accountability without allocating the appropriate resources or empowering middle managers with decision-making capabilities. Undoubtedly, this is a tough spot to be in. But even to accept such accountability reluctantly is to invite eventual disaster. As hard as it might seem, managers need to stand their ground and refuse to accept responsibility unless given the ability to control the end result.

Sometime back, and before the current corporate administration, Montgomery Ward had a problem with an excessive number of claims by shoppers regarding slips, trips, and falls. Exacerbating the situation, there were also many complaints that security personnel used excessive force. The situation became so bad that the television news show *20/20* aired a special feature on it. A new security management team was recruited and asked to lower both the number of incidents and the dollar amount paid out for claims. Although the security team could develop strategies for lowering incidents, control over how much was paid out for claims rested with the Risk Management Department and the Corporate Counsel's Office. Yet the security department was held accountable for this piece of the situation. Instead of challenging the situation, the security manager rolled over and accepted it over the objections of his staff. He wanted to demonstrate that security was a corporate team player; his staff wanted success. Neither got what they wanted. The manager lost credibility because he was perceived as not being able to deliver. Staff members lost because they were not motivated to give their mission their all when they felt that they could not control the outcome.

Have a Person on the Way

When a serious incident occurs, influential people want to see security demonstrate a sense of urgency. Equally important, they want to be assured that the situation is being properly handled and that a resolution is near at hand. Such expectations can put even the most seasoned manager into a panic. To counteract this, Murphy offers us the concept of "the person on the way." No matter where a situation occurred in the world, Murphy's first response was always to advise that one of his staff members was en route. By making this promise, he knew that he had bought an additional twenty-four hours, at a minimum, to assemble the rest of his staff, diagnose the problem, explore alternatives, and develop a game plan. This strategy of sending a security specialist made Murphy appear to be in control even though internally things may not have been so calm as his staff was gathering facts and assembling the necessary resources to handle the situation.

Being able to say that you have someone on the way shows the uninitiated that their fate is in the hands of experienced people. This alone dramatically lessens the stress and allows cooler minds to prevail. It also allows you to focus on the issue and not on individual competencies. In every crisis there is a time to determine who was or was not responsible for the event. Some may want that process to be on the front end because they are angry or embarrassed, but you will be more successful if you focus on problem resolution up front and attend to the finger-pointing later. Getting the right person to the situation expeditiously actually buys time and allows for a measure of rationality to take hold. Time can be one of your greatest management tools if you handle it in the proper way.

Empower Your People

In their book *The High Value Manager*, Florence Stone and Randi Sachs make the following observation:

> Leaner managerial staffs mean that those managers who survive the downsizing or right-sizing of their organizations have longer to-do lists than ever before. Many have greater spans of control. They either have absorbed into their operation responsibility once handled by a department that no longer exists or now oversee more than one operation, even operations farther removed than a few office floors. Which ever the reason, they don't have the time they once had to look over the shoulders of their employees. Delegation is no longer sufficient to allow today's manager to "manage." The need to truly "empower" their employees.[3]

Certainly Murphy's last maxim would support such an observation.

High-value managers are sought by senior executives because they have been able to free themselves through empowerment and focus on those parts of their managerial responsibility that are critical to contributing to the organization's strategic plan. Empowerment, in and of itself, is also a valuable management tool since it helps the company to benefit from the knowledge, insights, and experience of staff members. Since the concept of empowerment is critical to the success of a security manager, it deserves additional discussion beyond Murphy's maxims. Empowerment is discussed in more detail in the last chapter. However, for our purposes here, it is worthwhile to look briefly at empowerment as but one of the arrows in the manager's organizational quiver.

EMPOWERMENT

Stone and Sachs observe that some managers see empowerment as a threat to their position.[4] As the decision-making power shifts from largely a one-way street originating with the manager to a more collaborative and participatory style of management, these executives worry that they may make themselves dispensable. Conversely, insightful managers who have discovered the power of empowerment have found that it allows them to shift their time and attention to other more highly visible projects, thereby increasing their worth in the eyes of senior management. Ultimately this process can lead to promotion, or, at the very least, it can ensure that these managers are secure in their position—especially in these turbulent times.

Empowerment is manifested in the self-confidence that emerges within individual employees as they begin to test the limits of their abilities. Empowerment, however, is not something that can just be handed over to employees; they must be prepared. As Stone and Sachs point out, if you introduce the concepts of shared leadership and empowerment carefully to your employees, you can avoid being hit with the confusion or resentment that might follow, particularly if your style in the past has been more traditional. Preparing employees involves ensuring that they understand the mutual benefits for both parties as you shift operating gears and management style.[5]

Murphy's eleven maxims represent just the beginning for security managers who desire to discover strategies for accomplishing more with less. To go forward, however, we need to briefly back up and set the proper context. Those conversant with management can appreciate the fact that it is both a science and an art. There is no set formula for success within an organization. There are common denominators that can help establish a basis for eventual success, but there are no prescribed standards. If there were, there would be far fewer management texts in bookstores, and we would be introduced to the latest management theory every so many years. For now, let's explore where I believe the art and science blend together.

SECURITY MANAGEMENT AND THE ART OF FLY-FISHING

I have a good friend, Paul Franklin, who describes himself as a junkyard consultant to entrepreneurial enterprises. He characterizes himself this way because his clients can rarely afford conventional means of promoting their upstart businesses. Consequently, he is often forced to develop some rather unconventional strategy, or as he terms it, "scrounge around until he finds what works." Often this involves creating a mind-set for his clients that allows them to see beyond traditional approaches and to aggressively pursue the unconventional.

Franklin is also an expert fly-fisherman. If you can't find him at his Portland, Oregon, office managing the affairs of the National Training Center, you're almost sure to find him on the Deschutes River looking for the ideal spot to land steelhead trout. About a year ago he asked me to join him on one of his fishing expeditions. I had never been fly-fishing and didn't quite relish the idea of getting up at 6:30 A.M. to stand in the ice-cold waters casting a fishing lure, but somehow I thought it would be fun. My decision to go was one of the best management decisions I have ever made. When we first arrived, Paul pointed out that finding the right spot on the river was the first step to a successful fishing trip. To find that spot required knowing three elements: the speed of the water, its color, and its depth. Together, these factors indicate the section of the river most apt to attract and hold steelhead fish. Yet he cautioned me that this was only the beginning.

Once you have determined the spot, actually landing a steelhead requires knowing how to get the attention of the fish by systematically working the entire area. He pointed out, "These fish don't strike at a fly because they are hungry. Rather, they are very territorial and don't like intruders, regardless of their size. The trick, therefore, is to get the fly directly in front of the steelhead and make them mad. They will strike at the fly, thus enabling you to hook them and then begin the task of reeling them in."

Systematically working the spot requires a process of wading far enough into the river and casting your line out over defined sections. Using a measured approach of progressively extended casting distances and walking downstream, coupled with properly mending (that is, flipping the line over to position the fly where you want it) the fly line to cover the cast area, you will eventually fish the entire section. The result is that your chances of landing a steelhead are significantly increased, if the fish are there. Understanding these three facets of fly-fishing—choosing the right spot, knowing how to properly cast the line, and working the spot—I could begin to see the blend between the art and the science of the sport.

Those that have come to know me realize that I rarely stop thinking about business management strategies. Therefore it should not be surprising to read that while I was casting my fly over and over, I was asking how this art and science could be applied to the management of a corporate security program. After what seemed to be the one thousandth–plus cast, I began to enjoy the exercise of simply standing in the frigid water and casting this simple fishing line out over the river. Then it dawned on me. This was my "Zen" management consulting experience. Here is what I discovered:

1. Sometimes it's important just to get away and enjoy things so remote from what we normally do that new insights flow into our thought process. Mental retreats can be opportunities for breakthrough.

2. The process of fly-fishing for steelhead trout has applications in both the management and the marketing of security services. Your ability to cast the line to the right depth and allow it to float at the right speed blends the art of casting with the science of catching fish. Together they define a process that leads to success. The same can be said for managing a security program. We'll explore this more in a moment.

3. One doesn't catch fish with every cast. Just like when casting your program onto the organizational waters, sometimes a strike occurs and sometimes you strike out. If you persevere, however, someone out there will eventually take notice and hit your line. Regardless, your approach will have been consistent and well thought out.

4. There is a parallel between what is required of us and what we really enjoy doing just for the sake of its intrinsic value. Mainly, both require a commitment. Just as it may require dozens of casts and working several spots before you can successfully land a fish, the same can be said for proposing aspects of your security program to the right audience.

5. As with the fish, there is a motivator that draws each of us into action. Marketing specialists long ago discovered that without motivation, people are not going to act. The primary motivators, as we shall discuss below, are problem resolution, pain resolution, and opportunity gain.

Based on the foregoing, you can see how it dawned on me that the process of fly-fishing is parallel to the process of successful management. It was in the process of standing there, trying to improve my casting technique, that I realized why Franklin found it necessary to introduce me to the Deschutes River. I began to understand that the experience was truly related to a much larger issue—namely, how we can take one experience that is seemingly as remote as it could be from something else, yet transfer the principles from the first situation to the second—thereby enhancing the likelihood of achieving success.

Since finding the right spot and knowing how to work it are critical management tools, let us briefly examine our fly-fishing analogy in a little bit more detail. Recalling that the discovery of the right spot requires knowing the river's speed, color, and depth, let us examine how each factor applies to the management of a corporate security department.

Finding the Right Spot—The Art

The River's Speed—Organizational Timing
One of life's truisms is that every good idea has to have its own time or it will fall on deaf ears and not be appreciated. The same can be said for

security programs. We know that ideas flow through organizations at different rates of speed. Some can be introduced and be quickly adopted; others appear to languish, lost in the morass of bureaucracies and vested interests. Some plans never come to fruition simply because the organizational participants never develop a mind-set to accommodate the concept or its intrinsic value. Other ideas are modified to such a degree that only the core remains. Nonetheless, acceptance of the idea would be deemed successful if its central value remains intact.

As noted above, people are motivated to act when (1) they are experiencing a particular problem and require a resolution; (2) they are in pain as a result of suffering a loss; or (3) they believe that there is some personal or economic gain to be achieved. Absent any one of these three motivators, a program will most likely languish. Just as the trick to catching a steelhead requires getting the fly directly in front of the fish and irritating it, so, too, the presentation of a successful security program requires getting the idea in front of those who are motivated to act. This leads us to our second point—the water's color.

The Water's Color—Organizational Temperament

Historically, security managers and providers have lamented that they are typically the last to know when a crisis occurs. Over the years they have also complained that security is rarely brought into the planning process, particularly when new products are to be introduced or the company is planning to expand into new markets. Despite all of the rationalization that might be brought to bear regarding these two frustrations, the bottom line appears to be that senior managers have not been motivated (have not seen the need) to get security involved early on in the process. In short, we can characterize senior managers as being indifferent until they experience one or more of our three primary motivators.

Human nature is averse to conflict. This means that as human beings, we want to seek the tranquility of calmer waters. Change provokes anxiety and is therefore something to be avoided. Similarly, when problems do arise, we seek expedient solutions or try to avoid acknowledging problems altogether by ignoring the underlying causes and hoping that they will disappear on their own. If nonsecurity managers perceive the asset protection decision maker as contributing to the problem by pointing out controls, articulating various warnings, or generally taking a negative approach, it is not surprising that they will not seek the input of the security executive—or at least will significantly delay calling for his or her input.

Conversely, when the security manager is seen as a problem solver, people will quickly turn to him or her for assistance, and security may gain the opportunity for introducing long sought after programs, new technology, a change in corporate policies or operational procedures, and so forth. Just as for individuals, professional problems are unpleasant experiences that can either lead to more frustration and anxiety or be resolved satisfactorily, when the security managers are the agents of satisfactory resolution, their credibility increases, and they can count on a new level of advocacy.

When pain occurs as a result of an unexpected or catastrophic loss, people want the unpleasantness to go away as soon as possible. They are probably very anxious, and they will listen to and do most anything the perceived expert advises. In the case of corporate security, senior executives will seek out the security staff rapidly and place the resolution for the problem in their hands, thereby transferring their pain to someone else. Again, this may well serve as an opportunity for security to promote overdue programs. And, just as in problem solving, security's credibility will be enhanced if the situation is successfully resolved.

It is interesting to note that when people are in pain, cost is rarely an issue. Take, for example, a visit to the dentist to seek relief from a painful toothache. We do not typically go into the dentist's office and begin by asking what the fees are for extracting the aching tooth. Nor do we take the time to seek second and third opinions, because our focus is on ridding ourselves of the pain. We gladly welcome the dentist and will do almost anything we are asked including paying the bill. Afterward, because the pain is no longer with us, we are indebted to the dentist and can easily justify the dentist's bill.

This is in part what George Murphy's maxim Seize the Moment maxim is all about. Not only is taking advantage of an opportunity to demonstrate our expertise appropriate, but people actually want you to do so—after all, why else have they sought you out? If you conduct yourself in a professional manner and are responsive to the other person's need, that individual is likely to seek out your resources in the future. At the same time you are in an excellent position to remind the individual that just as preventive dental care could have eliminated the painful tooth extraction, advance involvement with security might eliminate or minimize the likelihood of a similar crisis occurring in the future.

The third motivator is often just as powerful as the experience of pain. Here we are talking about the opportunity to experience personal and/or economic gain. Marketing experts long ago understood the allure associated with perceived gains. Such gains might include increased visibility among senior management, an actual promotion, reassignment to a different position within the organization at the same or a different location, the potential for a bonus, and so forth. If any one or more of these motivators are present and an individual perceives that security can be instrumental in achieving them, then that individual is likely to call upon security or actively listen to an idea presented by security. Even if there is an associated up-front cost, the individual who perceives a potential gain has a willingness to accept the cost. This fundamental principle is particularly relevant when capital budgeting committees meet to discuss the allocation of monies over a set period of time. Essentially the concept of "return on investment" can be underwritten by the gain motivator. Financial decisions are made based on formulas demonstrating that the company's investment (expense) will return a profit or gain within a specified period of time. If the gain will not be realized over the short term to intermediate term, the motivation for expenditure diminishes significantly and rapidly.

The River's Depth—Organizational Positioning

Even though the timing might be right and the motivation may be there, if security programs are not presented at the right level within the organization, they will not have the backing necessary to achieve their full potential. There is no magic formula that prescribes at what level all ideas should be presented. Even though it is generally believed that ideas that are sold at the top have a greater likelihood of surviving as they are pushed downward into the organization, this is not always true. As organizations redefine themselves and more participatory decision making is involved, the selling of programs may just as well need to be presented at a much lower level in the company.

Even the seemingly most unimportant staff member can make or break a security program. For example, the district manager for a large contract supplier once confided that the success of his security program often relied on the cooperation he received from the janitorial staff at his various client sites. He explained that after normal business hours it is customary for the custodial staff to control master keys. Unless they understood the importance of locking doors or making themselves available to provide access to client employees requiring after-hour access, he found that it was his security company that took the brunt of both the criticism and the blame when things went wrong. As he observed, "Company presidents and department heads may well understand and support good security. However, at ten at night or two P.M. on a Sunday afternoon, they're simply not there. On the other hand, the janitors are, and if they have not been sold on the idea of good security, it becomes a tug of war between them and my officers."

It is one thing for nonsecurity employees to be aware of the potential problems associated with their personal safety and security. It is quite another for them to accept responsibility for the part they play in assuring that security practices are followed. Since there are two sides of the security coin—awareness and ownership—clearly security needs to market its programs and define its positions within the organization. Ideas that flow down may be met with resistance if they are not properly explained. To gain grassroots support for integrating something of benefit within the corporate culture generally involves a much longer time line. Therefore, it is incumbent upon security managers to target specific programs to selected audiences based on their expectations and needs.

Working the River—The Science

Covering the River—Organizational Coverage

Just as we discovered that successful fly-fishing relies on a prescribed methodical approach to covering the selected area, we can say the same about promoting security programs. Simply shotgunning an idea across the entire company is fairly ineffective. While those closest to the muzzle may experience the thrust of the blast, those farther away may not be affected at all. To be effective, the security program needs to be tailored to address the particular needs of a targeted group of internal customers. It is therefore reasonable to expect less than 100 percent compliance on the part of everyone associated with the company, especially when field operations are involved. What might work well in a corporate complex may well be completely unrealistic in a separate field location.

To illustrate, despite advances in technology, it is still fairly expensive to require electronic access control on all building entrances when multiple field locations are involved. Even though the cost for a front-end controller to govern electronic access control can be distributed on a proportionate basis, in some locations the actual use of electronic access control may be more operationally burdensome than the use of a mechanical key system. In other words, the security program must be adapted to serve to the functional, geographic, and operational needs of the internal work groups.

Security managers often create stumbling blocks for themselves by not distinguishing between the concepts of policies and the actual carrying out of procedures. The problem arises when security equates policy concepts with actual procedures across the entire organization, regardless of differing needs. Our example of access control is an excellent illustration of this mixing. The policy should begin and end with requiring access control. The procedure for implementing the how, what, when, and so forth can vary from one location to the next. By separating policy from procedure you create a mechanism that allows for complete organizational coverage while maintaining the integrity and respect for individual location differences and applications. While the argument can be made in this example that significant economies can be achieved through standardization, it is often just as debatable to point out the resulting operational inefficiencies that can arise based on the number of employees affected, the cost and quality of local servicing, and so forth. The answer is that each company is different and that a cost-benefit analysis needs to be conducted if universal procedures are to be implemented.

Successful fly-fishing requires the establishment of a pattern of one step forward and two steps sideways to cover the intended area. This approach requires deliberateness of thought and planned execution. Certainly the same can be said for managing a security program, which involves the creation of a plan involving a systematic and carefully thought through step-by-step action plan.

Not long ago I had the opportunity to address a group of security executives on the topic of *best practices*. During the session one of the participants asked how he could know whether or not he was engaging in best practices. After I had asked him a few questions, he blurted out: "Actually, I'm not certain we do much of anything right. We have been in the executive protection business for nearly two decades and haven't lost one yet. So I guess by that standard we are best practices. But what troubles me is that we don't employ any criteria, and we don't develop action plans. So who is right? Us, with our by guess and by golly approach, or you with your ideas about action planning?"

Pulling back and looking at his point from the perspective of end results, I can see that he might have a point. Unfortunately for his company, however, about two weeks after the meeting I heard that he had "lost one." A few days went by and he called and asked my assistance in developing criteria for when to and when not to accept assignments, an outline for action planning, and so forth. Absent a plan, his company's luck had run out—and unfortunately with a tragic consequence.

Mending the Line—Organizational Targeting

There is more to placing the fly than simply casting it out over the river. Depending on the conditions, the direction of the wind, and the speed of the current, it is conceivable that the fly will not land in exactly the intended spot. Therefore the fisherman needs to continuously adjust the line by mending it, that is, making continuous adjustments to direct the fly to the desired location once it's in the water. Likewise, the security manager needs to be making continuous adjustments to the program as circumstances unfold and prevailing conditions change. A shift in the company's business direction (the wind) can be cause for the asset protection manager to adjust the security program so that it flows in the new direction. This type of organizational targeting keeps the program relevant to end users.

In the dynamic environment of America's financial services community, changes in direction seem to occur almost on a monthly basis. This may be somewhat of an overstatement, but it emphasizes the fact that survival—and thriving—require a management style characterized by flexibility and adaptability. The security director for one of the West Coast's largest banks has a management style that underscores the concept of continuous mending. At one point he was informed that the bank was going to shift its business direction from largely commercial banking to full-service retail banking. He gathered his staff, and together they developed an approach aimed at meeting the security requirements for the bank's new direction.

Within months the security director was informed that there was going to be a change in senior management, and the bank was returning to its former focus. So he made a second change. Much to everyone's amazement, within a few months another change was announced to the management team—the bank's executive team had rethought its position and was going to make another change in direction. The security director adapted accordingly. When the fourth announcement occurred within less than a year, many of the business unit managers were growing exceedingly frustrated and angry. Several resigned while others became very cynical and lost confidence in the executive team. At one meeting a couple of unit heads turned to the security director and asked his opinion. His response took them by surprise. He said, "Certainly, this type of flip-flopping is frustrating, but I'm here to protect people and assets no matter what direction we go. I have to adjust. If I don't, I'm not holding true to the primary mission of what security is supposed to be all about. Do I wish they would make up their minds? You bet. But until they do, I'll just keep on adjusting. It's my job."

Was he successful? Clearly. He understood that the science of successful management entails flexibility. He left the business of banking to the bankers. He stayed abreast of what banking is all about, thus enabling his staff to contribute to the overall business plan, but he stayed focused on his core competency. For him bank security meant adopting different security strategies for different business approaches. He did not concern himself with matters he could not control.

Setting the Fly—Organizational Attention Getters

Once the fly is in the water, it is incumbent upon the fisherman to adjust its depth. If the fly is too close to the surface, the steelhead will swim underneath it. Conversely, if it is too low the fish will cross over it. In either event, the purpose of the fly will have been lost because the fly is not where it should be. For the security manager the lesson to be learned by this is that even the programs that can add the most value need to be brought to the attention of the most appropriate people within the company. One of the best ways to illustrate this point is with a discussion of the travel advisory programs that many security departments have developed for their traveling executives. Drawing upon the resources of several commercially available subscription services, security staffs have been able to develop profiles for certain countries and cities, as well as information about hotels and airlines. Yet it is not uncommon to find that traveling executives are unaware that this service is available, largely because the security department has been ineffective in marketing it.

As another illustration, I was recently asked to conduct a review of the security program at the head office complex of a large insurance company. In the course of this review I was informed that the security department provided escorts for employees to their vehicles after hours. When I inquired about how often security received such requests, I was informed that very few employees took advantage of the service. Ironically, a survey of employees showed that chief among their concerns was the lack of a security escort service during the hours of darkness. The officers were frustrated that few were taking advantage of the program, and the majority of employees were unaware that such a service existed. In other words, the program existed, but it had not been positioned well within the organization. The issue was easily and quickly resolved. Since most employees exited the complex through the main lobby, security placed a small sign atop the security console in the main lobby advising employees that the escort service was available upon request.

VALUE-ADDED OPPORTUNITIES

Between Murphy's maxims and the art of fly-fishing, we have seen that successful security management requires just as much an understanding of organizational behavior and strategy as a familiarity with the technical nature of asset protection. As we continue our journey we turn our attention to a fairly new concept within the management nomenclature, what is referred to as "added value."

Surviving and thriving is dependent on your ability to show that the service you are offering is more than just "what is required," and, equally, no longer can support units, including security, rest on the premise that the cost of protection is part of doing business. These days even the courts and legislatures are beginning to redefine limits on owner liabilities.

New technology, assumed higher levels of risk, affordable insurance premiums, and true reengineering all threaten traditional management approaches to safety and security. Unless you can demonstrate that your programs bring added value, the possibility of extinction is very real indeed.

Some of you reading this book may be able to readily recall friends or professional acquaintances who have already become the victims of wholesale elimination of the security function. Examples abound. One barometer I use is the number of resumes I receive monthly from displaced security executives. Even though I am not in the personnel placement business, I regularly receive resumes or calls from former security directors either looking for another position or exploring the possibility of becoming independent consultants. For the past two years, my file has contained no less than sixty resumes at any one time.

Survival tactics need to be replaced with strategies that allow you to actually thrive in today's lean and mean times. How do you continuously demonstrate added value? After all, isn't there only so much you can give before you reach the point of diminishing returns? Unfortunately, many security managers give up long before there is any cause to do so. Demonstrating added value is not always about reducing operating budgets.

Ten Ways to Demonstrate Added Value for External Providers

Here is a list of ten ways in which you can offer potential clients added value:

1. Promote the fact that you are an industry leader—a subscriber to world-class standards and principles.
2. Let it be known that you have access to other markets because of your business relationships.
3. No one can do everything themselves, so as a manager or executive be clear that your value is in operations, policy setting, consulting, investigations, and so forth.
4. Since your clients have access to your money and resources, by offering them monthly invoicing or alternative pricing strategies you can give them the edge.
5. Security is your core competency, not theirs. By trying to handle security matters, they are diverting valuable resources away from their core competency and therefore operating less efficiently than they could be. You can offset this imbalance through your efforts.

6. Using you as a strategic partner, the company stands to gain more than they will lose. As your strategic partner, they can transfer some—though certainly not all—of their risk to you.
7. Work that may be temporary or cyclical can be better managed by you. For example, systems design work, special investigations, executive protection, and so forth.
8. By creating strategic alliances with other synergistic service providers, you can achieve economic synergies for the company.
9. You can guarantee that greater management flexibility will be achieved relative to assignment of personnel, training costs, and so forth.
10. Because you believe in continuous quality improvement, your performance is not tied to profit alone. Thus the end users gain higher performance from your staff than they will from others.

These ten added values cover the spectrum of business opportunities for any potential client and go beyond the scope of traditional asset protection. By using these incentives as selling points you build a rationale for potential clients to consider contract services as opposed to a proprietary operation. Each of the ten added values can transfer risk, improve management flexibility, increase quality of service, and help a company operate more cost-effectively.

For third-party suppliers, the potential client has the advantage of drawing upon the provider's other customers as potential new markets, thereby increasing profits for the client. If there is any one theme that emerges out of these ten added values, it is probably the concept of leveraging. The client company has the ability to leverage your resources to tap their core competency while paving the way for expanded market position. Is the advantage solely with the outside contractor then? Not necessarily. In working with the resident security department from one of the country's largest companies, I was able to identify twenty ways in which that security operation could demonstrate its added value as an internal resource. In reviewing each item, ask yourself if your department or company (if you are the de facto security department) could make similar claims.

Twenty Ways to Demonstrate Added Value for Resident Security Departments

1. *Direct communications link.* Security serves as the conduit for resolving employee safety and asset protection issues and concerns. In this capacity it serves as the hub for three critical activities. First,

the security department has developed a network of experts and law enforcement professionals. Second, security is the linchpin for internal business units to resolve issues of physical protection and personnel security. Third, through research and analysis capabilities, security can provide state-of-the art solutions that reflect cost efficiencies and can be gauged by quality-oriented performance measures.

2. *Timeliness of response.* Security provides business units direct access any time of the day, any day of the week, to a core of competent professionals capable of resolving security-related issues. As an integrated part of the company's daily operations, security can respond to events as they unfold. Supporting the resident team, there is a group of external partners that can respond quickly. Each partner is prescreened based on his or her knowledge of the industry, proven experience, and professional expertise. In situations requiring that specialists be physically on scene, this typically can be accomplished within hours of security receiving the request.

3. *Company and/or country knowledge.* One of security's strengths is the knowledge base it has developed over the years. Security is composed of a cadre of professionals who know the organization and the markets it serves. Each staff person knows where to go and to whom when the need arises. This is essential because timeliness can make the difference between success and suffering a loss. In a crisis or a case of suspected wrongdoing, security knows where to go and how to deal with varying customs, practices, and regulations, assuring the protection of company interests and the individual's rights.

4. *Professional expertise and industry knowledge.* Proven experience is the hallmark of security's staff selection and retention program. Each staff member brings years of proven experience to the company in his or her specialty area. Security's senior consultants, field managers, and investigators have been recognized within the security profession for their contributions and routinely lead industry sponsored workshops or serve as guest lecturers.

5. *Established networks—external and internal.* The successful security professional needs an extensive network, both within the organization and outside. Security has invested the time and the resources to develop one of the widest security networks in the world. Through membership in some of the most select professional associations, as well as serving on national, state, and local governmental commissions, security has the capability of tapping the most appropriate resources anywhere in the world. By participating in a wide array of internal task forces and regularly meeting one-on-one with manag-

ers and specialists, security has established an internal network that provides security with access to all business and support units.

6. *Controlled confidentiality.* Security is part of the company's family. The corporation's interests are security's first priority. To protect this interest, security staff adhere to the highest code of ethics. Discreetness and confidentiality are the building blocks upon which they have built trust with end users; security's commitment to the company involves never taking either less than absolutely seriously. Confidentiality is a must, extending to written reports, verbal assessments, analyses and data collection, and investigations. Security's business operates on a need to know basis because the staff is committed to protecting company and individual rights.

7. *Extended capability.* Security is an extension of the organization's efforts to deliver the highest quality service and products. Through their resources, security can aid in conducting *due diligence* investigations and undertake other special inquiries, especially those requiring a proactive approach. This unique capability allows security to test the integrity of systems and processes *before* a loss occurs. Security also supports company efforts to host special meetings and events by providing an environment that is safe and secure. Security's field managers assist in conducting risk assessments and work with unit managers to design the most effective and least intrusive security designs.

8. *Understanding management's hot buttons.* Security knows the trigger points that are of primary interest to senior management. There is no learning curve delaying security's attention to the company's internal needs. Security can respond in a productive manner more quickly and at a lower cost. Security knows the culture, business aims, and the nuances of each business unit. As a result they can work with management, knowing what will be of particular interest to company executives and what will not.

9. *Expertise for strategic alternatives.* Security has the expertise to offer a variety of alternatives and solutions to asset protection needs. Security staff work with managers to develop a decision-making road map. By seeking alternative strategies, security ensures that the longer term needs will be met while addressing the immediate concerns. For example, in matters involving investigation, security can structure an approach to reflect criminal prosecution or civil litigation, or both. Field managers can help identify the advantages and disadvantages of one supplier or product over another.

10. *Image preservation.* Preserving the company's reputation in the marketplace is of paramount concern to security. By drawing on the

capabilities and discretion of its staff, security can help to maintain the fine reputation everyone at the company has worked hard to achieve. Security's professional staff can efficiently cut through to the issues involved and determine the most effective course of action to take whether it involves a sensitive investigation, security for a special event, or any of security's other service offerings.

11. *Awareness training.* If asset protection and employee/customer safety is to be successful, there must be an understanding that safety is everybody's responsibility. Security works with business unit managers to identify areas in which heightened employee awareness is required and in which strategies can be designed that will enhance the willingness of employees to accept greater responsibility for protecting company assets, regardless of whether those assets are physical or electronic. The same holds true for accepting mutual responsibility for the safety and security of other employees and/or company customers.

12. *Cost containment.* Security understands well the importance of cost containment. This awareness is rooted in security's knowledge and firsthand experience in corporate restructuring efforts and positioning strategies within the marketplace. Security works with executive and unit managers to identify security requirements that are based on business rationales and not on traditional assumptions about security. The goals of contributing to bottom-line performance and to safety for individuals drive decision making.

13. *Vested interest.* Security is committed to the company, first and last. As a partner in supporting the aims of the organization, security is both provider and service broker. When it is deemed appropriate for security to handle a situation exclusively, security is there to protect the interests of the company. When external resources are required, security screens service providers and chooses vendors based on their ability to represent the company's interests.

14. *Best practices provider/broker.* Security has been recognized as a leader in best practices within the profession. Security continuously benchmarks its programs and approaches by actively seeking out those recognized by industry experts for their pursuit of best practices. When approached by others and asked what they do and why, security converts this opportunity into an open and interactive forum so that the opportunity becomes as much a learning experience for security as for the inquirer. This two-way approach assures the company that security is committed to returning the best value for each dollar spent.

15. *Proven crisis management manager.* Security has proven itself over and over when the need arises for managing crises that affect the corporation. Security's commitment is to have the necessary resources at hand to dispatch immediately and to stay through the entire event. Knowing how to navigate through the company's businesses expeditiously, being familiar with local customs and practices, and having established resources allows security to respond confidently and quickly. Success is the result of experience and infrastructure. Crisis management is one of security's top priorities, whether one person or an entire business operation is involved.

16. *Cross-resource utilization.* Drawing on security's position within the company, security has access to the corporate support structure. This allows the team to quickly assess unit needs and to match them to the available resources. Direct access to other groups allows security to draw on the experiences of others so costly duplications and redundancies can be avoided. This means that security can direct managers to a more appropriate resource or assure that the crossover support occurs, allowing management to receive the best service delivery possible.

17. *Proactive orientation.* Security has long emphasized the importance of a proactive approach. Incidents happen, and unplanned events will always occur: security knows this is inevitable. However, by focusing on proactive strategies, security can help mitigate unwanted or uncontrollable events. Security is prepared to conduct proactive investigations designed to identify risks and exposures before they become realities. This level of preparedness allows security to work with unit managers in developing front-end strategies to avoid loss and injury.

18. *Earned trust.* Over the years security has earned the company's trust; security will never lose sight of its responsibility to protect the company's assets. Security knows that this requires consistent performance, positive results, and discretion. Consequently security places a high value on capability. Security carefully selects each external partner to assure that each staff person understands the importance of earned trust. Even in the most sensitive situations management can be assured that there will always be a proven security manager or specialist directly involved.

19. *Customer satisfaction directed.* Security has developed a formal customer satisfaction program, a process specifically designed to identify needs and expectations. Equally important, security has developed performance criteria to measure how the process is

managed. These same criteria are required of external partners. In this way unit managers can be assured that they will be satisfied when security's services—direct or indirect—are required.

20. *Continuous quality improvement is our hallmark.* Continuous quality improvement (CQI) is security's hallmark. Security does not, nor can it afford to, rest on past accomplishments. Security understands the need for continuous improvement and actively seeks it out. As a process, CQI serves as a barometer for measuring how well security is meeting management's needs. Security actively and formally solicits feedback, for in doing so security can push its team members to a higher level of performance—which serves the company better.

SUMMARY

Our journey toward successful management and customer service began with a discussion of what it takes for a security manager to survive and thrive in today's dynamic times. I introduced eleven maxims developed by one of today's most respected security professionals. His practical no-nonsense guidelines set the stage for a discussion that will be carried through to the end of the book. This was followed by a description of my experience with the sport of fly-fishing and how I came to apply the techniques of that sport to perfecting the art and science of security management.

Using the analogy of fly-fishing, we saw how an asset protection manager needs to understand how organizational timing, temperament, and positioning interact to define success in management. We extended the analogy further to illustrate how organizational coverage, targeting, and attention-getting strategies can help to ensure success in the science of management.

These discussions set the stage for our examination of how security executives, whether working within a company or as an external provider, can demonstrate their added value. Here we examined ten ways contract executives can position their contributions and twenty ways in which one in-house operation did the same thing. Next we turn our attention to the pursuit of another popular measure of success—quality focused performance.

2

In Pursuit of Quality

No one who lives in error is free.

...EPICTETUS

Venture into any bookstore today and browse through the business section. You will find a plethora of texts on quality management. It won't take long before you can "talk the talk." That's because much of what is written today about quality actually is not very complex. For that matter, among the many themes discussed, you'll discover some old concepts hidden behind some new names, yet they're easy to miss because the current terminology sounds very technical.

For example, what today is called "reengineering" is, for the most part, simply reorganizing. When asked why reengineering is necessary, organizational specialists will point out several advantages. They will begin by explaining the merits of "enhanced levels of productivity." We will read about how analyzing "cycle times"—a process initially developed for manufacturers to measure the cost associated with bringing a new product to the market—reduces costs while increasing quality. We'll also hear about structuring the workplace to achieve "added value for a greater return on investment."

These ideas and this new language may sound refreshing, but in many cases businesses are revisiting concepts and challenges that have faced managers, owners, and investors for decades. To illustrate, in 1937 an organization entitled the Institute of Public Administration published *Papers on the Science of Administration*. Edited by Luther Gulick and L. Urwick, this is a collection of essays by both academics and practitioners concerned about the art and science of organizational behavior and relationships. Just as today's experts in reengineering promote the process as a means of increasing productivity, Gulick and Urwick's authors were concerned with identifying strategies that maximize organizational efficiency and effectiveness. Moreover, like their 1990 brethren, these authors of the 1930s professed that quality is directly linked to morale, employee respect, and working conditions. What we today refer to as "empowerment," they called delegation.[1]

In 1928 John Lee, controller of the Central Telegraph Office for England, addressed a group of work directors, managers, foremen and forewomen at Oxford and detailed the pros and cons of functionalism. We can find relevance with his concepts in today's organizational gurus about the need to structure along functional lines as opposed to geographic boundaries. Many of today's Fortune 200 companies are restructuring themselves to consolidate business units based on the inner relationship of their functional utility and not demographic regions. In this respect America's three auto giants are most notable, but they are not alone. Financial service companies such as Bank Boston and energy leader Mobil Oil are actively pursuing realignment.

Simply put, today's emphasis on quality improvement is but the next step in the evolution of maximizing efficiency without diminishing effectiveness. Since early on, management theorists and practitioners have explored a wide variety of new approaches. We can follow the works of Frederick Taylor in the early 1900s, the Human Relationists, proponents of Management By Objectives, Theories XYZ, the Japanese approach of long-term commitment and team evolvement, to today's ISO 9000 and Baldrige processes. The inescapable undercurrent is finding the best way to best the two E's—efficiency and effectiveness.

Regardless of history or who is saying what, clearly today's emphasis is on achieving *quality*. In the context of customer satisfaction, quality can be pursued in a number of different ways. New concepts are being integrated with centuries-old approaches. Much of what is being advocated is an attempt to quantify quality. The mission is to establish criteria that can be measured empirically. And, in pursuing such criteria, we are somehow led to understand that we are engaging in quality efforts. Wrong! Quality is not something that can be pursued. It is an end result. Quality arrives when efficiency and effectiveness are maximized. Business executives can develop and pursue pricing strategies. They can achieve profitability and reduce production time and costs. They can do these things and more and still not achieve quality. Quality is a consequence. It has its own essence and comes only when certain elements occur in a proper alignment.

Understanding the nature of quality is critical to achieving quality. Many companies have become extremely frustrated in their attempts to pursue quality because they follow the mechanics, many of which will be discussed below. They work hard at achieving measurable, mechanical results. And when they are all done, they question whether or not their efforts were worthwhile since they fail to see quality. Others mistakenly believe that when they have completed a prescribed task list, they have achieved quality. They are convinced that completing the course means they now possess quality—whatever that means. After all, aren't they assured quality promised if they accomplish each task? Unfortunately, the answer is no.

Quality is a state of being. We know quality when we see a fine piece of furniture handcrafted by a master carpenter. We see it in art and in the design of such things as automobiles and buildings. We also see it in service performance. One of the central principles of quality is caring. People who are quality driven will accomplish improvement in carrying out tasks because they care—they want to do a good job. They take pride in their work and like the credit given to them, but they don't necessarily seek it. After all, they know that quality will be recognized naturally, and due credit will come.

I have said that quality arrives. What exactly does this mean? Perhaps an example will help. You go to a concert or a sports event. At some point in the process of watching you find that "you are into it." You are no longer just the disengaged spectator. The performer or athlete has engaged you. It's more than just cheering or applauding; you feel the experience. You're excited. You're uplifted. You identify with what is unfolding in front of you. The athletes on the field or the performers onstage have captured you because of their professional skill. Another way of putting this is to say that because they have efficiently and effectively maximized their skills, they have brought you, the customer, truer satisfaction. You know it's quality, but you cannot measure the quality you feel. It's there. It's very real. Quality is a phenomenon that emerges. It is the blending of the science and the art and transcends the mere mechanics of a process.

HOW DEMING VIEWS THE PURSUIT OF QUALITY

Quality guru W. Edwards Deming agrees that quality is measured in terms of the pursuit. Like Pirsig in *Zen and the Art of Motorcycle Maintenance*, Deming believes quality is not definable. You know quality when you experience it, and you can measure improvements in quality. How managers and supervisors align and motivate their people to contribute their collective efforts to achieve a common goal is the real challenge of quality.[2]

Credited as one of the central figures in bringing Japan to a position of world leadership in competitive pricing and quality, Deming has provided both a philosophy and a system for businesses to apply statistical methods to achieve higher quality and productivity in manufacturing and management. Organizational theorists characterize his approach as being of the camp of teaching people how to fish rather than feeding them. He believes quality is 85 percent the responsibility of management and 15 percent the responsibility of employees. Deming developed his fourteen points as a "charter for management" because he saw senior management's commitment as essential to the process. It is only within the past few years that his philosophy and methods have begun to gain widespread recognition for their impact on quality and productivity in U.S. companies.

Given his growing influence, it would be helpful to briefly review the highlights of his charter and how they can/need to be applied to the security profession.

Develop a Strategy for Constant Improvement

Deming suggests that organizations want a "quick fix," and in pursuing this they lose sight of the longer term and fail in the near term because quality is not something that can be achieved in incremental, individual efforts. Quality is a continuous, unfolding process. He offers this advice: determine what business the company is in and adapt to changing customer needs.

As a security decision maker, have you developed a process for continuous quality improvement (CQI)? Are job descriptions and performance objectives centered more on encouraging CQI as a way of doing business, for example, by keeping track of the number of doors found opened and unlocked, or the hours of investigative time spent, or the number of escorts provided?

Adopt a New Paradigm

We need to approach quality with a persistence that establishes the ultimate goal as an error-free operation. But unlike other experts, our goal will be to achieve quality over time through a process of continuous improvement. One of America's largest insurance companies has set up a Quality College, which stresses to its employees the importance of setting goals for error-free operation. Unfortunately they believe that creating error-free measures means assuring that tasks are accomplished the first time out. Their employees are understandably frustrated and find it difficult to feel good about themselves and their contributions. Why? Because they have been assigned an impossible task and have totally missed Deming's point about continuous improvement. Many security departments and third-party providers have entered into similar agreements. As we shall see later in the chapter, a number of security providers have created a high-school type of grading system to measure performance, with an A representing perfection. Since the compensation in such systems is unfairly tied to unrealistic performance standards, it is little wonder that many providers soon learn to shy away from such measures.

Replace Mass Inspection with Employee Troubleshooting

By their very nature, inspections have a negative connotation. The process involves an overseer acting independent of the process. Inspections need to be replaced by employees assuming ownership for their service and/or production. As a part of assuming ownership, there is a need to develop a means of empowering employees to troubleshoot the process when errors are discovered. It's easy to put off known deficiencies, placing accountability away from oneself and saying simply, "Well it's not my job."

For years I have described to audiences, clients, and even former bosses how effective security is accomplished. It requires both employee awareness and ownership. We know that security can't be everywhere, all the time. Unfortunately, for many years security professionals have preached that prevention begins with awareness. This is only half true. Prevention will not work until employees—including managers—assume responsibility for their awareness and translate this awareness into action (ownership).

END THE PRACTICE OF AWARDING CONTRACTS ON PRICE ALONE

I have elected to capitalize Deming's fourth principle to emphasize its current importance. Instead of awarding work to the provider with the lowest bid, which is often tantamount to accepting minimal quality at best, companies need to develop long-term relationships with suppliers. Deming's view is that as long as organizations see vendors as vendors, they will remain vendors. When they see them as partners, they will become partners. Creating this new perspective requires nurturing mutual respect, trust, and responsibility, and offering rewards.

Tom Marano, president and chief operating officer for Argenbright makes the following observations about the commodification of security: "In an industry that is nondifferentiated, the ultimate product is a commodity. With limited barriers to entry and no regulated standard of quality, competition is driven by pricing. As a result, little value is created for the client. Within the client's structure, the security function is a cost center that is not understood by the broader organization it serves. As a result, a new paradigm is needed." Tom's comments underscore one of the prevailing obstacles confronting the security industry. We'll address this in more detail in Chapter 5 when we tackle the issue of commodity-busting head-on.

Promote Leadership and Institute Training

Managers need to understand that their title, manager, means that they are responsible for managing processes and things, not people. Managers lead people. This is a very critical, but oftentimes misunderstood difference. Leading involves supporting, delegating, and empowering people to achieve their fullest potential. Leadership involves coaching and mentoring as much as demonstrating by example and pushing people in positive ways to accomplish more. As many management theorists note, the organization is in the business it's in, but managers are in the organization business—and that means the business of developing people. A manager's final product is creating an environment in which people can make their best contributions, and consequently the organization can be productive and successful.

Leadership also involves eliminating fear. Deming notes that companies that make it "unsafe" for employees to ask questions and learn to do things right are facing tremendous economic losses on the way to their own demise. Employees who are afraid are not free to create. An environment of fear is directly rooted in traditional performance evaluations where compensation is tied to "those who toe the line" as opposed to those who dare to challenge assumptions and seek to make meaningful contributions.

Deming, along with many others, insists that most performance problems can be traced to a lack of orientation and training programs. Management needs to set expectations for employees and demonstrate how workers can be successful in their jobs. This is especially true for people working in asset protection. Despite the emphasis third-party suppliers put on their ability to train, educating employees is still one of their weakest links. The same can often be said for resident security programs.

In Security, training is limited to primarily on-the-job learning. Initial officer training rarely exceeds twelve hours, and advanced officer training is done in a variety of ways, but invariably in the way determined to be the least costly. In short, the quality of training is largely determined by price, regardless of which side one considers. But real training is neither easy nor quick. Interactive communicating, group planning, and problem solving are the first stages. Deming believes that effective training is driven from the top down. When training begins at the top, managers and supervisors are aligned behind the same concepts and share a common language. Next, those in work groups or project teams on the pilot quality effort are trained in the new methods, teamwork, and statistical techniques. Eventually a training program is implemented for each area of work.

Eliminate Hype and Quotas

Deming rejects hype such as slogans, contests, targets, and other forms of internal competition. He thinks that such efforts have little meaning and impact unless they originate from within the workforce. I'm not convinced that he is right here. Nonetheless, Deming contends that internal competition works against the goal of removing internal barriers. He believes that organizations need to redirect the competitive spirit to their real competitors in the outside business world.

Oren Harari, a member of the Tom Peters Consulting Group and a professor at the University of San Francisco, would agree with Deming and consequently has argued very strongly against emerging total quality management processes. He believes that it is common for these processes to be so internally focused that the real business of workers' efforts—serving the external customer—is lost.

Deming also believes that quotas should be eliminated. This move can be particularly difficult for many businesspeople since we have all been conditioned since the advent of the Industrial Revolution to believe that businesses run on numbers. Profit and losses, production units, services provided—all share a common denominator: they are driven by numbers. Yet achieving the numbers alone does not necessarily equate with achieving quality, market share, or innovation. Workers who are held to quotas are held to yesterday's standards; they are not moving the company into the future. Worse, quotas merely guarantee that workers will do whatever it takes to make the mark. An excellent example of a counterproductive system is today's version of the old Detext guard watch tours. Although the Detext watch tours system is hailed as the definitive means to track security officers, an experienced officer can quickly figure out ways to effectively "beat the system." As one officer confided: "When I first started working at the mall, I worked the midnight shift. They had a guard tour package, and I had to punch in every fifteen minutes or so at various locations. Since I was going to school and used the time to study, it didn't take me long to figure out how I could ride a bike through the back service corridors and make the necessary punch-in time. By the time I left, I was really good at maneuvering around tight corners at high speed."

Remove Barriers and Promote Continuous Quality Improvement

It is up to management to begin to encourage the process of interactive listening. This means really listening to what employees have to say about what gets in the way of their performing well. To eliminate barriers entails making available the resources necessary to accomplish the task(s) at hand—by developing innovative operating practices, assuring proper levels of staffing, and providing the necessary technology. Deming is clear that a special top management team must develop a plan of action to carry out the quality mission. The organization is a holistic system, including all of its influencing factors—internal and external customers, suppliers and competitors—and the process needs constant perfecting.

As I pointed out at the outset, these seven points are only the highlights. Deming's total charter incorporates fourteen points.

The Seven Deadly Sins

Deming also points out that there are seven deadly diseases that can have a negative impact on an organization:

1. *Failing to develop a long-term purpose.* American businesses are driven by quarterly and/or annual results. Success is measured based on how well you perform this quarter or this year as compared to the previous quarter or year. The lack of a longer view makes employees and managers feel insecure in their jobs, and this problem then feeds directly into the second deadly disease.
2. *Focusing on near-term profits.* American businesses define their success based on quarterly earnings. Public companies are driven by expected returns from the investment community. This preoccupation with profit for the sake of profit erodes concern for and attention to the longer view. Quite often resources that are designed to feed the future are sapped for the sake of making the near-term profit.

3. *Conducting annual performance reviews.* Annual performance reviews rarely measure true annual performance. Instead they reflect the last "you done me wrong" or "attaboy." Employees soon discover that performance reviews involve more punishment than encouragement. Deming believes that the impact of these measurements on the morale and productivity of both managers and workers is the opposite of what is intended: performance reviews promote fear, inequities, internal competition, anger, and discouragement. After nearly thirty years in both the public and the private sector, I heartily agree that annual performance reviews create more negative effects than positive outcomes.

4. *Not discouraging management exodus.* Deming points out that the migration of high-level managers from one company to another is a tradition. Whether those who leave are dedicated executives who have become disenfranchised or opportunists, the fault is the company's for not developing managers with the "big picture" in mind. Over the past several years, corporations have unwittingly turned on themselves by collaborating in the wholesale elimination of middle and senior layers of management. In their pursuit of lower operating expenses and higher dividends for stockholders, they have lost both their own continuity and the talent once hired to create their future.

5. *Missing the hidden value.* A company's success is linked just as much to intangible values as to empirical, or "known," data. Unfortunately, many companies miss the former altogether in their pursuit of the latter. As Deming explains, some of the most important figures for a company are "unknowable," including the multiplier effect of a happy or unhappy customer, the absence of motivated managers and workers who are willing to go the extra mile that makes all the difference, and the hours saved down the line by front-end planning and proper communication.[3]

6. *Failing to emphasize health care prevention.* Even though many companies are turning to health care prevention programs, the vast majority of American businesses have yet to make the transition. The evidence clearly demonstrates that significant savings can be achieved in premiums when prevention becomes the front line. These programs include wellness programs, antismoking programs, paid workouts and/or health club memberships, and annual medical checkups.

7. *Substituting Continuous Quality Improvement for warranties.* It has become easy for companies to offer warranties. Yet the real value of their product and/or service is not based on "customer satisfaction

guarantees." While such guarantees provide an assurance that the company is concerned about the quality of its product, the real value to the company is in establishing error-free systems altogether. Companies that commit to quality and error-free work realize savings during a warranty period because they decrease the number of nonanticipated services. In other words, the warranty is the consumers' safety net; it is not the company's substitution for CQI.

On the surface, it would appear that these seven deadly sins have applications that are easily applied to security providers. Even though each has a specific lesson for the third-party supplier, the underlying principles apply to resident security programs as well. Security decision makers need to become focused on the longer-term strategy for providing asset protection, and this has special relevance to their systems purchases. I find that all too often the procurement process is driven by answering the need here and now. As the company grows or alters its course, today's "new" security system quickly becomes obsolete.

Similarly, focus on short-term profits can be just as deadly to security programs and organizations as well. In today's litigious society, premises liability has become big business for plaintiff attorneys. Companies that defer taking the proper precautions until better economic times are in swing are placing themselves at greater risk. There are many ways to creatively finance capital expenditures or to budget operating expenses. One of the more commonly overlooked approaches, for example, involves splitting the cost over a longer budget period, for example, by extending the budget cycle from twelve months to eighteen months.

Deming's belief that annual performance reviews work more against the employer-employee relationship than for it is worthy of particular note with regards to the security operation. He is not advocating that performance ought not be reviewed; rather, he, along with other quality specialists, finds the current approach troubling. More effective are peer reviews, group assessments, quality circles, demonstrable contributions, and so forth. These and other strategies are addressed later in our discussion of the journey toward future success.

One of the more difficult challenges facing corporate America, and in particular the security profession, is the issue of management mobility. It remains true that a company's success is linked to its ability to come up with fresh ideas and new perspectives on a regular basis. It is also equally true that a company's success is linked to its ability to maintain a balance of continuity. Longevity is not bad. As American Protective Services have discovered, establishing a track record for proven managers can be very beneficial, especially when clients are experiencing turbulent times. Likewise, managers at resident programs such as those at Monsanto, John Hancock, AMP, and Wells Fargo have also learned the value of balancing their security teams with experienced professionals and new management blood.

Security programs are built on earned trust and proven reliability. Whether the people are proprietary, outsourced, or a combination of the two, the success that is achieved is directly related to demonstrated capability. Such know-how is difficult to measure, but it is very much real. As an illustration, Tony Potter, the director of public safety for Crawford Long Hospital of Emory University, recently observed: "I think our program's success lies in the fact that the staff does a lot of things right the first time. They have taken ownership and in doing so, they really enjoy their job. This attitude carries over to the rest of the hospital staff and our patients. You can't measure it, you can't even see it most times, but you know it's there. You can feel it."

Deming's last two deadly diseases speak to a reliance on traditional approaches and their inherent traps. There was a time when the costs of health care benefits were an insignificant part of the compensation formula. With runaway costs, however, this is no longer the case. As opposed to shopping for lower premiums among competing carriers, companies should be changing their strategy altogether. By seeking an alternative health care approach, companies can attack at the root the cost associated with escalating expenses. The result is lower cost all around. The question to be asked is whether or not the same type of paradigm can be applied elsewhere.

In a like vein, warranties have become a standard business practice. There was a time when guarantees by their nature forced employees to think error-free. The corporation understood well the cost associated with having to redo or replace a defective product. Over time, warranties have become the employee's safety net. After all, managers reason, the company can afford a few mistakes. Besides, how many people really go through the effort to take us up on our warranty? Such misguided and what I would term "lazy" thinking misses the very point of offering a guarantee. From personal experience I have found this mentality even among my consulting colleagues.

To become an associate of my firm, a candidate needs to demonstrate a commitment to quality improvement. Part of what is involved is an acceptance that if the client is not satisfied (satisfaction being defined by the client), then neither of us receives our fee. Thus, the quality incentive is very high for both of us. The only way I can assure success is to do an excellent job myself and be very selective in choosing the right associate.

If compensation were the primary driver, we would not be successful. Being willing to accept such a risk shows a commitment to producing a quality product for the sake of a quality product. Stated another way, it's a willingness to engage in something where the intrinsic value of the process transcends the monetary value that can be placed on the service.

Obstacles to Quality

In our pursuit of quality strategies, I'd like to complete our discussion of Deming's contribution with a review of several obstacles that he has identified. These obstacles plague organizations because they are grounded in management mind-sets that work against their best interests. Yet because of America's obsession with short-term fixes, executives and business unit heads frequently find themselves heading down a path that leads straight into such obstacles, and not in the direction of success, as they had hoped. Security managers are no exception.

- ♦ *The quick fix.* Deming cautions that one cannot simply put a quality process in place overnight. When I was asked recently to assist a security services company in developing a corporate-wide quality assurance (QA) program, I suggested that the transformation would begin to bear its first fruit three years out. The president blanched and then rested back after a moment's reflection. It was then that he commented: "If then." That insightful comment demonstrated that he was on the right road.
- ♦ *Reliance on technology as the great problem solver.* Technology is an administrative tool. Nothing more. Real quality arrives when tools are used by skilled specialists. As one observer notes: "The future includes high-tech as well as high-touch."[4]
- ♦ *Following the leader.* Organizations that wait for "the other guy" to chart a new course and then follow the other's lead will always be behind. Each organization is unique. It is important to learn from those who have gone before us, but it is only when we take note of the nuances of our culture as well as study the maps of those who have gone ahead that we can make real qualitative progress.
- ♦ *Accountability for quality assurance is limited.* A security supplier was asked to describe her company's QA program to a client's selection committee. She proudly told the committee that her company had a great program. She then went on to describe how there was a QA director, a QA Council, and a QA mission. When pressed to describe the process, she said she would have to get back to the committee because that was something the QA people would have

to answer. And then she asked: "Why are you concerned about QA? We've done that and moved beyond." Quality assurance is a continuously unfolding process. It is not a commodity or one-time process to be left to those who specialize in it. It belongs to everyone, all the time.

I have chosen to dedicate considerable space to Deming and his ideas. That is because many of his ideas have been transformed into action with proven results. With his help the entire nation of Japan was repositioned within the business world. Yet Deming has been followed by many other business thinkers. Among them are other early pioneers such as Joseph M. Juran, Armand Feigenbaum, Philip Crosby, and Karu Ishikawa.

THE OTHER EXPERTS' POINT OF VIEW

Juran basically mirrors much of Deming's approach, although the two do have fundamental differences; for example, Juran places more emphasis on the influence of financial planning. He is noted for his early attempts to measure quality in terms of cost. Through his analysis he has demonstrated that it is possible to calculate the real cost associated with losses attributed to poor quality. Feigenbaum's nonconformance model, discussed later, furthered this approach.

Juran's ten steps for management have come to serve as the basic building blocks for an organization seeking to pursue CQI.

1. Build awareness of the need for improvement.
2. Establish improvement goals.
3. Organize to reach goals.
4. Provide the necessary training.
5. Set and initiate action plans.
6. Communicate progress.
7. Provide formal recognition.
8. Analyze the data.
9. Communicate results.
10. Integrate CQI into corporate culture.

Armand Feigenbaum began his pursuit of quality at General Electric. Through his early work he discovered that employees could become highly motivated if systems and methods were improved through cross-functional teamwork and an open work environment. Some organizational theorists credit him with paving the way for what would eventually become known as *focus groups* and *improvement teams*. One of his major contributions is his idea that the customer defines quality.

As noted above, Feigenbaum is probably best known for his non-conformance cost model, which can calculate the costs associated with poor quality. This model is divided into four parts:

1. *Prevention costs*, which include the costs incurred by failing to do quality planning and failing to adopt measures designed to prevent noncomformance and defects;
2. *Appraisal costs*, or the costs incurred when teams do not evaluate product quality to maintain established standards;
3. *Internal failure costs*, or the costs caused by the use of defective and nonconforming materials or by products that do not meet the company quality specifications; these include scrap, rework, and spoilage;
4. *External failure costs*, or the costs that result when defective and nonconforming products reach the customer; these include complaints and warranty product service costs, costs of product recall, court costs, and liability penalties.[5]

As was Feigenbaum's, Philip Crosby's experience with quality assurance was operationally developed at Martin Marietta and ITT. The author of *Quality Is Free*, Crosby is highly regarded for creating the concept of *zero-defects*. He has argued, It must be cheaper to do things right the first time. He stands nearly alone among quality experts in believing that quality can be achieved relatively easily. In *Business Strategies,* I raise the example of the Boston hotel Le Meridien and its approach to quality customer service. As I pointed out there, once the concept of quality has been integrated into a business's culture, not only is maintaining quality easy, but it can be done at minimal cost. This seems to confirm Crosby's point.

Karu Ishikawa is probably the best known of the Japanese quality gurus. His work in quality circles, though initially not fully understood by American business, has gained widespread recognition lately in the United States. Perhaps the best example was the introduction of quality circles by General Motors when they opened their first Saturn automobile plant. Like Crosby and Deming, Ishikawa believes that top management needs to provide the impetus and serve as the role model for employees to commit themselves to quality. He places the accountability for poor quality squarely at the top. He sets himself apart from his contemporaries by defining the customer as whoever gets the work next. In this way, employees begin to see better their relationship with the next person in the chain of the production process or the service. Ultimately, the last *internal* customer is responsible for handing off the finished work to the external customer, thus completing the chain. It was Ishikawa who introduced the concept of a vision of the company's mission and goal that unifies all people in an organization.

Thus far our discussion has highlighted the contributions of recognized quality gurus. Within the security industry there are many who have taken the QA baton as defined by these noted theorists and practitioners and applied it to their organizations.

These managers have translated the concept of delivering quality assurance through a very specific application of continuous quality improvement. What differentiates them from their security contemporaries is each embraced a strategy referred to as *best practices*, an approach that contributes to the *operationalizing* of QA. Before discussing the individual contributions of these security professionals, let us review what is involved in best practices, how they can be measured, some of the myths about best practices, and some proven tips I've developed over the years.

BEST PRACTICES—AN AVENUE TO QUALITY

Pursuing quality requires making a commitment to doing things in the best possible way. In today's organizational environment we would call this *pursuing best practices*. But what does this mean exactly? To properly understand the context of best practices we need to consider three fundamental realities:

- There is no set criteria for defining best practices within security today.
- Best practices do not necessarily have to be empirically measurable.
- Best practices can be common practices.

On the surface, each of the three considerations appears to fly in the face of the very essence of what best practices should be all about. Yet ironically all three embody the very essence of best practices for a security manager. Let's examine each briefly.

First, security is a noncodified profession. Unlike corporate safety with its guidelines as set forth by underwriters and regulators, the security industry has not subscribed to a set of standards. Consequently security professionals are pretty much driven by the codes of other professional business counterparts, and an occasional state requirement, underwriter prescription, or court decision.

Even though there may be no prescribed, empirical criteria for measuring the attainment of best practices, decision makers can determine if they are pursuing the right (that is, best) activities in a certain context—namely (a) such practices directly contribute to the organization's bottom line; (b) they are recognized for their added value; and (c) they demonstrate a maximization of both efficiency and effectiveness. To be effective, best practices do not necessarily have to have a totally empirical base. As we have seen in our discussion of the quality gurus, there are hidden aspects that contribute to the process of best practices. Achieving a level of customer satisfaction, for example, does not necessarily translate, in all cases, into neat and definable terms. For my own consulting company we let customers define their own level of satisfaction. If they are satisfied, as *they* define satisfaction, we have met a basic condition of our consulting agreement, and therefore we know that we've achieved a level of quality service. If we were to ask customers to put a quantitative value on the level of their satisfaction with our services, they might be hard-pressed to do so.

It is also important to note that best practices can involve the pursuit of commonly established practices. For example, having employees properly display a photo identification badge has become common for most organizations. Enforcement of this practice through a system of incentives and disincentives is a best practice because statistical evidence shows that this practice contributes to loss prevention and, therefore, reduces operating expenses. As a second example, detaining individuals based on the premise that reasonable grounds exist to warrant such detention is a best practice. Because of the legal implications associated with false detainments, requiring "reasonable grounds" is both a legal prerequisite and a common practice.

Given each of these considerations, when do you know that you are engaging in best practices? To answer this question, you need to address each of the following questions about your business practices:

Are You Getting the Job Done?

If your responsibilities include criminal investigations, one criteria for determining whether you are engaging in best practices is whether you are able to complete such investigations in a timely manner and at a reasonable cost. As we all know, there are no prescribed time limits and no set dollar amounts associated with one type of investigation versus another. On the other hand, there is a point at which we would all agree that the amount of resources spent on a criminal investigation has exceeded the bounds of reasonableness, in terms of both time and money. Likewise, too little time and too little money spent is a strong indicator that you may achieve a less than desirable outcome. The same can be said for any other security responsibility, for example, patrol operations, alarm monitoring, executive protection, workplace violence response, and so forth.

To get the job done using best practices the security decision maker needs to frame the individual security function within the context of each of the following strategies:

Challenging Basic Assumptions

Are the common assumptions associated with staffing levels and deployment, allocation of security systems and devices, and operating practices relevant in today's organizational culture? Or are there other opportunities available to be pursued that will yield the same result at a lower cost while actually maintaining or increasing the quality of the service delivered? As an example, with respect to criminal investigations, is it better to create a prosecutorial threshold (that is, no loss under an established value will be criminally pursued) rather than using civil litigation as a means of seeking appropriate remedies for all losses? By establishing such thresholds, both the manner in which investigations are pursued and the allocation of resources could vary significantly. Only those incidents involving a loss equivalent to a significant monetary value would be pursued from a criminal perspective, and those investigations would require an adherence to a higher standard of investigational pursuit. It is important to note that the best practice here is the establishment of a value threshold. The actual value you establish will vary depending on the type of organization and value of the assets.

Allocating Staff Resources

To "get the job done" how many staff people do you require? This is much different from the traditional approach of seeking authorized levels based on "the great what-if." Security executives, like many of their counterparts in other service-related industries, have traditionally defined levels above what is actually required. They want "the coverage." Usually they justify this judgment by pointing to their ability to provide a more rapid response or by giving the assurance that selected posts will not be left open. Unfortunately, neither of these "justifications" fall within the definition of services as "required."

Employing best practices means analyzing what it takes to meet the routine assigned tasks and then creatively identifying strategies to accomplish the nonroutine incidences. To address the issue of rapid response, you may need to develop a mutual response program with neighboring facilities or organizations, similar to what is done in the public sector.

American Commercial Security Services, a subsidiary of ABM Industries, employs a program of "overstaffing" to assure that posts are not left open and that advanced training is accomplished. This system entails scheduling one or more officers on-duty over what is actually required. If the officers are used by the client as a result of unplanned calls or an emergency, the client pays. If the officers are not used, the client does not pay, and ACSS absorbs the cost as part of its investment in officer training. In this way the client's needs are covered, and ACSS is diligent in its scheduling since it bears the cost burden.

Using Appropriate Technology

Accomplishing most assigned security tasks requires the use of some technology. Against the backdrop of today's continuum of available security devices, it is easy to fall into the trap of believing that the more sophisticated and electronic the security device is, the better it is. Best practices speaks to addressing the problem at hand with the technological resource commensurate with resolving the need. If a simple mechanical lock and key can suffice to prevent unauthorized access into an area, as opposed to an electronic card-access system, then the use of the lock and key should be pursued. Though locks and keys may not be as "sexy" as access cards and electronic readers, there are applications where locks and keys are more cost-effective and, therefore, demonstrate a commitment to quality assurance and best practices.

Conversely, attempting to address a security issue using outmoded technology when state-of-the-art devices are available is equally inappropriate. An example would be the use of radio frequency controlled closed-circuit television surveillance systems as opposed to hardwired configurations in selected applications. The wireless devices may be more expensive initially, but the cost of installing the wiring (that is, across parking lots, in marina locations, and so forth) for the other configuration may be more.

Challenging Basic Operating Practices

To get the job done using best practices also requires that the decision maker (e.g., generally the manager) challenge basic operating practices, especially when the common response from employees is "We've always done it this way." The best of a best practices approach recognizes that employing security's operating procedures is often the most effective and least costly way of accomplishing the security mission. By shifting the responsibility for good security practices to end users, the security management team is able to redirect limited resources to other areas requiring specific attention. Meanwhile, business unit managers and nonsecurity employees can not only be held accountable for the security and safety of those assets charged to them, but also share in the knowledge that they have promoted the well-being of their colleagues.

Is the Service Being Delivered Effectively?

Best practices demand that the results be achievable. The Royal Canadian Mounted Police (RCMP), have long adhered to the motto We always get our man. Perhaps the best example of the RCMP's single-mindedness was underscored at a workshop I recently attended where the guest speaker was one of their senior officials. When he concluded his remarks by saying, "And remember, we always get our man," one cynical member of the audience chided him by saying, "Yes, but you never tell us how long it will take." The RCMP commander was quick with his own retort, "As you know, time is relative. It's the end result that counts."

Best practices embody the concept of accomplishing what it is that we are setting out to do. As a part of measuring our effectiveness, security managers need to be in tune with the expectations of senior management and the overall corporate culture. Determining what their perception of effectiveness is and how this translates into security's service delivery is critical. Not only must the end result be clearly defined by security best practices but it must also be perceived by senior management as being in accordance with cultural values. All too often the result is accomplished, but the methodology or personalities involved have alienated enough key players so as to render the actual results less obvious.

Not long ago a security director for a large Southwest bank was asked to resign or face termination. He had alienated most of senior management with his gruff personality and obstructionist attitude. His boss saw him as a liability. Before he was asked to resign, I was asked to evaluate him. I found that his ideas were good, and his concern for the company was very high. To listen to him outside the corporate environment, you couldn't help but be impressed by how much he cared. Over the years, however, his disdain for many of the executives working at the bank had worn him down. He was no longer organizationally effective despite the fact that his department's losses were among the lowest in the area.

Best practices means looking for new ways to be effective. Using this strategy you assume nothing is so sacred that it cannot be improved upon—even if it means taking radical action. I have often cited the 180-degree rule as being one of the most effective tools for management decision making. Simply, the rule is, To maximize effectiveness, consider approaching the problem from exactly the opposite direction. Often we find that by simply altering our perception and looking at the problem from completely the opposite direction, an answer arrives—oftentimes the answer is better than what we might otherwise have come up with through conventional means.

For instance, there is the case of the company faced with renewing the labor contract of its security force. Over time, most of the officers had become complacent and developed actual disdain for many of the company's employees. The security workers' compensation was well above what was competitive in the marketplace, their union officials were under investigation for stealing dues, and several officers had recently been charged with sexual harassment of nonsecurity employees. The company was at a loss because it was afraid of facing a hard negotiating session and a strike. The answer to this dilemma: don't renew the contract and bring in another unionized external provider. The results of this course of action were immediate: lower costs, higher service, transferred risk, and more management flexibility. The company employees were thrilled, and the better officers were retained and incorporated into the new workforce.

Is the Service Being Delivered Efficiently?

Efficiency is often synonymous with cost. Whether such cost is measured in terms of time, dollars, or both, the bottom line is that dollars are spent to achieve results. Efficiency naturally translates into bottom-line performance. Best practices assumes that deciding to do something well means aiming at achieving the best value for the "best" total dollars spent. Further, by its own definition, *efficiency* means "the best way of doing something in the best utilization of time." As we have seen, time can be measured in economic terms (Feigenbaum and Ishakawa). There is a cost associated with identifying needs and expectations, defining appropriate responses, implementing programs, and measuring results. All of these require staff time, which means someone's labor expense.

Another quality guru, Genichi Taguchi, developed an excellent statistical model to illustrate how improper use of time can be measured in terms of actual loss to an organization. Known as the Taguchi Loss Function, it is a formula to determine the cost of a lack of quality. His principle states that for each deviation there is an incremental economic loss. The cumulative impact can be exponential if a number of areas are off by just a little.

Taguchi's concept has direct application to the management of a company. Consider the interrelationships and interdependence among support units, including security and other revenue-generating units. Each sector has its own procedures, which are necessary to achieve its goals. For each department to perform optimally, all work from the other departments must flow smoothly and in accordance with some defined schedule. This way the integrity of the whole is maintained. Following Taguchi's thinking, if any one system or schedule is slightly off, there may be little impact per individual event, but over the entire organization, the cumulative toll will be far greater. If each department missed a deadline by a day or two, the consequences for the end customer in the chain would be pronounced.

Achieving efficiency requires front-end coordination to gain a full understanding of goals and follow-through to delegate responsibilities. Benchmarking and identifying contingency plans are just a few routes that Taguchi recommends for determining how the batons should be passed. Cross-functional teams and on-line systems coupled with regular face-to-face communication among all the parties involved are also critical.[6]

Let's take a moment to summarize where we have been.

Earlier I described empowerment as another arrow in a manager's organizational quiver. The pursuit of best practices can be considered another such arrow. But what exactly is meant by the term best practices? Management books are quick to define the concept as those best-in-class practices that contribute directly to a company's bottom-line performance.

Because of the uniqueness of each organization, and the absence of a defined formula or process, there is no fixed checklist to follow to become a practitioner of best practices. Nonetheless, there are certain conditions nearly universally present among best practice practitioners that guide them—conditions that lead to enhanced profitability, increased productivity, heightened employee morale, and the delivery of better goods and services. These four conditions underscore an organization's commitment to positioning itself as a world-class organization.

Insider Tips for Pursuing Best Practices

Do One Thing Well

One of the myths about pursuing best practices is that to be a world-class organization all your departmental activities must be carried out from a best practices perspective. Best practices is an evolutionary pursuit. It begins with concentrating on one particular activity and doing it very well, focusing on the four conditions we've described previously. As you develop a best practices proficiency in any one area, the lessons learned can then be carried over to other areas. In time, if you pursue best practices diligently, several, if not all, aspects of your security program will be classified as best practices.

Leverage the Good, the Bad, and the Ugly

While there are many ways to measure the activities in your organization, it is not uncommon to describe tasks as those being done well (the good), those that were initially good but for any number of reasons have failed (the bad); and those that seem to "get the job done," but you're mystified about how it is accomplished (the ugly). Regardless of a particular outcome, there are lessons to be learned. The astute manager maintains the broad-based perspective and seeks to find the opportunities in each situation.

Develop and Maintain Employee Loyalty

In addition to empowering people, there are other techniques you can use to build employee loyalty, particularly when third-party providers are involved.

1. Develop a "we will" package. Items to be included might be a packet for newcomers including coupons for discounts offered by the company, a WELCOME ONBOARD card signed by other employees, a company T-shirt, a certificate suitable for framing or a plaque for posting, promoting the idea of the employee belonging to the company family, and so forth.
2. Recognize a security officer and his or her contribution with a gift certificate for $50 at Christmastime either to the nearest toy store to be spent on the officer's children or to a nearby department store.
3. Give a gift certificate for two to the security officer to a local medium-priced restaurant. Include an extra $15 to $20 for babysitting money for those officers with children to assure that they will be able to take advantage of the gift certificate.
4. Allow employees to leverage on your volume discounts for the laundering and dry cleaning of their uniforms by offering them discounted fees for the care of items in their personal wardrobes.
5. Extend employee award programs to staff members normally not eligible, such as administrative staff and security branch offices, as a way of recognizing their support and contribution to the security program.
6. Pay officers for as many as two hours per month for helping in community school activities or other charitable work programs.
7. Create employee support groups, such as parents with teenagers, dealing with aging, and so forth.
8. If security vehicles are used, stencil the name of the security officer of the year on the side of his or her vehicle.

These are all small examples of affordable options, yet they demonstrate to employees that management is willing to make an investment in them. Such gestures allow employees, proprietary or contract, to develop a measure of loyalty because they get a feeling of both acceptance and respect for the contribution they are making.

Quality Should Be Cultural—Not Supplanted

Quality, and therefore the pursuit of best practices, is not something that can be forced on an organization. It is something that is embraced naturally by both management and line staff. For them quality is a matter of identity and not just the latest management fad.

"We've Always Done It That Way" Is Changed to "We've Never Done That Before"

The pursuit of best practices is a journey involving the pursuit of alternative ways of doing things. In the process you challenge traditional methods, not for the sake of eliminating them, but in an effort to seek other ways that are better suited for the current climate. In my previous text, *Business Strategies for Success*, I made the point that the attitude "We've always done it this way" is an organizational cancer that needs to be surgically removed, because it is indicative of complacency, a major obstacle to pursuing best practices.

Challenge Every Existing Assumption— Don't Necessarily Change, But Challenge

As we discussed above, challenge does not necessarily equal change. Challenging the status quo simply shows a *willingness* to break away from the temptation to protect sacred cows or territorial boundaries that can get in the way of pursuing efficiency and effectiveness. As a young boy, my father once shared with me the saying "Never tear down a fence until you know why it was put up in the first place."

Define Your Operation as World-Class

Behaviorists have long taught us that you can only achieve that level to which you aspire. By defining yourself as a world-class organization you force new perspectives and a willingness to ask yourself questions such as How would a world-class organization respond? Would a world-class organization pursue this? If we do not pursue it this way, are we running the risk of losing our status as a world-class service organization? Only when you begin to define yourself as a world-class organization can you start to act like one.

Best Practices Are Top, Down-driven, and Supported from the Bottom Up

The achievement of best practices requires a commitment from senior management. Without their sign-off there will be an absence of budgetary support and a lack of leadership by example. Yet, the actual implementation of best strategies is the functional responsibility of those at the bottom of the organization. Without their willingness to implement and actively participate in such practices, best practices remain only a concept. In short, success can only be achieved when there is a convergence of involvement from both the top and the bottom levels of the organization.

Security Is Not a Commodity

Chapter 5 is dedicated to the topic of the commodification of security. For our purposes here, however, the security program is defined as a value-added contribution to the organization's well-being, because the business of protecting both assets and people is critical to the very survival and success of the organization as a whole. Just as we would not think of the function of marketing or personnel management as a product that can be contracted out to the lowest bidder, the same needs to be understood about the function of security. Unfortunately, many proprietary security directors and third-party providers seem unable to break away from defining their services as if they were commodities. The best illustration is in the procurement process, in which the overwhelming majority of agreements are reached following a process of identifying the provider who will provide the service for the lowest price. The very notion of competitive bidding suggests a lock on what I refer to as the *commodity syndrome*.

Best Practices by Its Nature Require Constant Change

Organizations are dynamic. The same can be said for the environments in which they operate and serve. It is only reasonable to expect, therefore, that the way in which security conducts its business needs to be characterized in fluid terms. Organizations that remain static discover that it doesn't take long before they are behind the curve and are at risk of losing more than they gain. The very nature of best practices connotes a desire to continuously evaluate your practices through established feedback mechanisms and to adapt accordingly. Best practices require the perception "We're in it for the long haul." Those who pursue best practices understand that it takes time not only to effect change, but also for change to have a measurable impact on the rest of the company. To be world-class requires an investment of both time and resources. Just as it requires more time to build a custom home or assemble an automobile by hand, the same can be said for pursuing strategies that are designed to assure that end users receive the best in quality service.

Don't Let Lawyers, Human Resources Pros, and Procurement Specialists Lead—Let Them Guide but Never Lead

Best-in-class practitioners understand the role of resource specialists and will draw upon them much as they would any other management tool in the decision-making process. The function of legal counsel is to avoid risks. Human resources professionals and specialists are there to serve as guides to assure compliance with corporate policies and regulatory agencies. These organizational functions are inherently risk averse, seeking strategies to limit liability and operate within fairly well defined limits. The best-in-class practitioner views each of these resources much as the head coach of a football team looks upon his assistant coaches for help in establishing a winning game plan. Regardless of their input, though, it is still the head coach who makes the final decision and is responsible for leading his team to victory.

Benchmarking Is a Staple of Best Practices

Continuously seeking ways to improve yourself and the way in which your company delivers services requires developing a network of comparators. This network is analogous to an underwater spring that constantly brings forth a flow of fresh water. Benchmarking, whether it's done with other in-house user groups, relies primarily on outside comparisons, or falls back on a combination of both, serves as a barometer for determining what works best under comparable circumstances. Just as we saw that you can gain mutual benefit through the process of empowerment, so, too, we see that you can achieve a similar gain through seeking out the experiences of others and discovering what works best for them.

Best Practices Requires a Continuous Loop

The pursuit of best practices is not done in a vacuum. It requires a four-step process that is configured as a continuous loop. It begins with the identification of the end user's needs and expectations—oftentimes referred to by management theorists as the research phase. This step is followed by an articulation of strategies designed to meet the stated needs and expectations, strategies involving some trial and error, data collection, the development of programs using comparator data, or the pursuit of bold initiatives generated from staff ideas.

The third phase of the process consists of soliciting and receiving feedback from end users/internal customers. Even though a security executive may believe that best practices are being achieved, the real measure of security's efforts is not taken until customer feedback has been received and evaluated. The final phase of the process involves the development of changes or modifications in the best practices strategies generated from the internal customer feedback received.

Once the process has been developed, it is incumbent upon the security manager to begin all over again by identifying expectations and needs to assure that the changes and modifications as reflected in phase 4 are still relevant and in sync with the research gathered in phase 1. This four-phased process is a continuous loop designed to enhance the security manager's commitment to best practices.

Despite All Else, Cost Is a Primary Driver

It is easy to get caught up in the process of bold thinking. Exploring new ideas is invigorating and exciting. The reality, however, is that putting new ideas into action must be done against the backdrop of cost-effectiveness. In a world of highly competitive markets, it is paramount that today's security managers keep a sharp eye on the bottom-line contribution. If bold thinking and new ideas cannot be framed within the context of profitable performance, then senior management, despite their enthusiasm and initial support, will reluctantly withdraw support in deference to the pressures of cost containment.

There Is Nothing in Security That Is Not Measurable

When pursuing best-in-class practices, assume that any support function can break its contributing parts down to activities that are measurable. The same holds true for corporate security. Although many security managers attempt to take solace in the mistaken belief that there is more art to security management than science, in reality, there is nothing within the operational management of asset protection that cannot be measured in one way or another.

From guard operations to sensitive investigations, you can develop measurable performance objectives as a means of demonstrating added value to the company's mainstream business plan. For example, guard tours and deployment schemes can be measured based on response time and the outcomes of specific guard operations. Similarly, investigations, regardless of their level of sensitivity, can be measured in terms of the cost associated with work that is done from the time the case is opened to when it is closed, the identification of potential and real risk exposures, recoveries as measured in terms of asset value, and referrals to either criminal prosecutors or the human relations department for personnel action.

Awareness Is Only the First Half; Ownership Is the Second Half

The pursuit of best practices recognizes the two-sided nature of asset protection. Even though a given person may be aware of security risks, that doesn't mean that he or she accepts the responsibility to act in a manner that takes into consideration such awareness. Take for example the individual who is fully aware of the fact that he lives in a high-crime neighborhood but refuses to lock his front door when he goes to work. When asked if it's reasonable to expect that upon his return he will find his house burglarized, he will say yes. In other words, it isn't until he merges his awareness of the burglary potential with the willingness to lock his door that he will accept the responsibility of protecting his assets.

Best Practices Recognizes Expectations as Realities

It is easy for the disenfranchised security manager to disregard an end user's expectations as existing in the end user's mind and not necessarily being a reflection of reality, such expectations are *in fact* realities from the end user's perspective. Best practices acknowledge that there is very little difference between what the end user expects and the reality of the situation for him or her. In short, there is nothing wrong with attempting to meet the expectations of the end user, provided that such expectations are within the capacity of security to deliver. If such expectations are totally unrealistic, best practices demand that the security manager clearly articulate why they are beyond the current scope of capability and what is required to achieve a more realistic perspective.

Here's a quick example to illustrate the point. Department heads are quick to challenge security managers when an unauthorized person is found walking through a restricted area without an escort or a valid reason to be there. Nonsecurity managers assume that as long as security is responsible for access control, it is security's responsibility to see that an unauthorized person will not be allowed to leave a public area such as the main lobby and enter into restricted work area. While the nonsecurity manager's perception is that security is responsible for access control, the reality may be that there are competing elements operating within the lobby that make it impossible for the security officer to control access into restricted areas 100 percent of the time. Such demands on the officer's attention can range from responding to radio transmissions to answering telephones to registering visitors or regular employees who have forgotten or lost their access control cards. Given these competing demands, it is not unreasonable to expect that unauthorized persons will at times slip by the security officer unnoticed and enter into a restricted area.

When such a breach occurs, instead of becoming defensive and trying to protect the officer on duty, security managers who are interested in pursuing best practices need to seize this as an opportunity to explain such limitations and solicit support either to change the lobby officer's duties or to create other ingress procedures that will be effective in limiting access to authorized personnel only.

Just as Cost Is a Driver, So Too Is Empowerment

In our previous discussions, we have had a great deal to say about the strengths inherent in the process of empowerment. For our purposes here, we need only add that employee empowerment makes an essential contribution to the pursuit of best practices. Employees who are empowered to think critically will bring new ideas to the table that will have a direct impact on the company's bottom line.

Best Practices Require an Ongoing Commitment on the Part of Everyone

Pursuing world-class recognition is clearly not a one-shot deal. To achieve enhanced value, each employee needs to demonstrate an individual commitment to pursuing best practices. The customer services chain is only as strong as its weakest link. Therefore it is essential for both line and management staff to demonstrate an ongoing commitment to the pursuit of excellence. While we should expect bumps in the road or unanticipated potholes, the test of true commitment is our ability to move beyond such obstacles and remain focused on delivering the highest quality of service despite the occurrence of unplanned events.

Best Practices Means Stepping Outside Your Area of Expertise

It is far easier to pursue those things with which we are most comfortable. Over time we become proficient in those things we do every day. Best practices managers look well beyond their own area of expertise to see if there is a way they can transfer their expertise into other areas. Pinkerton typically does not benchmark within the security industry. It looks to other service sectors and seeks those that are recognized as best-in-class. This allows Pinkerton to bring a much wider array of ideas to its operation.

Security Applications in Best Practices

Success is the diploma awarded from the University of Hard Knocks to each person who is committed to the pursuit of best-in-class practices. Thus far we have looked at the underlying principles associated with the concept of best practices and at some insider tips. Following are several quick illustrations of how best practices are being manifested in security programs today.

Competitive Pricing and Brokering

The Global Security Department for one of the country's largest energy firms has begun a process of defining value beyond conventional asset protection. Perhaps more impressively, security has identified its true cost of providing services and is competitively biddings its services against those available in the open market. When it is to the advantage of the business unit to use third-party providers, Global Security serves as the internal broker to assure that best-in-class services are hired.

Electronic and Self-Sealing Money Containers

One of Seattle's major bank's security department initiated a program to bring added value to its major internal customer, retail banking. The program involves the introduction of safety packs, which are self-sealing caches filled with paper currency. Through a process of electronic locking mechanisms under the control of its central console, security is able to coordinate the removal and replenishment of money within ATM machines with the assistance of a third-party armored car carrier service. This arrangement eliminates the need to inconvenience branch personnel during nonbusiness hours or to incur the expense associated with overtime or compensatory time.

Hospital Greeters

In an effort to improve customer service, a few years ago Christ Hospital in Cincinnati initiated a program involving security officers greeting arriving patients at curbside and escorting them to the admitting window. After the hospital completed a patient survey and discovered that the admittance procedure was rated unusually low from a customer service perspective, the security department offered to have its officers provide the dual role of offering coverage at the main entrance and serving as patient greeters; no other aspect of the admitting procedure was changed. A later survey demonstrated that customer service perceptions improved by more than 67 percent in the ensuing six months.

Leverage Security as a Marketing Tool

Heitman Retail Properties' management is committed to positioning their security operation as making a positive contribution to the marketing of their retail malls. They have created a national security steering committee composed of representatives from their security providers. The committee regularly meets with Heitman's senior management, including the president and marketing director, to discuss ways to incorporate security into the marketing and business plan for each mall.

Some of the committee's suggestions have included integrating the promotion of security services into television and radio commercials for the mall (a panoramic video shot of the mall with a passing patrol vehicle or a man on the street type of interview incorporating the comments of the security officer) creates a positive image while subtly suggesting to the consuming public that security is present on the premises; or leveraging CCTV monitors to include advertisements from local merchants and suppliers—a way to generate revenue given the money sunk into such security devices. Not only are such marketing approaches ways to generate revenue as an offset to security's operating cost; they also put a positive spin on the business of asset protection.

Combining Security with Medical Emergency Response

Mary Kay's security department was looking for a positive way to define their department's added value. By creating a program for certifying officers as both security specialists and emergency medical response personnel, security has begun to change the perception of employees and external customers about security, helping them see security in customer service related terms.

As part of the planned outcome, individual officers not only enhance their own professionalism but also participate in a career development program. This increased training of security employees translates directly to increased compensation and leads to new opportunities within the company. The program's strength is that security is defined within a broader service context, and security is seen as providing personalized services to its customers. Because security personnel are seen as resources, employees seek them out for other needs.

OTHER TECHNIQUES FOR THRIVING

Jim Harris has written a book for the American Management Association entitled *Getting Employees to Fall in Love with Your Company*. He steps through, in a no-nonsense way, a process for managers to access organizational needs, particularly those of their employees. After reading his book, I was struck with the similarity of applications that a manager could employ to enhance employee loyalty and those techniques that can help a manager to thrive in these turbulent times. In his book he provides thirty-five examples of how companies have demonstrated their best practices approach when dealing with employee needs.[7] Reflecting on them, here's a sampling of his ideas, intermingled with my own.

Going the Extra Mile

In an earlier discussion I cited the advantages associated with having employees be a part of the collaborative management decision-making process. The Ritz Carlton Hotels have probably taken this notion the furthest in their pursuit of the Malcolm Baldrige Award for quality customer service. They have empowered each employee (including the housekeeping staff) with the ability to authorize payment up to $2,000 on the spot to resolve any customer complaint.

Let me share with you a brief experience I recently had at the Ritz Carlton in Chicago. After checking into the hotel, the desk clerk walked around the front desk and escorted me across the main lobby to the elevators. As we made our way across the main lobby, she pointed out many of the hotel's features, including the dining facilities and health club. While we waited for my elevator to arrive, she extended her hand, welcoming me to the hotel, and wished me well during my stay. After thanking me, she went on to tell me that when I exited the elevator on my floor, I was to turn right and proceed down approximately seven rooms before I would come to the one assigned to me. This attention to detail and the extending of the role beyond that of the traditional desk clerk to hostess not only impressed me but reinforced the impression that I was a guest at a world-class hotel whose staff was intent on providing the highest quality of customer service. The enhanced interaction of the Ritz Carlton desk clerk with customers has some powerful lessons for the security manager intent on demonstrating added value.

The Three- or Four-Word Motto

The Disney Corporation has created a motto that each of its 36,000 cast members (employees) recite when asked: "We create happiness by providing the finest entertainment to people of all ages, everywhere." As Jim Harris points out, even if audience members only remember the first three words, "We create happiness," the message is clear. Creating a simple three-word motto that all of your employees can remember and probably recite is an excellent technique. Some examples for security might include "We secure assets," or "We protect people," or "We make people safer," or "We prevent crimes," or even "We help people." Each of these three- to four-word slogans succinctly and clearly tells everyone the primary purpose of corporate security.

Employee and Business Enhancement Programs

To demonstrate your added value as a contributor to the company's overall concern for employee performance and your ability to think beyond the limits of asset protection, propose to your senior management for their consideration any one of the following employee recognition and employee enrichment ideas:

1. A charity day one day a year when employees volunteer to work for free (on one of their days off). The proceeds of their day's pay are dedicated to a charity of their choice.
2. Leverage on the distribution of payroll checks to employees by enclosing promotional items granting employees discounted prices on the company's products.
3. Negotiate discounted prices with local handymen, electricians, plumbers, and so forth, for company employees. In today's two-income families, it is difficult for employees to identify qualified repair personnel for routine home maintenance needs. Knowing that their employer has already created a vetted list of qualified contractors, employees are more likely to turn to these people in addition to appreciating management's gesture.
4. Likewise, depending on the size of the organization, senior managers, through their procurement process, could negotiate volume discounts with local merchants such as snow and water ski rental companies, bicycle companies, camping suppliers, and so forth.
5. Leverage your professional network. Whether you are a proprietary security manager or a contract provider, think of the added value that inures to you if you are able to arrange a reciprocal agreement with other security directors for your employees or clients to take advantage of the other company's services or products at a discounted rate. For example, you might know the security director of the local museum. What a wonderful idea it would be if your employees or clients could take in a local museum show at a discounted rate by virtue of their association with you and your connections with the security director of the museum. Similar discounted rates might apply for high-tech companies, entertainment centers, and even supermarket chains.

6. Create a charity fine program. Getting employees to wear photo identification badges can be both difficult and frustrating. One way to encourage full participation is to assess a "charity's fine" for non-compliers. Anytime an employee is found not wearing his or her photo identification badge, the violating employee would be assessed a $1 fine, or more, the proceeds of which would be donated to a local charity at the end of the year.

7. Review the top twenty-five versus the bottom twenty-five. For a number of years now Wal-Mart Stores have assembled the top twenty-five performing stores within a district along with the bottom twenty-five stores every Saturday. As a company they celebrate the performance of the top companies and work on ways in which they can improve the performance of the bottom twenty-five. For contract providers, there is a significant lesson in quality assurance and customer service to be learned here. Those units that are not meeting performance expectations are able to learn both successful techniques and obstacles associated with bottom-line profitability and performance.

8. Create forgiveness notes. As Jim Harris points out, great organizations understand that the freedom to fail and try again applies to both operations and customer service. Success is built on failures. As a consequence, some companies such as Alabama's natural gas distributor Alagasco have distributed to all of their employees GET OUT OF JAIL FREE cards. When an employee makes a mistake in his or her attempt to deliver outstanding service, he or she goes to a corporate executive, discusses what he or she has learned from the experience, turns in the GET OUT OF JAIL FREE card, and is forgiven. This simple initiative has spurred a tremendous turnaround in the quality of service delivery to Alagasco customers. Think what could happen in your department if your employees realized that they had an opportunity to make an honest mistake without punishment.

9. Nordstrom's golden rule. The Nordstrom Department Store company has developed one performance rule: Use your good judgment in all situations. Almost as an afterthought, they have attached a rider to this rule: "There will be no additional rules." In other words, employees are expected to always use good judgment, and as a result there is little reason to develop the typical three-inch binder of additional rules and regulations.

10. Got an idea? Give it away. One of the principles behind thriving is continuously pushing yourself to do something different. By encouraging your suppliers or employees to give away their best

ideas, this forces them to push the envelope to try out new ideas. In other words, you cannot become complacent, since eventually you will become but one in a sea of penguins. By giving ideas away, you make room for bold thinking, thereby creating an opportunity to thrive in unsettling times.

11. Sometimes career development means moving on. As organizations trim down, more and more demands are being placed on the surviving staff. Companies need to be able to expand beyond the limits for which employees were originally hired. For some, the transition will be made regardless of whether it is easy or difficult. Unfortunately for others, the transition will never be made. Consequently, a thriving-oriented manager owes it to those struggling employees to suggest that their professional development may be better enhanced by moving on to another organization.

12. Create a professional library for others. Security services provider Arko Executive Services in Atlanta, Georgia, has developed an extensive library, which they make available to their clients and local college students. It is an excellent way for Arko to demonstrate added value to its clients and a concern for the surrounding community.

13. Ask "Why not?" One of my closest friends, Dave Armstrong, is an executive for one of the country's largest radio station networks. Although he did not understand the technical aspects of the Internet, he had a vision of being the first radio station to offer worldwide live broadcasting of his radio station on the Internet. As he began to explore the possibilities, he was continuously confronted by specialists saying, "Well, we can't do it that way." Dave responded by continuously asking the question "Why not?" As he continued to press the point, the specialists eventually began to relent and asks themselves the "Why not?" question. It didn't take long after this mental breakthrough for them to realize that what Dave wanted was achievable. Within a period of months Dave had established his radio station as the world's first live-broadcast station on the Internet. The lesson for security managers is that gains can be made by continuously challenging traditional approaches and asking the great "Why not?"

14. The brain problem syndrome. As noted earlier, thriving means having the ability to translate past mistakes into learning opportunities. I recently had an opportunity to work with a security director in the development of a new program for his company. As a contract provider, he had managed to bridge the perception of being an outside provider and was seen, for all practical purposes, as a member of his client's management team.

In the process of implementing the operation of a closed-circuit television monitoring function, we discovered that a number of his officers were unfamiliar with the equipment. Initially I was surprised because the officers involved were veteran employees with an average tenure in excess of five years. When confronted with this situation, the security manager said that he would look into the matter and report back to me shortly. Later that afternoon he sought me out to report that the problem seemed to be rooted in what he termed a "brain problem syndrome."

When I asked him to explain, he stated that he had made the assumption that tenured officers were experienced in the operation of CCTV systems, so he had not included them in the initial training program. This ability to acknowledge basic mistakes and quickly correct them when they were brought to his attention reinforced my perception that he was a thriving-oriented manager; a perception that was also shared by his clients.

15. Create on-line teams. With the explosion of electronic mail and the Internet, staff members located anywhere from a few feet to thousands of miles away can be electronically connected and communicate at rapid speed. The thriving-oriented manager fully understands the power associated with the ability to communicate with his entire staff, irrespective of physical distance. By putting an issue out on the Internet or company E-mail system and soliciting feedback from a variety of staff resources, the manager is able to take advantage of the multiplicity of resources available in the resident staff.

16. Creating reserve resources. As companies experience fluctuation in their labor pools, retaining experienced staff can sometimes be challenging. Consider the value of actively participating in helping employees seek temporary work assignments outside of the organization. The strategy is to position valued employees so that when circumstances change you'll have the opportunity to reintroduce them into the organization. By working out alliance relationships with companies that have high turnover rates, security companies can move their employees between employers to the advantage of everyone. The security department literally cross-trains employees with another profession, thus enabling both employers to take advantage of swings in their business cycles.

These sixteen examples illustrate how security managers, whether proprietary or external, can integrate themselves and their programs into the overall business plan of the organization. They underscore the fact that success is tied directly to an ability to demonstrate an aptitude for thriving as opposed to struggling to survive in uncertain times.

WHEN PURSUING QUALITY MISSES THE MARK

The pursuit of quality initiatives has taken hold in every business sector. Over the past few years many of the security giants have also developed their own programs. Pinkerton was one of the first to develop a true total quality management (TQM) program. Wackenhut, American Protective Services, Stanley Smith, Ogden, and First Security have also proceeded down the path of quality assurance (QA). Others have professed to adhere to "high-quality standards" and aggressively position their marketing efforts around the theme of quality. These companies would fall into the category of "talking the talk." What makes it possible to come to this conclusion? A company is only talking the talk if it has no mechanism in place to promote quality continuously throughout the company. Regardless of how an organization frames its program, it needs to develop the following elements in order to have a true QA program:

- An articulated set of quality values;
- An action plan for accomplishing each quality value;
- A mechanism for soliciting customer expectations and needs;
- A program that actively involves employees at each level in the decision-making and feedback process;
- A program for training all employees, including managers and supervisors, in the principles of best practices and quality customer service tailored to meet the customer's needs and expectations;
- A customer satisfaction program that measures satisfaction and includes a complaint resolution component;
- A timely customer feedback mechanism; and
- A data analysis strategy that provides a springboard for continuous improvement.

These eight components serve as the basic framework. If any one is missing, the program is incomplete. One of the clearest ways to test whether such a program is in place is simply to ask yourself to describe each of the components. If the answers are generally anecdotal, this strongly suggests that your program is either in the initial phase of development or really doesn't have a QA program at all.

Asking security providers about their QA progam is especially important because they may have developed a program that is limited in that it serves only those clients that require a QA program. This means that pursuit of QA is not really an integrated part of their corporate culture; instead the provider may view QA as something that is client specific and therefore a commodity rather than a process for seeking continuous quality improvement. To determine whether a company is committed to QA or not test its ability to demonstrate that values have been identified, action plans developed, feedback received, results measured, and that plans for revision or adjustment are in evidence.

Many high-tech companies have implemented some very elaborate programs. Unfortunately, several have fallen victim to the advice of so-called QA specialists who subscribe to a philosophy that says "If it can't be measured, graded, and forced into some formula, it can't be worth much." Tragically, their approach is fundamentally flawed when it comes to implementing the quality process. This may appear to be a somewhat harsh judgment. Unfortunately for those companies, it is. Their misguided pursuit of quality assurance has caught the attention of many critics, and rightfully so. These companies unknowingly have put themselves into a position that Tom Peters describes as being out of touch with *customer focus*. This is because total quality management programs are more often run by technocrats. It's also interesting to note that those who seem more likely to miss the mark are those who profess an allegiance to the Malcolm Baldrige process.

For those readers unfamiliar with the Malcolm Baldrige process, this is a U.S. Department of Commerce award process for selected companies who subscribe to rigorous criteria in implementing quality improvement. Named after a former commerce secretary, the Baldrige process has become synonymous with excellence in customer service—at least according to one school of thought. The problem for many companies is the misconception as to who is the true customer.

In the two examples that follow—Company 1 and Company 2—the security managers assume that they are the customer. Wrong! Rarely is security the customer. Security is the conduit for delivering a service to customers. For some reason security managers—whether they employ a resident staff or rely on external partners—believe that they are the end user. Their error is further exacerbated when they measure success in terms of turnover, response time, E-mail messages and pages received, and so forth. Although these factors are critical to achieving operational success, they reflect infrastructure issues and not true QA.

As the end users of security, internal customers want to know that their expectations and needs are being met. But are these expectations realistic? If one of the customer expectations is that each security officer will know the name of certain employees, then that becomes a QA measure. If officers don't know certain names, dinging then for not knowing is unfair and unrealistic.

This leads us to another aspect of a misguided QA program—namely, the way in which programs are measured. As we shall see, both of our example companies have implemented grading systems that have been taken right out of the classic high-school grading system. Security personnel receive numeric scores in the first and letter grades (A+ through D) in the second. As a quick aside, it is interesting to note that in the second company a failing grade is not possible (there are no F's). Why not? Are companies and individuals not allowed to fail? This is not a point to take lightly. Part of true QA is the recognition that programs can, and do, fail. When I asked one of the managers why he didn't use F's, he responded, "We think F's send a negative message. We don't want people to see themselves as failures." Let's stop and think about that for a minute. Such a perspective, taken to its logical end, would mean that if a security officer deliberately stood by and watched while a customer/client was brutally attacked and did nothing at all, the officer would not have failed to provide quality customer service. Failure is part of the continuous improvement process and should therefore be built into the QA program. Failing to recognize failure limits the value of the program and undercuts the seriousness of the effort.

Before proceeding it is important to note that our purpose in reviewing these two companies is to learn from their experiences and not to embarrass either. Consequently, we will refer to them generically.

Company 1: A Major Manufacturer

Company 1 has developed what some observers refer to as the alphabet soup of QA. Its program is often called TQRDCE after each of its major components: technology, quality, responsiveness, delivery, cost, and environment. The program is designed for "partnering" with third-party providers. The basic approach is fundamentally sound insofar as the managers talk about partnering and providing a climate that promotes customer focus. Yet, as discussed above, the managers miss the mark by concentrating on the infrastructure of providing security and do not at the same time focus on the deliverables as defined by customer expectations and needs.

Within each of these six major functions of TQRDCE, the supplier is given anywhere from twelve to twenty-one criteria to meet. Each criteria receives a score according to the following system:

4—Consistently exceeds expectations
3—Consistently meets and occasionally exceeds expectations
2—Consistently meets expectations
1—Occasionally meets expectations
0—Consistently does not meet expectations

As we cross the boundary from a score of 2 to 3, value is being added by the supplier.

Thus far the information suggests that the process is designed to identify progress in continuous improvement. But the breakdown in the system occurs in the actual criteria and in the application of numeric scores. Let's look at two criteria drawn from each area and comment accordingly.

Technology

First we'll comment on two criteria drawn from twenty-one technology criteria.

> Supplier uses electronic mail as a tool to communicate internally and with XX on a daily routine.

> Supplier is an expert in all aspects of security, that is, surveillance, violence in the workplace, theft of ideas, burglary, terrorism, vandalism, and so forth, and makes recommendations.

To begin with, E-mail is a valued communication tool. Many would characterize its use within a company as evidence that the company is pursuing best practices. But should the use of E-mail be one of the measures determining whether the company is delivering quality customer service? In Company 1's case, E-mail is widely used, but it is not the exclusive mode of communication. The goal of effective communication has been lost in emphasizing one communication tool over another. The point here is similar to what we have seen in our previous discussion in which we concluded that universal procedures cannot be universally applied.

Regarding being an expert supplier of security, this is an area that is supposed to focus on technology alone. Yet "expert in all aspects of security" sets a performance criterion that is overly broad and open to interpretation. What company could ever meet this tall order? Moreover, the examples—violence in the workplace, theft of ideas, burglary, terrorism, vandalism, and so forth—don't match up to the technology requirement.

Quality

Now let's look at the quality component and two of its nineteen criteria.

> Supplier prioritizes security.

> Supplier management schedules routine meetings with XX's management to address TQRDCE in general.

The first objective makes the provider the party to set the agenda. What happened to the customer? In the second objective both parties have agreed to meet and "address TQRDCE in general." What does this mean? This criterion is so overly broad that we miss out on any specific meaning.

Responsiveness

Here are two among the fourteen criteria of the responsiveness component.

> Supplier response time to emergency situations and extra coverage is predictable.

> Supplier has resolved concerns not addressed explicitly in this matrix.

Response time is a critical component of a security operation. Customer satisfaction is based on successful past performance and an expectation that the good service will continue. Having response time and predictable extra coverage as criteria demonstrates only half of the issue. What about past performance specifically? What lessons have been learned? What mechanisms are in place to assure predictability? None of these issues are addressed. Likewise, how does one resolve concerns that aren't addressed in the matrix? If those concerns haven't been identified, how can we know that they will be addressed?

Delivery

From among twelve criteria in the delivery component, here are two criteria.

> Supplier quality of service will not degrade when customer needs increase.

> Supplier maintains accurate and current post duty descriptions.

The first indicator is weak because it is vague and open to interpretation. The second appears to be out of place. Although it is important to have current post orders, the topic of service delivery generally refers to capability and not to instruction.

Cost of Ownership

The cost of ownership component had seventeen criteria. Here are two of them.

> Supplier is proactive in looking for ways to reduce rework—waste—and changes. (e.g., reworking assigned projects to achieve

the desired result, wasted efforts and resources, and unnecessary changes in programs)

Supplier provides trained personnel with no training cost to client.

The first criteria is excellent. It addresses the broad concern for controlling costs that arise out of misallocating resources. Unfortunately, the second criteria is both unrealistic and unfair to the supplier. Training is a cost of doing business. If this were a proprietary operation, the security director would have a training cost. Why put this burden only on the supplier? Under such an arrangement the supplier will either have to hide the cost of training somewhere else, which works against the very concept of partnering, or will suffer a loss when entering into such an agreement.

Environmental
The environmental component had eighteen criteria. Here are two.

Supplier seeks out and supports programs to reduce, reuse, and recycle.

Supplier has established a working link with all contractors for emergencies.

In this last group, the supplier is expected to participate in the client's environmental program. This is an appropriate objective and should be seen as a measure that helps achieve customer satisfaction. The second indicator, like several of those before, appears to be out of place. Would working links with contractors for emergencies not be better placed under the responsiveness category?

Company 2: A High-Tech Company

Company 2 really doesn't understand the concept of partnering. After awarding the security contract to a supplier, the company scheduled what was billed as a preconversion strategy meeting (the supplier was taking over for another). When the supplier managers arrived, they were prepared to talk about the transition plan and identify the client's specific expectations and needs. As they entered the room, they were greeted by a team of five client representatives, four of whom represented corporate security. The fifth, though not technically a security employee, was indirectly responsible for security.

The meeting started with a formal presentation by the lead in-house security representative who informed the supplier that the purpose of the meeting was to introduce the company's strategic partnership measurement program, and that the next four hours had been set aside to "negotiate" with the supplier regarding seven key measurement areas. Afterward the program would be set.

From the outset it was obvious that the company's security team was composed of inexperienced technocrats who believed that they were enlightened QA specialists. The lead security representative's credential was that his former company had been a Malcolm Baldrige recipient. Yet during the lunch break he laughed at the process, pointing out that most employees abandoned it six months after receiving the award. He concluded, "No one really bought into it. They just went through the motions to get the award." Ironically, the process he was introducing at this meeting was a knockoff of the Baldrige process.

At the meeting's end I couldn't determine who to feel more sorry for: the clients and their total misunderstanding of what partnering and QA are really all about? Or the supplier for agreeing to the conditions? It was clear that such a program would cost the supplier a lot of money to implement, yet the supplier managers had never been warned about it during the selection process and therefore had not priced their services accordingly. The client didn't care. Unfortunately there could be only one outcome given the circumstances. The relationship would end just as did the previous client-supplier relationship—tragically. No one wins in this environment because the client is imposing conditions that should not be imposed. Remember quality emerges; it cannot be implanted.

Compounding their mistake, the client's security representatives also defined themselves as the customer. When the mistake was pointed out to them, the lead representative argued that before internal customers could be served, the security company had to demonstrate to the representatives that its infrastructure was in place and that it had a program designed to make this happen. How foolish. The client was intruding into the operations of the supplier and therefore risking potential claims of co-employment (an arrangement they openly said they wanted to avoid "at all costs"). Further, the selection process must have been flawed since the issue of demonstrated infrastructure support should have been a primary criteria during the initial stages. In other words, demonstrated infrastructure should have been among the factors driving the selection process, and not something to be tested after the contract was awarded.

The seven key measurement areas as outlined by the client company were individual performance, responsiveness, flexibility, technical support, professionalism, training, and turnover. The first three key measurement areas will illustrate how all seven criteria were presented.

Individual Performance

♦ Ten percent of the workforce may receive oral counseling, 5 percent may receive written counseling, and 25 percent of the workforce may receive termination during each measurement period.
♦ Internal quality audits will be determined by sample audits of individual performers relative to their job knowledge and skill assessments. Sample quality assurance testing will be conducted on a weekly basis.

Both indicators were given a scoring range based on percentages that equate to letter grades. For example, if all officers passed the weekly spot audits the company receives a grade of A. If less than 75 percent of the force passes, the company receives a D. Note the underlying negative current in the first indicator. Where is the coaching, the employee input, and the recognition for a job well done? In the second performa, who is going to absorb the cost for weekly testing, let alone provide the administrative support necessary to track the testing?

Responsiveness

♦ Branch management/administrative support personnel response to calls, voice-mail messages, or pages
♦ Branch management/administrative support personnel response to E-mails
♦ Ability to provide information or related material as requested, and attendance/promptness at meetings, training sessions, or other scheduled events

Like the first indicator, success in the realm of responsiveness is measured based on the amount of time it takes to respond to a given situation. Less than two hours translates to an A, anything over four hours is a D. When the supplier pointed out that these times would be fairly easy to accommodate, the lead client representative laughed and said, "Well, I guess you'll get a free A, won't you?" If this is so, why not revise the indicator? Quality assurance is not about "getting free A's."

Flexibility

♦ The ability to staff unplanned posts with quality performers or to modify specific post instructions in a timely manner
♦ The ability to modify duties/responsibilities of an individual post or posts; the ability to grow and develop posts or positions as required

As with the first company, here we see an adherence to operational issues as opposed to internal customer expectations and needs. Staffing qualified people and maintaining current post orders should be considered part of standard operating procedure. If the supplier cannot do this, it shouldn't have been selected. It's as simple as that.

SUMMARY

In this chapter we continued our exploration of what it takes to be successful in today's dynamic security environment. We began with a review of one of this century's pioneers in quality assurance, W. Edwards Deming. Deming's ideas serve as the foundation for many of the practices of corporate executives today. In this review we examined his fourteen-point charter for management and saw how it can be applied to asset protection.

We also examined Deming's seven deadly diseases—those practices that organizations fall into that lead to a loss in market share and profitability. We saw how these diseases can be translated from the company as a whole to individual business units and the relevance of these failings to security. We concluded with a review of four obstacles to effective management that Deming has identified. We concluded this section with an overview of additional ideas offered by other recognized quality gurus such as Juran, Feigenbaum, Crosby, and Ishakawa.

From there we launched into an analysis of one of the most important QA tools—best practices. We found that even though there are no established criteria for defining what is and what is not a best security practice, there are three discernible measures: contribution to bottom-line performance, recognized added value, and demonstrated effectiveness and efficiency. In this discussion we also looked at twenty *insider tips* developed over years of experience and at the lessons learned from those that have pursued best practice activities within their organizations.

Afterward we turned our attention to several security practitioners and saw how they have applied the lessons given by the quality gurus for improving their operations. Drawing from both the corporate security side and the supplier side, we discovered that these security practitioners pursued quality through the initiation of best practices. We concluded our discussion by looking at several examples of how other companies have taken on their own thriving initiatives, with a primary focus on getting employees involved in the process.

We ended the chapter by highlighting what can go wrong when the underlying concepts of QA are missed. We examined two high-tech firms and their approaches to partnering with outside security providers as part of their attempt to achieve continuous quality improvement. We saw what can go wrong when security directors see themselves as the customer as opposed to the conduit for security service, and the effect that this misperception can have on their credibility and ability to survive. Next we turn our attention to matters beyond the pursuit of customer satisfaction.

3

Moving Beyond Customer Satisfaction

Perseverance is a great element of success. If you only knock long enough and loud enough at the gate, you are sure to wake up somebody.

... Henry Wadsworth Longfellow

In continuing our journey toward successful management and the art of quality customer service, we need to step beyond where the misguided technocrats would like to lead us in their pursuit of quality. For us the challenge is to set forth an alternative quality model that is responsive to our true customers. I could lead you directly there, but then we would overlook several critical variables that need to serve as the foundation for a strong and responsive management strategy.

To appreciate the strength of our quality-focused model, we begin by examining what John Guaspari calls the *value force* and its impact on how security decision makers define who their customers really are and what is expected of security.[1] Along the way we will look at strategies for moving beyond customer satisfaction. Initially, this may seem like a rather strange concept—how does one move beyond customer satisfaction? After all, isn't that the ultimate measure of success? No. There is a level beyond customer satisfaction—customer loyalty. For it is by developing a loyal customer that you maximize return on your total investment. We will go into this idea in more detail later in this chapter.

Our journey will also take us through specific strategies that will enable resident security managers and third-party providers to compete with other corporate forces at work. We will examine what I refer to as the *customer-supplier gap* and see how a customer's perception of quality is equal to what the manager delivers relative to what the customer expects. Finally, we will go over a number of strategies designed to deliver excellent service as we make our way toward a pragmatic quality assurance program.

THE VALUE MATRIX

To establish a more meaningful quality assurance model, let us begin by examining a conceptual management tool developed by quality expert John Guaspari. Referring to it as his value matrix, Guaspari gives us the opportunity to see how to illustrate his value force concept (Figure 3–1).

The horizontal axis refers to the degree—high or low—of process mastery within an organization. The vertical axis shows the degree to which the organization has a clear sense of purpose—how in tune is the organization with the marketplace and the expectations and needs of its customers, internal or external?

Guaspari has produced a videotape that leads the observer through the entire concept of value force. It begins with the main character, Al, who is in frantic need of a quarter to feed a parking meter. Concerned that he is going to be late for an important appointment, he spots a man

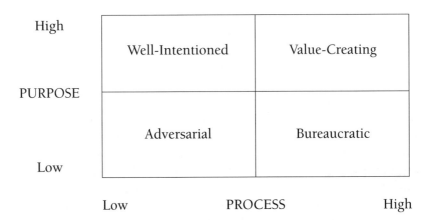

Figure 3–1 Guaspari's value matrix

nearby wearing a sign that reads A QUARTER FOR A DOLLAR. Al gladly exchanges the dollar for the quarter, feeds the meter, and is off to his meeting feeling very happy.

On the surface, one would be quick to assume that Al was taken advantage of by the sign-bearing individual. On the other hand, if we look at Al's transaction from what Guaspari calls the got/cost = value equation, Al actually received quite a bargain. In other words, if one considers that Al was able to get what he needed for the nominal cost of a dollar, he actually made out quite well. Why? Consider his alternatives. He may have run the risk of not feeding the meter and receiving a $15 parking ticket, paying at least $10 to park in a garage, or spending the time it would have taken to find another parking spot, and surely he would have been late for his appointment.

Guaspari's formula for value sets the groundwork for each of the subsets within the value matrix. Beginning in the lower left-hand corner, Guaspari identifies the adversarial organization (low purpose, low process). This is an organization that is so inner directed that it is totally out of touch with customer expectations and needs. Over the past several years many municipal law enforcement agencies have been criticized for falling into this category, as the pendulum has swung way over to the "we" side of the we-them continuum. One of the most notable examples of this phenomenon is the criticism received by the Los Angeles Police Department for their loss of police-community relations, despite their efforts in community policing.

Continuing along the horizontal axis, the next type of organization is the bureaucratic organization. There was a time when I would have cynically referred to this type of organization as reflecting the DMV, or Department of Motor Vehicles, syndrome. Many states have attempted to lessen the bureaucracy of their DMV offices and make them more customer oriented, yet they still suffer from a long-standing reputation of being overly bureaucratic and uncaring.

The third type of organization in the value matrix is what Guaspari refers to as the well-intentioned organization. You might recall that at the outset of this book I referred to the bad experience my wife and I had with America Online. Clearly America Online is a well-intentioned company, but it has grown so fast that it is unable to keep up with customer demand. The company has created layer upon layer of well-intentioned departments that are unable to resolve simple accounting problems. Customer service has even created its own Escalation Department, whose sole purpose is to attempt to resolve problems that should have been solved at the level of the customer service representative.

Finally, the value matrix includes those organizations that have mastered both high process and high purpose. These are the value-creating organizations. Examples could include any one of the best practices companies we reviewed in the previous chapter.

The value force helps security managers and suppliers understand that to achieve and maintain customer satisfaction they need to demonstrate a sensitivity to defining what customers want and need. It also assists them in developing those processes that will enable them to deliver the appropriate level of service. To achieve this dual capability, security decision makers need to begin by knowing exactly who their customers are.

DEFINING YOUR CUSTOMERS

As Allen Meisel, vice president for Consumer Advocacy at Pfizer, Inc., points out, "It may sound trivial, but it's not. Most of us have focused on maybe one customer segment, but there are a lot of different customer segments. In the pharmaceutical industry, the physician is not the one who is in control anymore. Increasingly there are hospitals, managerial organizations, employers and insurance companies that are getting into the process of deciding what medications patients can take."[2] What Meisel is underscoring is the fact that there are many customers beyond those assumed as primary. With respect to the security industry, I'm reminded of the president of a large security services company who lamented the loss of a major client. When asked how this had occurred, he confessed that the true decision maker (the customer) had changed, and his company was not astute enough to realize soon enough that the change had occurred. In an effort to justify his loss, he went on to point out that working on customer relations is like walking a tightrope. Even the slightest misstep can cause you to lose your balance and meet with a disastrous end since most service contracts do not have a safety net.

I would challenge this rationalization. Business managers should be constantly ahead of the marketplace and able to detect the shifting winds of change far enough in advance to be able to make the appropriate adjustments. An inability to do so is evidence that the manager is not truly in touch with who the customer really is. Robert Geiger, general manager for Nashua Tape Products, reinforces this concept when he notes, "We're also struggling to deal with dramatic shifts in our customer base. As customers shift we need to be ahead of the power curve so that we can continue representing added value to those that represent new relationships."[3]

The same advice holds true for resident security managers in that they need to define who their internal customers are. Experienced security managers understand well that there is an ebb and flow to internal customer demands. As business cycles change and emphasis is placed in new and unfolding directions, the internal customer base will also shift. What might have been yesterday's primary driver for security services may no longer be a primary focus today. Conversely, yesterday's customer-in-waiting may be today's primary focus.

Given the dynamic nature of customer relations, how does one develop a strategy that is customer focused? The answer lies in your ability to allow your agenda to become their agenda. In other words, if as a security manager you attempt to impose your agenda across the organizational continuum, you are ultimately destined to become frustrated. True customer satisfaction, which leads ultimately to the higher good of customer loyalty, is expedited when you are able to put your individual agenda second to the needs and expectations of your fluid internal customer base.

Despite changing customer bases, there are a number of similarities from one customer to the next. By developing strategies and practices that address these common denominators, you can learn to address specific end-user needs while maintaining continuity in customer satisfaction. Specifically, nearly every internal customer wants the following:

Their security department to demonstrate a high level of professionalism. This translates into appearance, demeanor (confidence), initiative, and a knowledge base that positions security as the experts in asset protection.

A proven business approach. Whether the security program is administered by resident staff or through a third-party supplier, today's internal customer wants policies and procedures, staffing allocations, and technology applications that reflect proven business practices based on added value, reasonable cost, and appropriateness to individual customer requirements.

The expectation of continuity in the delivery of service. Whether it's at the corporate, regional, or local level, business unit managers want to be assured that their needs will be addressed with the same degree of intensity and interest at every level. What happens if security is unable to deliver? From the customer's perspective the answer is quite simple: the customer will seek alternative sources.

As Brian Hollstein notes in describing how Xerox Corporation approaches its corporate security requirements, "To survive within a large corporation, a security department must be able to demonstrate its worth and prove to senior management that it can provide company services more efficiently than an outside contractor."[4] If security can't do so, he goes on to note, given the decentralized nature of many large organizations today, the internal security department will be pitted against third-party providers in a competition for security services. Security providers who fail to understand who their real customers are within their client base also run the risk of being replaced by a proprietary workforce or some other alternative.

Many companies are experimenting with developing their own subsidiary security company (a strategy more commonly found among property management companies), or seeking nontraditional providers, including temporary employment agencies, large consulting houses, or upstart entrepreneurs who are known to local managers.

Mary Beth Merrin, a former vice president for marketing research at Marriott International, notes that another element in the value force is an organization's ability to transform employees from simply "friendly" people to "thinking doers." By this she means that customers go from being content to having a higher level of loyalty when employees demonstrate that there is a rationale behind their actions that drives them to do what they do, that they are not merely being robots carrying out prescribed procedures.[5]

David Fagiano, American Management Association's president and CEO, reinforces this idea by pointing out that success comes when employees at all levels are willing to move beyond "silo thinking." By this he means that employees should have a desire to think in broader terms, well beyond limits assigned to them in their specific organizational role. As he points out, companies have traditionally created departmental walls that appear to have been cast in titanium. Today's successful manager can bust these walls down and help employees to think beyond the limits of their assigned departmental responsibilities. As we shall see in the final chapter, when employees are allowed to think beyond the narrow limits of their assigned duties, they invariably retain a sharper focus on customer needs and expectations, and this attitude translates directly into wanting to help customers in a broader sense. This in turn translates into an interactive relationship between customer and service provider. As Marilyn Zuckerman, a senior consultant for AT&T Bell Laboratories, notes: "A number of studies prove that a customer who has had a problem that has been successfully dealt with is a more loyal customer than someone who has never had a problem. A problem is just an opportunity to show how much you care. Those kinds of things often create enduring relationships between customers and suppliers and between people."[6] Wanting to help, however, only positions an employee as well-intentioned; the real measure of success is to develop a mechanism that empowers employees to respond to customers quickly and effectively.

DEVELOPING A RAPID RESPONSE STRATEGY

Slashing response time and thereby enhancing value is a four-step process according to S. E. Toth, founder of the Toth Productivity Institute and a twenty-six year veteran in the aerospace industry.[7]

1. Find out your customers' definition of timeliness.
2. Map out the existing process.
3. Identify an improved process.
4. Install the new process.

He suggests that the first step is finding out your internal customers' definition of timeliness. It does not do department heads or third-party suppliers any good if their definition of what is timely is at odds with their users' requirements. Remembering that ensuring customer satisfaction is continuously driven by identifying customer expectations and needs, the same should then apply to understanding how customers define timeliness in terms of response.

Given the multitude of service offerings within the security function, response times will vary considerably. Just as law enforcement has found that a response time greater than five minutes for a 911 call is generally unacceptable, security professionals need to determine similar guidelines for responding to company emergencies. Administrative services will typically have a much longer response time requirement, however. Regardless, success should be measured by the security department's ability to consistently meet, or come in under, deadlines.

Toth's second step for reducing response time is to describe the existing process. This allows employees to create a baseline from which to measure future progress. Reviewing each action step allows the security decision maker the opportunity to study what steps serve more to obstruct a timely response than to facilitate it. Today there are many different types of mapping charts you can use for this type of analysis. These range from Pareto to Fishbone Analysis and Gant charting, all of which have been converted to computerized software programs for ease of use.

Toth's third step is to find an improved process. By identifying deficiencies and brainstorming the causes and effects of potential lags, staff members can begin to develop corrective steps, up to and including the elimination of unnecessary steps. According to Oren Harari, the Boston Consulting Group surveyed a diverse group of U.S. businesses and concluded that 95 percent to 99 percent of their internal activities had little or no relevance to the customer.[8] My personal experience as an asset protection executive for three large multinational firms would confirm these results.

It is not uncommon for larger internal security organizations to become mired in personnel matters, internal budgeting issues, systems development, and so forth. These internal operating functions, while critical to the overall operation, can often become burdensome and self-serving, and often they can contribute to an internal department's or a supplier's inability to respond to emergencies in a timely fashion. The consequence is a loss of credibility and a reduction in customer satisfaction, both of which threaten customer loyalty.

Toth's final step is to install the new process. Those who have found success in managing asset protection programs report that the installation of new processes is more easily achieved if the implementation is preceded by a test application. The test allows staff members to make adjustments in a test mode. Moreover, internal customers are usually more open and tolerant if something doesn't go exactly as planned during a test application. They are also more willing to participate since there is an expectation that if the new process is found to be workable, it will yield future benefit to them.

Thus far we have been talking about the necessity of defining the security agenda based on the expectations and needs of internal customers. The reason this is so critical is that security managers can easily fall into the trap of believing that they "know what's best" for the company concerning asset protection and employee/customer safety. Even though they may have the expertise, their ideas may not be in sync with the business unit heads' definition of what is operationally appropriate for their area. This creates a tug-of-war between expertise on the one hand and customer wants on the other. If this impasse is not addressed, more often than not the result is that the unit managers will deliberately circumvent the security manager in the future.

If they do not circumvent security, unit managers are just as likely to escalate the confrontation in the hope of derailing security's concerns altogether, because most nonsecurity executives know that asset protection managers are generally ill prepared to defend their position in strong business terms. Even for those security executives who are astute enough to fend off either strategy, the end result is a feeling of alienation for both parties. As an effective preventive strategy, security managers should define what the customer wants or needs in advance. In this way they can cooperate with unit managers rather than engage them in a confrontation.

PURSUING CUSTOMER SATISFACTION

Customer satisfaction is directly tied to the customer's perception. The smart business manager understands well the concept that a customer's perceptions are also that person's realities. Whether proven factually true or not, until the perception is changed, people will believe what their perceptions tell them. Consequently, Harari offers us the following formula: $CP = D/E$. Harari believes that CP represents a customer's perception of quality and that CP is equal to what the supplier delivers (D) relative to what the customer expects (E). Consider Harari's anecdote about service providers' and customers' perceptions of what makes a coffee break great.

> A Tale of Quality
>
> *You are attending an all-day conference in a hotel. The schedule calls for a periodic coffee break, which you look forward to gratefully. Here is the sixty-four-thousand-dollar question: What makes a good—that is, high-quality—coffee break? Here's how a diverse group of hoteliers responded when asked this very question: Timely availability of hot coffee, extras (buns, fruit, and so forth), attractive display, clean china, and clean table dressing.*
>
> *Sounds reasonable enough. Who could possibly dispute that? Only one small insignificant group, I'm afraid: the customers. At least there wasn't 100 percent disagreement between customers' and hoteliers' responses; both groups did agree that a quality coffee break should include hot coffee. After that, however, the differences were marked.*
>
> *Here's how customers responded to the same question: "Hot coffee, or equivalent, fast line (especially for refill), close and high-dash capacity restroom, close and numerous telephones, and plenty of room to chat."[9]*

Customer expectations are most often grounded in common sense. When confronted with an overly bureaucratic procedure or an inability to get their most basic needs met, people can become frustrated very quickly. As Harari points out, how often have we been driven to the verge of apoplexy when faced with some poor soul who cannot provide us with the most elementary information or make the most commonsense decision without getting a sign-off from his or her absent "superior"?

The AT&T Universal Card division understands this well, and as a demonstration of their commitment to best practices, their customer service representatives are allowed to fix most customer problems on their own without clearance from their boss. They raise credit limits and issue additional cards without supervisory approval. They meet among themselves to adjust both policies and procedures that they know adversely affect customers. The end result is that customer concerns are resolved in one phone call 95 percent of the time.

In addition to the strategies about defining timely response and empowering employees who understand what the meaning of common sense is all about, Harari points out that customer satisfaction is also grounded in the service provider's ability to go the extra mile. He tells the story of a family who went to Disney World in Orlando, Florida. While there, they were viewing a huge fish tank when the children became upset because they thought that some of the fish looked unhappy. When the father sheepishly brought this concern to the attention of one of the staff members, that staff member took the parents and youngsters backstage. The staff member sought out one of the professionals who tended to the tanks, and the specialist in turn spent more than two hours with the children not only explaining to them why the faces of happy fish may have appeared unhappy to them, but also giving them a little tour describing how he and his staff tend to the tanks. Harari closes by noting, "If you think that anecdotes about empathy and respect have little to do with quality, I'm afraid there's not much hope that you'll ever attain it."[10]

DEVELOPING STRATEGIES FOR CULTIVATING CUSTOMER LOYALTY

Why is customer loyalty of a higher order than customer satisfaction? Simply put, loyalty is built on satisfaction. Whether your customers are internal or external, it is only when they are absolutely and totally satisfied with you that they will be willing either to send additional business/ service your way or to refer others to you. Loyalty means your customers will continuously return to you as a positive resource when they have a problem. Harkening back to our previous discussion on fly-fishing and its parallel to management, remember that people are motivated by the need to resolve a particular problem, the experience of pain owing to a loss, and the belief that they can reap a personal or economic gain. They will seek you out only because of one of these three motivators and only if you have enough credibility that they perceive you to be a reliable resource.

I'm loyal to my auto mechanic because I know he fixes problems when I bring them to him. Similarly, people are loyal to a security department when they experience a loss and see security as a solution, because of either a previous experience or a referral from another satisfied customer. If your department doesn't have such a reputation, your customers will seek alternatives such as calling the police directly or writing off their loss as a "cost of doing business."

To build customer loyalty for your security program, your customers need to have the following needs met: show that you understand them, show that you respect them, help them feel important, and provide them a comfortable environment. The first three are self-evident, but the last is frequently overlooked by those who are responsible for planning security facilities.

Despite the significant gains made by many security departments, there are still a high number of departments that have been relegated to boiler rooms, oversized janitorial storage facilities, back-lot shacks, and so forth. Individuals seeking security's services cannot be satisfied if they have to make their way to the security office by some circuitous route through service corridors, basement passageways, or across storage yards to an unheated facility in the wintertime.

When I find such deplorable conditions among my clients, I am both quick and stern in pointing out to senior management the obvious duplicity of professing a commitment to quality service and relegating security personnel to such unprofessional facilities. I recall asking the president of a large Texas-based financial services institution if he had ever visited his security department. When he said that he hadn't, I asked if he had a few minutes and agreed to accompany him. He consented, and after taking him down to the sub-sub-basement and through the boiler room, he stopped and asked, "Is this a joke?" When I assured him that it was not, I led him to the security office, situated between two very large and extremely hot boilers. The room measured less than seven feet by seven feet and was so overcrowded that spare uniforms were literally hung on hangers that were hooked over ceiling-mounted piping running to and from the boilers.

After seeing the conditions, the company president said that he had had no idea, and he asked if I had any suggestions about where the security office ought to be located. I jokingly suggested that we could begin by considering his office. He laughed and assured me that something more suitable would be arranged immediately. Much to the security director's amazement, he was relocated within two days to a more appropriate office on the fourth floor adjacent to the vice president for human resources. Within a few days, he received a memo from the president directing him to submit for budget consideration his plan for a new complex, complete with locker rooms for his officers, a report-writing room, and necessary storage space. As I looked over the memo the security director pulled a document out of his desk and said: "I've submitted this very plan seven years running. Somehow or other I think this time it will receive the attention it deserves."

THE CUSTOMER-SUPPLIER GAP

One of the major obstacles to achieving customer loyalty is the gap that often exists between the customer's expectations and the supplier's perception of what it means to deliver quality service. I refer to this disparity as the *customer-supplier gap*. The difference will vary from internal customer to internal customer depending on several factors, among which are:

♦ Past experience. Perhaps security has not had an opportunity to work closely with the customers and therefore does not understand their requirements;
♦ Believing that they know the customer's business when in fact they do not;
♦ Conflicting corporate reporting lines. Security lacks credibility because it is not in one of the more favored business units;
♦ A lack of organizational advocates for a strong security program.

Over and above each of these contributing factors, it is not uncommon for security managers to define asset protection in terms that are completely different from those of their end users. This is an easy trap to fall into. Because they are the experts, the security managers assume that they know what is best for their customers. They would be just as amazed as the hoteliers in Harari's anecdote were to learn the degree of disparity between their perception of what constitutes good service and what customers consider good service.

To close the customer-supplier gap, First Security Corporation of Boston, Massachusetts, has devised a series of questions that managers can use to define the degree of disparity between service providers and customers and ways to close it.

♦ How do clients define service quality?
♦ How do other constituencies, for example, client employees, executives, other security organizations, and so forth, define service quality?

♦ How does First Security management and field supervision define service quality?
♦ What are the elements of service quality?
♦ What additional resources or practices are needed to develop and improve service quality?
♦ What must we, as a company, do that is different from what we have been doing?
♦ What road should we follow to go from where we are to where we want to be?
♦ What should I, as a manager, do that is different from what I have been doing?

These are very thought-provoking questions, and they need to be asked continuously. They speak to the core relationship between the service provider (resident or contract) and the internal customer. The questioning process begins with the agent for the service provider actively listening to the needs and expectations of customers. From there it builds on what the provider's definition of service is, thus identifying the gap. The exercise is not complete until the individual manager and the company at large redefine their approach. It is also important to note that the gap is not defined solely at the management level; it must also include perceptions from the operational level through to the supervisory level.

SERVICE EXCELLENCE STRATEGIES

To help us better understand how customer satisfaction can be used as a basis for gaining customer loyalty, in *Service Excellence* Price Pritchett offers us the concept of "service excellence strategies."[11] His first overall strategy centers on the management of the relationship between service agent and client. For Pritchett the first and highest priority in customer service work is to build good relationships with your customers. There are three important reasons:

If your customers don't like you, the odds are a hundred to one they're not going to like your service. Experience bears this out. When I first began my career as a security manager for Crocker Bank in San Francisco, I remember the director was having difficulty with one particular vendor. My initial impression was that the vendor was okay, so I naturally asked what the problem was. My boss explained that the vendor had a long-standing relationship with the bank, and that recently some of the bank's executives had come to dislike the local vendor representatives. That company simply couldn't do anything right in the minds of the bank's executives. Their service was suffering—or at least that was the perception—and within a short period the company lost the account with the bank, despite the vendor's best efforts.

Problems are a lot easier to solve when you're on good terms with the customer. Many times I have heard security suppliers lament the fact that one of their staff members has made a serious mistake, and now they fear that their relationship with their client is in jeopardy. The first question I ask is how strong is the relationship? If they say it was good up until the incident, I tell them that the relationship is far from broken. When people trust you they measure you more on how you resolve a problem than on how the problem occurred in the first place. Customers want to see prompt corrective action and an assurance that the incident will not recur. If the business relationships are good, service agents are allowed several strikes before they are out.

If the relationship doesn't go well, it not only complicates the basic problem but also creates new headaches. When the relationship becomes rocky, it is likely to get even more rocky before it gets better. I recall a time when Pinkerton and I shared the same client. I hadn't met their CEO, Denis Brown, yet, but I called to advise him that there was a problem with the client. He exclaimed in frustration: "How come whenever I hear their name in a sentence, it is always accompanied with the words 'and there is a problem'?" At that time Denis was fairly new to the security profession, but certainly not new to the concept that problems often beget other problems. Instead of walking away from the situation, to his credit he set out to change the course of the relationship and succeeded. Today the client is very satisfied with Pinkerton's attention to its concerns.

Managing a Customer Relationship

It is very wise to invest the energy it takes to start a relationship off on the right foot. Just a little extra effort in the beginning can prevent some real hassles later on. There are three steps involved in managing a relationship, and they are so simple, but so powerful. As W. Clement Stone has written, "Success comes from doing common things uncommonly well." Here's what Pritchett believes are the keys to building a good relationship.

1. Take the initiative.
2. Be positive.
3. Make the customer feel special.[12]

That's it. Three steps, but mighty big ones when it comes to execution.

Taking the Initiative

When it comes to service, asset protection managers need to understand that they must make the first move. They must position themselves as the end user's logical choice for resolving problems and/or handling incidents. If you seize the initiative you are in a better position to wield early influence over the other person's behavior. Here's a lesson drawn from the world of sports. At the beginning of the game, would you rather be in a position to act or react? Most people want to establish themselves and set the tone by their own actions.

Being Positive

The second choice involves your attitude. A positive attitude entails being upbeat, affirming, personable, interesting, respectful, and considerate. Each of these factors creates the basis for customers wanting to do business with you; ergo, if you have the right attitude, loyalty begins to emerge. Pritchett postulates that when you take the initiative and act positively, you put psychological pressure on the customer to react in a positive fashion.

Making the Customer Feel Special

Loyalty emerges when customers are surprised by your actions. The aim is to build an approach within the service delivery system that catches the customer off guard. Dr. William Martin, in his series *Quality Customer Services*, reinforces this idea by suggesting that satisfaction that leads to loyalty is measured by each extra bit of service the provider is willing to give. To be success driven you should treat each customer as if he or she were your *only* customer, as if this were a person you *must* get to know, satisfy, and keep happy.

Managing the Transaction

Pritchett's second overall strategy is to manage the transaction. After setting the stage for a good relationship with the customer, the service agent still needs to conduct the business. If the business transaction is not managed effectively, sooner or later the relationship will be damaged. To assure that this need is addressed, Pritchett suggests three additional steps:

1. Listen and understand.
2. Be helpful.
3. Deal with the uniqueness of the situation.[13]

Listening and Understanding

Customers want to be assured that you understand their situation. At the outset most end users believe that their problem is unique and requires a special approach. Even if it is not unique, you can explain this later. Similarly, customers want to talk about why they need your service, and they don't necessarily want to listen to how good you are or what your capabilities are. This information will come out in due course anyway. Rather, at the beginning customers want to be assured that you know what they need, and they want to know whether or not you can resolve any problems that come up. To achieve this understanding you need to begin by asking what the problem is and then listen—simply listen.

In working with my clients on how to market their services, whether they are proprietary or a third party, here's a strategy I recommend that not only differentiates you from other service agents but also shows that you care about your potential customer:

> *Begin by saying that you want to hear why they have sought you out. You'll be glad to share with them your credentials later, but for now it's more important to understand why you have come together. During the course of discussing the problem, you can always work into the conversation past experiences or similar events. This assures them indirectly that you are experienced and that their situation, despite their perception of its uniqueness, can be resolved.*

Being Helpful

This second step in managing the transaction means taking action. Listening leads to understanding, which leads to action. Customers want to know that the security manager has taken personal responsibility for satisfying them. As an asset protection professional you should be aware of the value of creating mutual ownership while leaving the impression that you are "in charge." By taking part in the problem solving the customer becomes a partner. The customer will feel as though he or she has a role and will seek you out again and again.

Pritchett adds, "The idea at this stage of the game is to fix things. So there's a problem? Take care of it, even if it's a problem the customer caused. No finger-pointing, no runaround, just an effort that clearly says, 'The buck stops here.' You'll always be able to help the client in some way. So even if you can't give what the customer wants, give as much as you can."[14]

Dealing with the Uniqueness of the Situation

People want to be treated as though they are special. Loyalty is built on their belief that you fully understand their uniqueness. They need to seek you out over and over because you have invested the time and resources to understand their particular circumstances. The truth of the matter is that there is some aspect of their situation that is unique. When you have spotted the unique aspect of their situation, all of a sudden you have an angle on how to handle it. Now you can customize your approach. With this third step you personalize your approach to managing the transaction. This strategy really sets you apart from the competition in the service experience you create for your customer.

A CUSTOMER-DRIVEN APPROACH TO QUALITY ASSURANCE

We have examined Guaspari's *value force* and how it affects an organization's ability to move beyond customer satisfaction; we also reviewed Harari's formula, CP = D/E and the notion of the customer-supplier gap. Collectively, these models have laid the foundation for defining a pragmatic approach to quality assurance. These, like Pritchett's *service excellence strategies,* are critical building blocks for sustaining internal customer business over the long term.

Each of the foregoing concepts also underscores another important point, namely, that the pursuit of quality-oriented programs need not be complex or burdensome. For many operation managers, the idea of continuous quality improvement (CQI) is an immediate turnoff because they see it as "just adding to my workload." Even though they are intellectually committed to the idea of pursuing quality, they cannot enthusiastically support it because they feel that the effort they'll need to make will compete with other responsibilities.

As some of the more experienced organizational theorists point out, the failure of most QA programs is not inherent in the plan; rather the failure is directly related to the execution of the program. As we saw at the conclusion of Chapter 2, when a program is full of measures aimed at operational infrastructure, it can become overly taxing. Sadly, such efforts miss the mark entirely and achieve exactly the opposite results—loss of credibility, customer dissatisfaction, and no long-term commitment—that is, a loss of customer loyalty.

Does this mean that QA is doomed to failure? Like reengineering, if it is thought to be the blueprint for success, then it has been dead for some time; it was stillborn. On the other hand, if it is pursued as a commonsense approach to improving customer service and enhancing loyalty, then it is very much alive—and projected to live a long life. QA does not have to have its own unique organizational niche to be successful. For that matter I would suggest that security managers need to be leery of those who propose such structures. Let me hasten to add that I'm not suggesting that we do away with quality assurance directors—just the bureaucracies that tend to build up around them. An effective program is woven into the very fabric of daily operations. American Protective Services (APS) has adopted such a program. Their QA program is effective because it is designed to be integral to their culture and part of their service delivery system. In short, it has literally become a way of life.

Let's examine what I call the pragmatic quality assurance (PQA) model.

Step 1 Articulating Your Service Values

Just as with any worthwhile venture, PQA begins with an articulation of what your organization stands for. Quality service values are different from mission statements and goals. They serve as a set of guidelines for your staff and your customers, establishing your definition of QA. At the core of these principles should be a recognition that service is defined in the context of the customer's expectations and needs—not yours. Further, accomplishing QA requires a collaborative effort between provider and customer to provide a business environment that is as safe and secure as possible.

Quality service values should also aim for achieving the best value and not the lowest price/cost. You need to stress your commitment to managing the process as opposed to simply executing the program. This postures you, the security decision maker, as a problem solver willing to complement your approach with state-of-the-art technology and best practices.

Step 2 Establishing a Quality Assurance Strategic Oversight Group

To assure that QA is an ongoing process, you need to develop an oversight group consisting of a cross-section of employees from throughout the organization— horizontally and vertically. The role of this oversight group is to set the direction for the QA process. Tasks include setting service values, identifying specific QA tools, establishing incentives, and ensuring top management's personal and direct involvement.

Step 3 Establishing Your Service Delivery System

Security managers and providers are prone to falling into the "we serve everyone" trap. In its concern for the well-being of its customers—internal and external, employees and assets—understandably security defines its universe fairly broadly. In doing so security runs the risk of becoming "good," at best, in a number of areas, but failing to become excellent in any. Undertaking quality-oriented customer service means learning to set limits. For the resident security group this means limiting your service offerings to those areas that are truly within your core competency. This translates into defining what you do best and then redefining your program accordingly. For example, in one large insurance company the security director realized that corporate security's role should be defined within the context of major fraud investigation and serious corporate policy violations. He then reassigned other traditional security functions to support units whose service offerings were more synergistic.

For third-party providers limiting your service offerings means being selective about your customer base. Despite the temptation to offer services to virtually anyone who calls, companies focused on QA have found true value in defining their market segments and adhering to them. To follow their lead you will need to acknowledge the fact that you are not a company for everyone; nor is every potential client the right match for you. You will need to conduct your own assessments to ensure that you have a solid match. Among the criteria you can use are officer compensation, degree of risk, and reasonable margin.

Step 4 Establishing a Single Point of Contact

Customers want a designated resource. They want to be assured that when they call for security's assistance they are not going to be handed off to someone else or hear "That's not my job. I'll have to have someone else get back to you." Therefore it is critical that customers have direct access to the security staff and level of service that can best assure rapid response and resolution of a problem. Client confidence is won and retained based on responsiveness and personal attention. Consequently, your employees must be empowered to respond accordingly. For external suppliers this means that your local account manager will become the pivotal point of contact.

Step 5 Customer Focused Employees

There's an adage: You can't win the race unless you have the horses. The same holds true for customer satisfaction. Unless your employees are customer focused, as security manager you have no chance of winning customer loyalty. This means that you should seek out candidates who can exhibit customer sensitivity in the recruitment process. Ironically, few security programs highlight this asset when they are selecting new hires. Security people are traditionally screened based on more technical merits.

Typically resident managers and providers alike believe they are recruiting customer-focused individuals when in fact they are not, largely because they misunderstand the distinction between consumer focus and interpersonal skills. They are operating with the mistaken belief that if a person is cordial, friendly, and so forth, he or she is therefore customer service oriented. This is a myth. To be customer focused a candidate needs to have a desire to serve, a desire to help, an inherent supportive personality. One can be very friendly and still be a very controlling individual. A person can be respectful, but indifferent to people in general. Get to know your candidates before hiring them.

The same attention to customer orientation needs to be reflected in your selection of candidates for supervisory and management positions. In order to be selected an individual should demonstrate proven past customer satisfaction accomplishments. Absent this built-in managerial orientation, the manager candidate will not be an appropriate role model for lower-level employees. To be considered for promotions, employees need to balance proficiency with the appropriate orientation. Likewise, employees should be disciplined if they fail to demonstrate customer focus when the opportunity presents itself. In other words, customer satisfaction orientation needs to be sought out and groomed just like any other necessary skill.

Step 6 Customer-Focused Training

Having the right caliber of staff is one thing; training your staff is another. Asset protection managers often talk with pride about their training programs. They will expound on the considerable time and money they spend on training. Few, however, have actually developed courses specifically designed to carry the concept of customer service throughout an employee's entire professional development.

By this I mean that customer service training should begin with the training of new hires and then carry through to on-the-job training, annual advanced officer training, monthly publications and performance coaching, and specialized courses. It should continue through supervisory training and management assignments. To be absorbed, customer service needs to become a consistent theme. In addition to developing specific courses, you will need to weave the concept of meeting end-user requirements into other topics as well.

As an example, when designing a course on search and seizure or on report writing, frame some examples in terms of customer satisfaction principles. This is rarely done. When an officer receives initial training at the time of being hired, it is customary for him or her to receive from one to two hours in *public relations*. When questioned about course content, marketing representatives for third-party suppliers will commonly attempt to explain that this module is their customer service relations training. In examining the actual curriculum, however, it is obvious that the training isn't centered on customers; rather, it focuses on press relations, complaint referral, and so forth. But customer service is not public relations.

Step 7 Customer-Focused Performance Measures

Are job descriptions written to suit the concept of customer loyalty? In reviewing hundreds of position statements around the country and across the business sector, it is highly unusual to find one that is customer focused. The same can be said for performance indicators. Take a moment to review yours. Do you even have performance measures? Most managers do not. Assuming you have one or both, are they written to reflect customer expectations and needs? Or are they centered on the technical aspects of the position such as meeting specific post assignments? This concept carries over to other positions, such as investigators, safety specialists, console operators, photo identification clerks, data security personnel, and other professionals.

Step 8 Customer Feedback

Effective programs have built-in feedback mechanisms, which serve to measure the program's continued relevancy. Feedback is only effective if it is ongoing and targeted to issues at hand. Typically feedback becomes personal only when a series of failures have occurred or customer expectations are consistently not being met. I have found that there are four tiers of feedback. Each serves as an important link in assuring quality performance over the near and long term.

Daily Operational Feedback.   This type of feedback involves verbal and nonverbal cues, ways to solicit responses that tell security staff whether they are on track or not. This feedback can come from a variety of sources. Sometimes it's from client employees or end-user staff. Other times it comes from colleagues and supervisors. Through coaching, daily operational feedback becomes interactive. Supervisors and managers elicit from employees ideas that can generate more efficient operations, and employees learn firsthand how they are performing.

Customer Status Meetings.   An effective but often overlooked tool is the use of regularly scheduled status meetings between security (for example, the designated single point of contact) and its end users. More than just project status meetings, these interactions serve as an opportunity to review ongoing concerns and special projects as well as to solicit directly customers' level of satisfaction. The frequency with which you hold such meetings will vary depending on the client's needs and availability.

The status meeting should be an interactive forum where both parties exchange ideas, receive input, and give feedback to each other. This is a good opportunity to measure how both you and your clients are doing and to make continuous adjustments. It creates an avenue to ensure that surprises are kept to a minimum.

Midyear Review.   Every 180 days each customer should receive a short questionnaire asking them how the relationship is progressing. The feedback from their answers should be integrated into the next status meeting to assure that security and the internal customers take the time to review the document. This feedback loop should remain at a set level unless there are major concerns or additional resources are required, at which point the clients or the security representative should escalate the feedback to a higher level.

Annual Client Satisfaction Survey.   Generated by either corporate security or the third party's home office, this is a survey that is intended to rate overall performance. The purpose is to provide a more in-depth review of how the relationship has been managed as well as to assess the infrastructure that supports the relationship. The survey instrument need not be overly detailed. It should solicit narrative responses that reflect the customers' true feelings. It should also be aimed at identifying both strengths and weaknesses, since both serve as critical barometers for fostering a long-term relationship.

In recapping this pragmatic approach, the emphasis has been on incorporating quality as a way of life in your operation. Absent are the mechanical aspects that accompany most other programs. The approach is client focused as opposed to inner directed. Quality is measured based on the service delivered and not on whether security officers are late for work, investigators are not utilizing 100 percent of their time, or safety specialists are not finding their quota of industrial hazards. Operational matters are important but ought not be confused with delivering QA. Customers assume certain infrastructures are in place, and they want attention and results; they do not want to be burdened by processes. Under the proposed approach, quality is encouraged and not used as a hammer to force compliance by your staff members.

SEVEN CRITICAL MISTAKES

When pursuing customer loyalty, security departments and third-party providers can make mistakes. Here are seven common—and unfortunately critical—ones. I share these with you because they provide an opportunity to learn from others.

1. *Disinterested sounding telephone answering techniques.* Want to test how customer directed your employees are? Call them on the telephone. What is their initial response? On several occasions I have called prospective suppliers regarding a multimillion-dollar contract, only to have a security officer mumble some incoherent salutation. Commonly security personnel answer by barking into the telephone, "Security Officer Jones." It is as though they have been taught or inherently believe that professionalism means sounding militaristic. We have all heard that first impressions are lasting impressions.

2. *Thinking customer service means doing anything the client wants.* Security providers are particularly prone to believing that customer service means never being able to say no. A friend of mine describes this as the welfare mentality. In reality, customer expectations can often be unrealistic. Good customer service means being in tune with what customers want, not necessarily blindly accepting everything they say. If their expectation or need is beyond your scope or, worse yet, inappropriate, it is to be hoped that your relationship is

sound enough that you will feel comfortable indicating as much. If the customer still insists, perhaps it's time to reassess the relationship and move on. If you don't take a firm stand, not only do you jeopardize targeted profit margins, but you set up everyone else in security for eventual failure.

3. *Being slow in handling customer complaints.* Complaint resolution can make or break a relationship. When something goes wrong, customers want a resolution—quickly. This demand is not unique to security, but in security the stakes are different in that sometimes loss or injury is involved. People expect that mistakes can happen. One of the tests of whether a relationship will continue is how rapidly corrective action was taken.

4. *Being reactive and not doing a root cause analysis.* There are generally two ways to resolve a problem. Attack it on its merits or go for the root cause. Most managers will attempt to resolve a problem on the surface level. They may put out the fire, but until they have determined the cause, there is no assurance that the problem will not flare up again. Root cause analysis brings about true resolution and prevention. Without it, the security manager is doomed to a career of repeating the same mistakes over and over.

5. *Not having your executives meet with regularity with client executives.* This mistake is often experienced by third-party providers, but it can apply to resident security executives as well. Customers, whether internal or external, want the senior ranking team member to pay them some attention. This makes them feel that their business is important to the service agent. Even if it is a simple periodic telephone call, end users want—and expect—that senior management is aware of them and their needs. One service company president lamented the fact that his style was such that he rarely called on his clients. After five years with one of his largest accounts, his firm lost the opportunity to expand its business with that client by more than threefold simply because he failed to nurture the account by calling on the client on occasion.

6. *Not knowing when to say no.* Not being able to say no is like the second critical mistake, only here the issue is more one of timing. Every organization has its limits. Sometimes it is simply ill advised to say yes or agree to do something. If the resources are not there or the infrastructure is not in place, failing to say no is tantamount to accepting failure. It takes a brave manager to know when and how to say no. Yet doing so can often be the best decision. Customers respect honesty just as much as they respect performance, because they know that performance is based on ability.

7. *Making promises you can't keep.* Customers expect that once a commitment has been made by a service agent, the commitment will be met. Failure to perform leads to an immediate loss of credibility. It doesn't take too many disappointments before customer satisfaction waivers and loyalty is eventually lost. Here's a simple rule to follow: if you promise you had better deliver.

SUMMARY

In this chapter we pushed our journey toward achieving organization success further down the path. The task was to explore what lies beyond customer satisfaction—customer loyalty. To better understand the hierarchy of customer service we began by examining the value force matrix. We discovered that companies can be sorted into one of four categories ranging from a low of process oriented and mired in adversarial interrelationships to a high of process oriented and focused on creating value.

We also found that end users make decisions to stay with security service agents, resident or external, if a given security organization demonstrates professionalism, a proven business approach, and continuity in the delivery system. Customers expect rapid responses. To help us understand the dynamics for achieving better response times we examined Toth's four steps. This led us to consider Harari's customer service formula: CP = D/E. Harari believes that CP represents a customer's perception of quality, and that CP is equal to what the supplier delivers (D) relative to what the customer expects (E).

Our exploration of customer loyalty also led us to consider the customer-supplier gap, or the differences between the perceptions of customers and those of their service agents. Security managers need to learn to listen to their customers and respond accordingly instead of generating their own agenda. To help close the gap we reviewed the ideas of Price Pritchett and his two service excellence strategies.

These discussions helped to set the stage for an analysis of what I call the pragmatic quality assurance (PQA) model. Contrary to other approaches that focus on internal processes, the PQA model concentrates on integrating quality customer service with the supplier's company culture as well as in its service delivery system. Beginning with the hiring process and continuing through selection on the management team, PQA principles reflecting a customer focus should be ingrained in staff and managers. As a final guidepost, we looked at seven critical mistakes that security managers commonly make when servicing their internal client base.

PART ONE SUMMARY

With the conclusion of this chapter we come to the end of the first part of our journey. Our purpose has been to review concepts and experiences from many recognized experts in quality service management. These ideas and concepts have allowed us to set a foundation and to get a clearer understanding of what it takes to survive and contribute in meaningful ways in today's dynamic business world. I was heartened to read Eric Harne's ten survival techniques in the April 1996 issue of *Security Management Bulletin*. His list summarizes what we have been discussing thus far. It's gratifying to read others espousing the same concepts and concerns that I have been writing and lecturing about for the past fifteen years. Through Harne and others such as Bill Zalud, editor of *Security Management Magazine*, John Fay at British-Petroleum, and consultant J. T. Roberts, there is a collective validation that success for today's security professional can be summed up as follows: Corporate success comes when we see ourselves as business managers first and security specialists second. Here are Harne's ten survival techniques.

1. Don't be an isolationist.
2. Embrace the essentials, not the time-consuming minutiae, of today's "quality" movement.
3. Don't let company politics make you the company cop.
4. Make your written procedures reflect good priorities.
5. Shine when the company audits.
6. Be a business manager, not just a business security manager.
7. Groom your support staff.
8. Be aware of trends, but don't give them more importance than they deserve.
9. Be an obvious expert in your own field.
10. Embrace innovation (real innovation, that is).[15]

True success is measured in terms of the efforts we make and the attitudes we adopt that reflect a strong desire to thrive in uncertain times. But who are today's pursuers of such strategies? This is the next leg of our journey.

Part II

Today's Security Manager—
A New Approach

Part II

Today's Security Manager—
A New Approach

4

The Eclectic Manager

Riches get their value from the mind of their possessor; they are blessings to those who know how to use them, curses to those who do not.

…TERENCE, 163 B.C.

There was a time when defining a security manager's background was fairly easy. The slang expression *corporate cop* leaves little doubt as to the individual's background. Other expressions are equally simplistic: *corporate gumshoe, security chief, captain of the watch, corporate snoop,* and *big brother.* Regardless of the label, one quickly understands that the individual has had a previous career in law enforcement or has been associated with an intelligence agency.

Although private enterprise has been a part of the American scene for over four hundred years, the concept of private security can be traced only as far as the Civil War era and the exploits of Alan Pinkerton. Other notables followed, such as William J. Burns, who was active in the early 1900s. As we near the twenty-first century, it's fair to say that as a profession corporate security, which has become synonymous with "private security" in the business world, is fairly young and still very much evolving.

Although corporate security is an evolving industry, it is difficult to arrive at a consensus as to what is included in the term, let alone who manages the endeavor and/or who should be held accountable for the services. For some organizations the notion of private security translates as uniformed guards whose primary responsibility is protecting people and physical assets. For others it means the first line of defense in today's world of cyberspace. For still others it is limited to protecting VIPs or valued corporate secrets from the competition.

Regardless of who defines corporate security, how they define it, and what background experience they believe security professionals should have, the likelihood is that they will be correct. Security, in essence, is one of those support functions that reflects the values and business aims of a given organization. *Support* is meant here largely as a back-office function, but it also reflects the notion of advocacy. For example, as we have seen with Heitman Retail Properties, their executive group is a strong believer in security. Therefore, it is a high priority in the company's planning process and integral to their operating approach. Conversely, the president of one of the country's largest banks recently confided in me that he rarely thinks about security at any level or, for that matter, when considering any aspect of his company's products or services. He then asked to be reminded about why I was conducting an assessment of the security program—little wonder, I concluded, that the security director lacked even the most fundamental support among business unit heads at the bank.

As security's role within business evolves asset protection officials can experience confusion. This is especially so for the traditionally oriented manager who finds himself caught up in the dynamics of today's turbulent and uncertain corporate life. The same can be said for the security provider who has been asked to step in and assume a much more active role in meeting the daily operational needs of the organization. The role of security is in flux. Of this we can be certain.

Against a backdrop of changing roles and a definitive shift from an exclusive reliance on traditional public sector management, let us examine more closely the changing role in asset protection management.

THE EMERGING NEW ROLE FOR SECURITY MANAGERS

As today's companies search out new paradigms for corporate security, the roles of resident managers are changing. As we saw in Part I, the role of security is changing. For some security professionals this change means that they need to assume broader responsibilities and concentrate on only those threats that are considered high risk. In other settings security's roles are being defined more in collaborative terms. Sometimes security managers' skill set is defined within the context of marketing the need for security and/or providing in-house consulting services. To illustrate, consider the following two recently developed job descriptions. The first is for a major oil producer; the second is for one of America's largest health maintenance organizations.

Job Description, Company 1: Manager, Security Services

Responsible for managing security services group, providing leadership and vision, and setting standards for the security function. Consults with senior line and staff managers on strategic and emerging security exposures/risks. Establishes functional priorities, guides ongoing benchmarking activities, and ensures cost-effective service delivery. Manages security personnel servicing all company business units throughout the world.

Key roles:

♦ Manages company-wide security plan and operations,
♦ Manages development and ongoing application of key security performance measures,
♦ Manages research into and development of new security initiatives and programs,
♦ Manages professional development of security staff,
♦ Manages major security crisis management operations, and
♦ Chairs Security Management Council, which oversees resource management and evaluation

Job Description, Company 2: Director of Security Consulting Services

The director of Security Consulting Services heads a team of professionals and support staff that provides technical support and guidance in the development of standards and protocols for protective and preventative security systems, security operations, and investigative services for the protection of individuals and properties. Along with security staff, the director provides the means, methods, and practices to support all security services. The team is also a resource, providing technical support and guidance for security contracting throughout the program.

The director of Security Consulting Services provides functional leadership in coordination with regional security directors across the facilities' service regions for security delivery. The objective is to provide an appropriate level of guidelines and standards such that security is executed consistent with industry best practices, with appropriate management of risk, and with superior standards that address the security needs of the program.

The director of Security Consulting Services also leads certain initiatives to create programwide savings and/or service improvements. All standards and protocols must take into account the specific needs of different health care markets, evolving trends in health care delivery, existing and pending legislation/regulations, and marketing efforts.

The director of Security Consulting Services will work closely with the other national technical and administrative support managers. The work of the director of Security Consulting Services will be supported by a facilities services council that provides strategic input from senior program managers, facility administrators, controllers, associate medical directors, and so forth.

The director of Security Consulting Services will organize and work closely with technical advisory groups of customers, and experts that provide input and decision making for security systems, security operations, and investigative services. The director will provide staff support and process management to both the facilities services council and the technical council.

Major Responsibilities (listed in order of importance).   Leads a staff of technical and support personnel who support the security process throughout the program, carrying out the following duties:

1. Organizing and leading an ongoing process of security and investigative standards development and updating that actively address the operational, staff, member, business, and marketing needs of the program. The standards must be developed with maximum input from facility users and other key stockholders and must provide for a variety of applications in different markets and for different durations while maintaining the security of people and properties.
2. Actively participating, with the regional Facilities Service directors, in the review of means, methods, and practices of security and investigative service delivery across the program to provide technical input, to validate consistency with established standards, to ensure that an appropriate image is maintained for the program, and to cause an interregional flow of ideas and learning.
3. Providing a wide range of security consulting services directly or through appropriate external strategic alliances and support to the regions to include review of practices/plans, technical support, advice on application of standards, and troubleshooting during the course of security and investigation delivery.
4. Developing and maintaining a comprehensive productivity model consistent with the standards used and applicable to the variety of

markets and geographic locations in which security services are to be provided.

5. Developing and maintaining a comprehensive set of security procedures and guidelines that will provide ongoing support and guide the practice needs of all aspects of security, ensuring that consistent, superior, and cost-effective delivery practices are utilized throughout the program.
6. Providing a program of results analysis and review to ensure that practices/standards are effective and that appropriate levels of compliance are met.
7. Managing and developing a program of standards to create national contracting opportunities for security services and to serve as a resource for the selection of qualified providers.
8. Providing consulting services to customers external to the organization, including international engagements, to the extent that the engagements bring cost, quality, capability, or knowledge improvements to the organization.

The job description for Company 1 reflects an organization in transition. This company had followed a traditional asset protection approach. In today's organizations there is a decided shift away from operational issues. As the director and the staff move more toward the internal consultative role, the emphasis is more on strategic planning and program development. The shift away from operations and toward expert consultation is reflected in such phrases as *development and ongoing application of key security performance measures, research and development of new initiatives, chairs Security Management Council in its roles of resource management and evaluation.* Ties to security operations are still reflected in such duties as assuring individual professional staff development and crisis management. It is also interesting to note that the job description is straightforward and is not burdened with a lot of excess language. It is simple but comprehensive. The scope of responsibility is clearly established. It is interesting to note that the job description is for one of the largest companies in the world with multinational presence in every sector of the globe.

The Company 2 job description reflects a radically different approach. It concentrates on the consultative skills of the individual. Here the director of security is both corporate policy setter and program collaborator. Despite its verbosity, it delineates the interrelationship between the director and end users. Success for this position lies squarely with an ability to "sell" security as opposed to an ability to "provide" asset protection.

The emphasis is on standards development, participating as a team member in the decision-making process, working with strategic alliance partners, monitoring for compliance, and measuring productivity. The director is expected to bring to the job a base of technical knowledge that will serve well in analysis and program development. Note that the candidate must demonstrate through prior experience skills in influencing and collaborating, establishing priorities, managing change, and leveraging purchasing opportunities.

The job descriptions for both companies call out capabilities that are significantly different from those required for classic security management. The emphasis is on development over enforcement, planning as opposed to execution, and collaboration instead of dictating. As many security managers will candidly confide, the business of asset protection can be taught; the art of managing security effectively resides within the very character of the individual. Some will succeed in these new roles; others will find it necessary to step aside. Since there is need to find individuals capable of delivering on these expectations, the door is open to candidates beyond those reared in traditional security training and experiences.

MAKING THE TRANSITION
FROM THE PUBLIC SECTOR

I recently had two separate and unrelated conversations with a couple of my clients. The first was a thirteen-year veteran of private security who had served as an administrator for one of the industry's leading associations. Prior to that she had been an educator and corporate trainer. The other client was a security director for a large multinational company who had been in his position for over twenty years. His prior career had been a combination of military and law enforcement. Both are highly respected by their contemporaries, and "having been around the block" a few times, we were all commenting on the changing nature of today's security executive.

Their observation was that *today's security decision maker is evolving into a business manager.* This statement may appear to be less than flattering considering that private security executives define the very essence of their job function within the business community. In short, wouldn't their observations be somewhat of a paradox?

For some there is a paradox. Unfortunately for many others there is not. Regardless, the matter of the role of the security manager is one of the longest running debates in security. Over the years those who have followed the profession have read and listened to the ongoing dialogue regarding the capabilities of former public servants in private security. One school of thought holds that former police and military commanders have actually held the profession back because of their myopic perspective on how a company's security program ought to be run. Another school of thought suggests that for every police or military leader who has held the profession back, there are at least two who have advanced the profession, especially in terms of demonstrating business acumen.

I entered the "private security ranks" in the late 1970s. My decision to leave law enforcement was somewhat unique since I was only twenty-eight years old and still had enough time ahead of me for an entire career or two. Most of the other folks entering the profession, like the overwhelming majority of those who had preceded us, had already retired after spending a career in law enforcement or the military.

Despite the debate on the question of whether or not a police officer or military commander can make a good security director, it is safe to say that for years your credibility as a "security professional" was measured by the length of time you had spent in the public sector, who you had worked for, and how large your command had been. The more people you had under your supervision, the more important you were assumed to be, and therefore the more prestige you commanded.

I'm sure the debate will continue to ebb and flow for years to come. For there is no one right answer; nor should there be. Your success should not depend on whether you were or were not in the military or graduated from the FBI academy. True success is the result of your ability to translate your background and past accomplishments into the skill set necessary to survive and thrive in today's turbulent times.

Nonetheless, it is important to recognize that most of today's security executives do not have the luxury of a business degree. Nor have they had the opportunity to test their classroom theories in the open market immediately upon graduation. Rather their experience has been gained in the public sector. And even though many of today's management principles can be applied in both the private and the public arenas, there are some very significant differences between the two arenas. The successful asset protection manager is the one who readily accepts this reality and adjusts accordingly.

When I'm asked to host a workshop or seminar, I am frequently asked to address this very issue. It is little wonder, then, that I would use this issue as the platform for all of what follows. Over the last several years I have been invited to speak before large numbers of security executives to work through the issue of organizational survival. Most of the time such survival is defined as protecting the integrity of companies' programs, but it is not uncommon to be asked to address specifically the issue of personal survival.

There is also the need to recognize that senior managers have their biases too. For many executives believe that prior public service experience is a handicap. I recall my first meeting with a bank executive client a few years back. Within minutes he was telling me about his security director. He described him as being very bright, so bright that he was the youngest police chief ever appointed in his home state. But the client went on to tell me that he was very concerned about the security director's ability to grasp the significance of the bank's intended conversion from in-house security staff to a third-party provider. As he commented, "You know how these cops are. They can only define themselves by the number of men working for them."

He went on to add that despite his admiration for the security director, if he had it to do over again, he wouldn't hire an ex-cop. He concluded that former law enforcement personnel just don't seem to have the ability to make business decisions. A short while later I had the opportunity to meet the director privately for the first time. When I asked if he knew why I was there, he responded: "Boy, I hope it is to convince these guys the value in converting my guards. We're paying an arm and a leg for them, and as a group, I think we could do a lot better in terms of quality."

Without a doubt, I could fill the remaining pages of this book and several others with similar anecdotes. Conversely, I could also tell of situations in which it was painfully obvious to everyone, including the security manager, that because the security manager was a former military officer or police executive, the transition to private security was a total disaster. Why is this so? The answer lies within the individual. Some people can make the transition; others cannot. The same can be said of those who can make the change from one management style to another. Over the years I have found that success or the lack thereof has little to do with the public sector/private security relationship. Instead, it centers on the person's ability to adapt to the change.

Executives, especially American executives, are quick to look for simple solutions. We look to affix blame as fast as we can, and we're focusing on what appears to be the most obvious answer. There is an old adage that has always intrigued me: If it walks like a duck, sounds like a duck, and looks like a duck, it probably is a duck. If that were so, why is it that sporting goods stores sell so many wooden decoys? The point is that the reason that someone is not successful ought not be so simplistically explained away by saying, "Well, what would you expect from a former cop?"

I can make a few observations about public sector recruits. The evidence would suggest that a person coming from the public sector has more than the hurdle of bias to overcome. Although I can provide no scientific proof to back my assertion, I have come to conclude that it takes even the most sophisticated public servant nearly three years to become "corporatized." That is because to make the transition there are cultural and organizational differences security professionals need to learn, cultivate, and experience.

I recall sitting in the audience of a large gathering of security managers next to a security manager for a large company who was widely regarded for his business acumen. We were listening to a speaker address the very issue of making the transition from public service to private security. The speaker was making several excellent points when the man sitting next to me leaned over and commented on how much he could have used this advice when he first left the military and joined his company. I looked at him and smiled, recollecting how I, too, could have benefited in the same way when I accepted my first corporate position.

Several years ago, I developed a workshop entitled The Corporatization of the Public Servant in direct response to a number of requests from police and military officials who were considering retirement and wanted to pursue a second career in private security. They had talked to enough security directors to know that they were going to need some front-end coaching if they were going to be successful in their new role, not to mention learning how to bid competitively for a security manager's job with a for-profit organization. The seminar was designed to address a wide variety of contemporary issues from the employment process through developing the skill sets necessary to survive. I explained how the transition involves learning how to acquire the corporate image, to choose the proper attire, and to read important, but not always plainly visible, organizational signs. In my previous book, I dedicated an entire section to reading the handwriting on the corporate wall. All of this is important because it serves as the foundation upon which you build for your ultimate success.

The New Perspective

Thriving requires the right orientation. No longer are the assumptions of yesterday valid. Defining your organizational importance based on the size of your department or operating budget, once-valued criteria, is no longer apropos. For that matter, the real measure of success has nothing to do with *bigness*, per se. Today's competitive marketplace seeks the value of "less is best." Senior management's challenge is to find ways to meet program goals and objectives with far less than what has historically been allocated.

In other words, you can become a hero by accepting the fact that quality of service can actually be increased while reducing the level of resourcing. Many security managers believe that quality is linked to maintaining current levels or increased levels of resourcing. This is simply not true. More often than not, it is quite possible to achieve higher quality with fewer resources. The first step to busting the "it can't be done" myth requires a shift in conventional thinking.

We are all capable of changing our perspective. Paraphrasing Jeremy Tarcher in his book, *The New Paradigm in Business,* The key to our inner resources is self-knowledge. Self-knowledge is gained by personal development and leads to success. By gathering experiences, new insights and wisdom arise.[1] Therefore, whether our personal background is rooted in the public sector or in the ranks of corporate life, there are experiences we need to draw upon as building blocks for new ways of thinking.

To gain this new insight, Tarcher suggests that we begin by recognizing the limitations of a system built on hierarchies and structured subordinates. Such a system is inherently rigid and requires multiple levels of resource allocation. It assigns specific tasks to groups of people. Often this leads to redundancies across organizational lines and competition for limited resources. The end result is a system that works directly against the values of quality service delivery and affordable pricing. For resident managers with a background in the military or law enforcement, this sort of system can be very troubling. After all, their primary orientation has always been within the context of a hierarchical system.

To survive, let alone thrive, a manager needs to understand that there is a new expected role. This involves the ability to coordinate and not dictate. It also means seeking support and collaboration with those outside the traditional boundaries of departmental units. Coordinating as a way of managing needs to replace giving orders. Moreover, in a hierarchical system it is not uncommon to push problems upward to be solved at the higher levels of the organization. We call this *upward delegation.* It does not always work out quite the way one expects.

There is the case of a group of middle managers who, when given almost every assignment, would delegate the final decision to their boss. This went on for a number of weeks. One day the boss called a staff meeting. Shortly after it commenced, he began issuing orders to those in attendance, giving them specific direction on how to resolve a number of outstanding issues. It didn't take long before staff members began complaining about their assignments.

Despite the protests the boss kept right on handing out the assignments. After a while one staffer said that he didn't understand what was going on, and he asked for an explanation. The boss seized the opportunity and calmly said, "Over the past several weeks each of you has been giving me one problem after another. Well, when you made your problem my problem, I naturally assumed that my resolution is your resolution." In other words, as staff members gave up ownership of their problems, they also gave up ownership of the resolutions.

Hierarchies, as a reflection of a traditional management approach, have their place. But in many of today's organizational environments, classical hierarchies may not be appropriate. Security managers who insist on adhering to these traditional systems face the likelihood of being criticized by those above and below them.

CHANGING ROLES IN SERVICE MARKETS

If we were to divide security service markets into broad categories I would suggest that those categories would be corporate head and field offices, property development, and specialized operations.

> *Corporate head and field offices.* These would include sales facilities, manufacturing complexes, processing centers, financial operations, and professional firms.

> *Property development.* These include developer- or investor-owned properties under the direct management of security or of a fee manager. Examples would include multi-tenant, mixed use, and residential properties.

> *Specialized operations.* Within government-owned properties, these would include embassies and consulates, correctional facilities, nuclear establishments, and judicial buildings. Other special use operations include schools and universities, health care facilities, retail centers, and entertainment complexes.

Traditionally security service providers have assumed more of a security management role within the property management sector than in any other business arenas. Over the recent years security providers have moved rapidly into many specialized operations within both the private and the public sector. For example, in the late 1980s it was fairly common to find a proprietary security operation within a large regional retail center. Within five years, the number of retail centers had significantly shifted such that today it is estimated that 50 percent or more of retail centers are now managed by third-party providers.

In a recent symposium for security provider executives, a health care security executive stated that security for the health care industry would be largely outsourced by the turn of the century. Less than ten years ago the use of a security company as a facility's primary asset protection resource was a rarity. He predicted that by 1998 the security for more than 60 percent of today's medical facilities will be contracted out.

Another major growth opportunity for contract security management has occurred within the public arena. Wackenhut Corporation serves as an excellent example of how a private company has infiltrated the prisoner control business. In times recently gone by, it was widely believed that only sworn police personnel could effectively deal with prisoner control. Today Wackenhut's success in correctional management is measured in terms of shareholder value because Wackenhut is a publicly traded company on one of the major stock exchanges.

It is also interesting to note that private security and local police agencies are developing some interesting alliances. Driven by the need to lower costs or provide more services for the same dollars, city and county governments are beginning to integrate private security with public law enforcement. Today it is common to find private security being used as a resource in airport security, county-owned hospitals, court buildings, and city-owned properties.

I firmly believe that before the turn of the century we will see private security serving as police dispatchers, lockup specialists, traffic control officers, and as investigators responding to cold crimes such as auto and residential thefts. In many communities these services are currently performed by civilian personnel on the police department's payroll. Yet as the compensation requirements of these workers continue to rise, city officials will look more to the private sector to backfill these assignments with professionals with the same degree of capability but at lower costs. In short, just as police personnel have bargained away these positions to civilians, so today's police civilians are unwittingly dealing themselves out of employment tomorrow.

Even though security companies have been taking over corporate security operations for years, the current wave is unprecedented. Over the past ten years the pendulum has clearly swung from a reliance on proprietary security operations to contracted third parties. It is not unusual for someone to be introduced to a corporate security manager only to discover later that the individual is actually an employee of an external business partner. The conversion to external security providers is particularly evident at the middle management and operational levels. Many large corporations have opted to retain their security director and outsource most if not all of the operation below the director. This switch has frequently been accompanied by a shift in the director's full-time responsibilities. Instead of being dedicated to asset protection alone, today's security manager will often have a variety of other competing responsibilities.

All of this has given rise to what I refer to as the *eclectic manager.* By this I mean that the current environment is much different from that of the past, requiring that security managers be more versatile and have a wider range of skills. Businesses are seeking alternatives in both approach and management resourcing. The field of security is no different.

MODELS OF SECURITY MANAGEMENT

Present-day security management is as varied as the business sectors security serves. What was once the exclusive domain of retired military or law enforcement today is as diversified as any other profession. Although it would be possible to profile the average asset manager through a national survey, to do so would not do justice to what is really unfolding in the profession, because business decision makers are systematically challenging the need to have one type of security person versus another. Some have elected to stay the course with a security manager whose background reflects traditional experiences. On the opposite end of the continuum, there are others who have elected to introduce security managers who have no background in private security or public law enforcement.

Against this backdrop three security manager models have emerged: the resident security manager, the contract security manager, and the nonsecurity security manager.

The Resident Manager

My first experience with corporate security was in 1979 with Crocker National Bank. I had just left law enforcement as a civilian administrator for a progressive municipal police department in the San Francisco Bay area. During my tenure with the Fremont Police I had the opportunity to interface with a handful of corporate security directors and attend the local chapter meetings of the American Society for Industrial Security. From these experiences I assumed that nearly every organization of any reasonable size had someone on staff serving as the resident security manager. This notion was reinforced early on at Crocker. At the bank our staff actively interacted with other security departments in an effort to share what today would be termed world-class operations based on best practices. In security we were interested in turning around our reputation as the most robbed bank in the most robbed state. To do so required finding proven strategies by seeking out resident security managers and soliciting their input. We found that their experiences and approaches ran the gamut from very effective to nothing or little at all.

As a result of these experiences, I learned firsthand that the value of a resident manager is directly proportional to his or her level of commitment and understanding of the job. The latter is particularly critical since many resident managers, even to this day, don't really understand their primary duty as an asset protection manager. They think they do, but often they miss either the nuances of the business they purport to protect, or define their responsibilities according to their agenda as opposed to that of their end users. We'll have a great deal more to say about this in Chapter 5 when we discuss strategies associated with third-party providers. Suffice it to say, today competent resident security executives have a critical role to play.

Over the past few years the notion of having a resident manager has come under severe attack, especially in organizations attempting to downsize in order to achieve greater competitiveness in the marketplace. In such cases, jobs that are not considered to bring true added value are eliminated. Since many of today's security managers do not have the background or skills they need to present both their programs and their individual capabilities in value-added terms, it ought not come as a surprise to hear that many of them have had their position eliminated. Effectively defending this assault is something we will address shortly.

Emerging growth-oriented companies have a real struggle with the idea of employing a full-time security manager. For them making such a commitment means breaking through the barrier of "We're too small and can't afford a full-time director" to the recognition that without a dedicated resource their level of risk will continue to escalate, and actual losses will go unchecked. Clearly there is a need to acknowledge that in any business venture there is a window of risk associated with any aspect of the operation. The questions for each organization to answer are, What is our level of tolerance? and Can we afford to leave the window open, and how much?

In 1995 I had the opportunity to participate in an interesting research project with members of the senior class of the Criminal Justice Department at California State University at Hayward. The objective was to survey businesses of all sizes in all sectors of the San Francisco Bay area to determine at what point they developed a formal security program. We targeted sixteen cities, including the Silicon Valley communities and the metropolitan areas of the East and West Bay, San Jose, and San Francisco, including Marin County. Organizations were grouped by reported size, based on sales or asset base. The sectors included service, product manufacturers, and professional firms. The results were fascinating. Among other findings, we determined the following:

♦ Companies under $400 million in sales typically did not think about physical security and were only casually interested in intellectual property and data security issues.

♦ Companies between $500 million and $600 million in sales or assets actively discussed the need for a formal program among their senior management group and often had some form of security. Typically this involved the use of a contract agency.

♦ Companies over $1 billion in sales or assets had fully established security programs including dedicated staffing, formal practices and procedures, and supporting technology.

♦ Companies in the manufacturing and high-tech arenas, followed closely by service providers in the areas of health care and finance, were the most sensitive to the need for security.

♦ Companies located in multi-tenant high-rises, irrespective of their size, had very little physical security and relied on building management as a tenant amenity. (This explains in large part the tragic outcome of the infamous 101 California Street, San Francisco, shooting: A mad gunman freely entered the offices of one of what was then the largest law firms in the city and eventually killed several people and wounded many more.)

Is there a basic business rationale for employing a resident security manager? Depending on the size and nature of the organization, there are four traditional considerations for employing an asset protection professional:

Administrative accountability. Given the size of the organization, its complexity and the number of people who frequent the facilities (for example, employees, customers, visitors, vendors, and so forth) there is a need for someone to manage and oversee the three critical components of any security program, namely, policy development and compliance; staffing, whether it is dedicated or integrated into the general employee base as an added responsibility; and systems and technology management.

Establishing employee awareness and responsibility. Without accountability, it is easy for widespread indifference to develop among most employee groups regarding basic security procedures and practices. Central to the prevention of security-related occurrences is establishing both a comprehensive program of employee aware-ness and a willingness on employees' part to assume greater respon-sibility for personal safety and asset protection. In today's climate, with middle managers being inundated with added responsibilities, absent a central point of focus, increased loss and a breakdown of safety are being reported in both the trade journals and the general media.

Systems management. Beyond the administration of such devices as access control, photo ID badges, and so forth, there is a need for someone with experience to oversee and manage the daily opera-tional concerns and activities for all security systems. Included in these responsibilities is interfacing with suppliers and service pro-viders charged with the responsibility of maintaining existing sys-tems. Moreover the security professional should be responsible for researching state-of-the-art technology to assure that the company is receiving the best value for its money.

External liaisons. The very nature of asset protection requires that the security manager interface with a variety of external sources, ranging from suppliers and vendors to public law enforcement and regulatory agencies, or sometimes with private insurance adjusters and litigant counsel representing action filed against the corpora-tion. Regardless, there is often a requirement that the company have a resource dedicated to investigating the incident, communicating with the appropriate agencies, and analyzing the root cause behind individual incidents to determine preventive strategies. As a part of this process, the security manager should meet with other security directors in the immediate area as well as conduct individual research to determine how others deal with like incidents within their own organizations.

There are other factors that need to be blended into the overall deci-sion. A summary of the responsibilities for the resident manager might look like this one, developed by Applied Materials, Inc.:

The director of corporate security is the senior security manager for the corporation and charged with responsibility for the protec-tion of the organization's personnel, assets, and loss prevention. The director is responsible for addressing security risks, internal and external, to the corporation. The director should have exper-tise in all security disciplines under his/her supervision and should manage all security activities in the company's global operations.

The director should also maintain a professional presence in the local and national security community to benefit the company through the sharing of information and expertise with other security professionals and law enforcement groups.

Beyond these general precepts, specific areas of responsibility that fall to a resident security manager might include the following:

Corporate Security Policies. The resident manager might be charged with developing, obtaining approval for, and promulgating corporate security policies. Policies should address all key security issues covered in the corporate security statement—all that is important to the consistency and effectiveness of security operations. Among the resident manager's policy responsibilities is providing guidelines and counsel to ensure that corporate security policies are implemented in accordance with their intent. Moreover, the resident manager should ensure that security policies are implemented, which also means providing recommendations for modifications as required by a changing risk environment and corporate operations. Staying abreast of legislative enactments and judicial rulings that would affect the company's security program would also be important.

Management Responsibility. The resident manager should function as a member of the corporate staff. In such a position, the resident manager should provide counsel to all levels of the corporate management structure on security matters. He or she should manage the corporate security department to ensure successful achievement of security goals and objectives, and assist in the development of emergency plans to ensure orderly response to security-related events such as protests, intrusions, attacks against facilities, threats, kidnapping, and other extortions.

Security Operations. The resident manager should prepare and update, as necessary, an annual corporate security department budget reflecting anticipated requirements in terms of personnel and capital. He or she should oversee the daily operations of the security program by employing other resident staff or relying on the services of a third-party provider. Also the resident manager should act as the primary liaison with security consultants who supplement specific aspects of the overall corporate security program and complement the functions of the director of corporate security.

Physical Security. Another responsibility of the resident manager is developing standards to define the minimum protection that should be provided for the company's personnel and assets in all facilities or at all corporate-sponsored events. Periodically he or she should review the overall security program to ensure its practicality and effectiveness, and then revise the program as changing risk and operational environments require. The resident manager might develop a program to provide security surveys of facilities; such surveys should include checklists to be used by facility personnel on routine audits and actual visits by members of the corporate security department and internal audit to the company-owned facilities. Other tasks might involve maintaining an in-depth awareness of the state-of-the-art security systems, and developing security systems specifications for corporate facilities and subsidiaries. The resident manager might also coordinate with engineering and facilities management on construction projects to ensure that security is incorporated into initial planning for facilities.

Employee Protection. Systematically assessing the security risks to corporate officers and high-profile employees is another responsibility of the resident manager. This assessment should be conducted for personnel involved in both domestic and international operations. When circumstances warrant, the security manager should develop and implement an executive protection program. The program should involve, at a minimum, security awareness training for involved personnel, residential security, security in executive offices, travel security, and maintenance of a risk database. When appropriate, this should include providing for special security arrangements for annual shareholders' meetings, off-site board of directors' meetings, and special events.

Protection of Proprietary Information. The resident manager might develop a corporate security policy concerning the protection of proprietary information. This ought to include implementing the proprietary information policy for the company by issuing procedures, by conducting awareness training, and by offering educational programs. Also it should include providing ongoing monitoring of the proprietary information protection program by conducting periodic inspections of various offices, product development areas, and computer facilities. Further, the resident manager might want to coordinate with the organization's information management division concerning the design and implementation of the corporate data security program.

Investigations. The resident manager should coordinate all investigative activities, including internal investigations of corporate personnel who have violated local, state, and federal laws. He or she should personally oversee or conduct any investigations of a highly sensitive nature as requested by senior corporate management.

Loss Prevention.   Another task of the resident manager is implementing a program that will provide a means of regular and exceptional reporting of security-related events. This work might involve developing a security information database concerning loss and all other security-related incidents that can be used to justify preventive programs and resource allocations. The security manager will want to maintain close liaison with the company's risk management group, internal auditing, purchasing, controllers, and the legal department to ensure a timely exchange of information regarding losses. He or she should develop loss prevention programs to reduce loss by theft, misappropriation, embezzlement, and fraud, and submit a summary of losses to management for appropriate consideration and/or action.

Human Resources.   Coordinating with the human resources department, the resident might work up a program of pre-employment investigations. The objective of the program would be to check the validity of an applicant's credentials and to preclude the hiring of a candidate whose background is incompatible with the position. In conjunction with human resources, the security manager might enhance specific programs such as the company's substance abuse program, workplace violence program, and employee assistance program (EAP) through review and modification, if required, of policies, procedures, and work rules along with appropriate protocols such as EAP and disciplinary practices.

The Pros and Cons of a Resident Manager
Following are the advantages of hiring a full-time resident security manager:

- Your security department can develop a core competency directly tailored to meet the business needs of the organization.
- The company has direct control over the employment and assignment of the security manager, as opposed to the potential for the manager to be reassigned by a third party.
- The company can promote performance-based results by directly controlling both incentives and disincentives; senior management can control outcomes based on merit to raise performance requirements.
- The company can better control the loss of confidential information by requiring nondisclosure and non-complete agreements. Breaches can be better litigated when action is directed at employees by the company as opposed to through agents of third parties.

The disadvantages of hiring a resident manager, which also parallel those of hiring any other middle manager include, but are not limited to the following:

♦ Generally speaking, hiring an in-house manager involves a higher expense, as reflected in the need for paying a starting wage that can run as high as 15 percent over comparable fees paid to a manager from a third-party supplier.
♦ The company loses the opportunity to transfer risk by engaging the services of an external supplier.
♦ Security will be slower to address turnover since third-party providers generally have better access to the industry and can meet turnover more rapidly as a result of promoting or reassigning someone from within their company.
♦ Employing an in-house manager restricts the organization to the skill set, capabilities, and other limited resources inherent within the manager and the company. This disadvantage can be offset by using a third-party provider, whose own core competency is security, and who generally has a wider array of supporting resources, such as system design, engineers, trainers, research capabilities, and so forth.

The Resident Manager's Background
Today's resident security managers typically reflect one of the following backgrounds:

♦ They entered the security profession from a career in law enforcement or the military,
♦ They came up through the security ranks; either as an employee of their current organization or from another security department or provider,
♦ They arrived in security from another business unit within the company, having no previous experience in security.

The Contract Provider as Security Manager

It is not unusual to find that the management of the security function has been taken and assigned to a third-party provider. In an era of developing strategic partnering, many corporations are opting for the *virtual organization* approach. For the security services industries this presents an interesting challenge, the outcome of which is far from certain.

For years the service industry has complained that its clients have categorized security as nothing more than a supplier of limited services.

Security professionals have charged that rarely are they given the opportunity to enter into a true partnership. If allowed the chance, they contend, they would have the expertise to manage the client's program. "Just give us the chance!" has become their unofficial battle cry. Given the business forces presently facing corporate executives, the opportunity is here. Some providers are ready. Others are awakening to this new reality. Still others are only talking the talk and haven't a clue as to how to step up to the challenge. And then there are those who haven't even given the issue much thought.

So just as we have seen with resident security managers, for contract security providers the ability to meet today's challenges is a direct reflection of their commitment, experience, and willingness to adapt. In Chapter 7 of *Business Strategies* we examined the various relationships between client and contractor. Here we will revisit the three basic types of relationships.

The first is the buyer-seller relationship, whose distinguishing characteristic is its one-way nature. The client chiefly determines the scope of the work, provides direction, and makes nearly all the decisions, especially those governing business considerations. The second type of relationship is the preferred vendor relationship. Here the supplier is given a certain amount of latitude, but the client is still clearly the driving force. The last type is a relatively new dynamic requiring that a strategic partnering take place between the two parties. It is this latter relationship that we need to concentrate on since it is rapidly replacing the former two as the "relationship of choice" for both client and supplier.

In a strategic partnership the supplier becomes the managing arm of the security function. The client sets the parameters for what is expected, and the supplier is charged with carrying out the operational requirements. Considerable discretionary decision making is given to the provider. Often the provider is called upon to establish operating budgets, assist in the development of related capital projects, and take the initiative in scouting out cost saving opportunities. Typically the company's fee is fixed, with incentives available to encourage bold thinking and approaches. Since the provider's profit is not tied to the number of guard hours billed, the provider can afford to make recommendations that could well mean a reduction in the hours of coverage.

This background is necessary since it frames the need for a different type of account manager. Corporations electing to make the provider their de facto security department recognize the need for the account manager to be first and foremost a business manager, much as they would expect their resident manager to take the same role. The notion of a security manager being a *captain of the watch* is simply no longer valid.

A few years back I was asked to review the security operation for a large independent refinery. Security for this particular facility was provided by a well-known and highly regarded security service provider. The primary objective of the review was to assist the refinery management in determining current security requirements, since they were concerned about the lack of management direction being given by their provider.

At the same time the third-party supplier was concerned and believed the root of the problem was a lack of direction from the refinery. As a result of our analysis we concluded that the root of the problem was the account manager. In reality he had "retired on the job" and was beyond his level of competency. When he had first arrived, the position had been significantly less than what it had now evolved into. Because of his tenure and personality, everyone knew and liked "good ol' Jack." Most employees and managers had accepted Jack's limitations over the years.

But as times changed and the refinery became more concerned about employee safety and security, a group of people became frustrated with Jack and blamed the security provider. Assumptions about one thing or another were made on both sides, and it wasn't long before frustrations began to mount. To the credit of everyone involved, the refinery management and the security provider sought the assistance of an independent third party before the otherwise long-standing and solid relationship could disintegrate. The solution was simple. Jack wanted to stay on at the refinery but in a diminished capacity. The security provider wanted Jack to stay, and so did refinery management.

Jack accepted a lower position, and a new contract security manager was hired. His replacement was an experienced, business-oriented security professional who understood the refinery business. The end result was a positive outcome for everyone. Unfortunately this is not always the case. All too often frustrations and misunderstandings are allowed to fester until an event occurs, and then it is too late. The relationship is finished.

It's surprising how many long-standing relationships are terminated over what would otherwise be considered a less than significant event. The incident may be nothing more than a flash point resulting from an accumulation of episodes that could have been managed better. After reviewing hundreds of provider-client relationships, I have found that the common denominator underlying a change in provider is the contractor's inability to manage the account at the local level. Adept local management is the key to a successful relationship. While many argue that price is the determinant, in reality confidence in the security supplier's management ability is more often the key. As Tom Marano, president of Argenbright Security Services, comments, "Security companies need to understand that we are selling customer relationships and not guard hours." This is an incredibly perceptive comment, because it goes to the heart of what security service is really all about. Commonly both clients and security providers believe that more than 90 percent of the contractor's responsibility is customer service. Therefore it is essential that the local management team be well versed in the business of offering customer service in the most effective and efficient manner.

Being an account manager has never been so challenging as it is today, because client expectations are very high. As service providers step forward and willingly accept the added responsibility of truly managing the security function, the skill set required of their account managers continues to increase. Traditionally security providers had been used to providing an individual who was little more than a supervisor or lead officer. But the playing field has changed. Business leaders now look to the security provider to assign a manager with proven business management skills. Over the course of a year I typically assist several organizations in the selection of a third-party provider; this has been ongoing since 1979. In the past two years an interesting phenomenon has begun to emerge. If it is determined that an account manager is required, it is not unusual for the client to specify that the manager have proven business management experience. Ideally the client wants a mix of hands-on security experience and mid-level business management experience. The typical expectation is that the account manager have a minimum of two years of experience in a manager's role, the reason being that the client wants an individual who can assist the company by actively participating in the business decisions associated with the security program. The client expects that the manager will have the ability to set operating budgets, participate in capital budgeting projects, and represent the organization to tenants, clients, customers, and vendors. Even the most sacred of sacred organizational cows is no longer kept away from the third-party provider, for example, the press.

Historically companies have absolutely prohibited security personnel from talking to the media, particularly if an event or incident is sensitive. The rationale is that the company wants total control over what is said, how it is said, and to whom it is said. Corporate counsels and media relations people are typically resolute in this. Yet with companies relying on more external providers and fewer corporate staff, this is not always possible.

Consider the following example. Corporate management for a chain of retail malls was conducting a national meeting of center managers in Albuquerque, New Mexico, in late 1995. The management team for one of the premier properties was in attendance. A sensitive security situation involving a customer occurred late one night while the center managers were away. After security notified them, the center managers advised security that corporate management would address the media early the next morning and instructed security to handle the matter accordingly. By the time everyone retired that evening, all appeared to be well in hand. Unfortunately, and totally unexpectedly, early the next morning the center was overtaken by the local press. The only management member on-site was the contract security manager. Immediate action was required. He assessed the situation and called the center managers at the national meeting and advised them of the unfolding events. He was given the briefest of briefings and instructed to address the media. He did. Center management was confident in him because they knew his ability, background, and commitment to the property.

As corporate management held its breath, the account manager demonstrated his experience and ability. His knowledge of the mall, its rules, and the mall's policies made the press meeting a success. Most reporters assumed he was a corporate employee because of his knowledge of the mall and the way he handled the situation.

It is true that such success stories can be offset by any number of other less than successful press encounters. My point in raising this positive example here, however, is to underscore several important issues. First, the outcome of this situation is a direct result of the account manager's experience: he was not just a security professional; he knew his client's policies and their concerns. Second, he understood the sensitivities involved, and that he represented his customer, not his own company, and certainly not his own ego.

Other lessons to be taken from this example include the company's trust in its account manager. Admittedly it was a risk, but one they were willing to take. This confidence is the result of a proven relationship developed over time and with the successful handling of other incidents in the past. Therefore, account management is a reflection of continuity, proven capability, and commitment to the client.

These are the hallmarks of competent security management by a third-party team. Absent them, there can be no opportunity to truly partner. In an era of great competition for both client and supplier, account managers need to be capable of relating to business needs that transcend the requirements of asset protection.

Before leaving our discussion of contract account managers, we will look at the particular benefits associated with the use of a third-party manager as opposed to a resident manager.

Reduced Cost.   Generally speaking, a resident manager costs more. The outlay for a contract security manager typically runs 10 percent to 15 percent less, despite the service provider's need to charge overhead, inclusive of a profit margin. Some caution is required here, however. As corporations move to a greater dependency on external managers, the job requirements of account managers are increasing, thereby driving up the cost of employing them. In time, it would not be unreasonable to expect that the economic advantage of using a third-party provider may fade away. For the present, however, the economic advantage remains with the third-party provider.

Transference of Risk. With the use of an external account manager, the corporate client is able to create an arm's-length distance between itself and any potential liability claims. This is one of the classic reasons for outsourcing the security function. Although no corporation can totally delegate its security responsibility away (in the legal community it has been a long established legal opinion that security is considered a nondelegable duty), it is possible to create an arm's length relationship between the corporation and any potential injured party, thus reducing the company's liability.

Reduced Turnover Time. It is possible to decrease the amount of time associated with replacing a security manager. Resident managers are not recruited overnight. It is not uncommon to experience a six- to eight-week turnaround time or longer. It is possible for client and provider to reach a contractual agreement assuring the provision of a new security manager in significantly less time. The provider can transfer a manager from another account, promote a lower-level manager to your account, or temporarily backfill your position with another manager until a permanent replacement can be found.

Management Flexibility. Employing the services of a third-party provider gives corporate management the luxury of not having to deal with conventional personnel issues, including conducting evaluations, training, promotional/demotional actions, and so forth. The greatest advantage is that the client can request the immediate removal of a security manager from the account and have the action happen expeditiously. Although this demand may create a challenge for the provider, the client then escapes the hassles associated with an extended disciplinary process for a manager who is not working out for the company.

The Nonsecurity Security Manager

There was a time when selected middle managers were asked to wear multiple organizational hats. Oftentimes operational staff were asked to assume the responsibility for security. Largely businesses employing these generalist managers were small corporations. Some businesses no longer have this luxury. Community banks, small savings and loans, and credit unions, like their larger counterparts, have been required to designate a security officer since 1968 as part of federal regulations designed to reduce bank robberies. Financial services is one of the few business sectors that has such a requirement. With the advent of downsizing and management models designed to flatten the organization, some of the private sector's largest corporations that are not required by law to have a specialized security officer have adopted the generalist manager approach. Over the course of time, those companies that have experimented with lumping the security function under the umbrella of someone who does not have an asset protection background have had mixed results. Not surprisingly, those business sectors that have specialized security needs—such as health care, financial services, and public utilities—find that having a dedicated security professional onboard is essential.

The Upside/Downside of Using Nonsecurity Security Managers

Upside 1: New Insight.   I have found that one of the chief arguments for using a nonsecurity manager to administrate the asset protection program is that such a person brings a new insight to the position. He or she is not burdened by past assumptions or jaded by previous experiences. When considering this advantage, I'm reminded of Mike Foil at Mellon Bank. Very well regarded among bank security circles, Foil took his first security post as the bank's security director. Prior to that he had held a number of positions within the bank.

Because of Foil's business orientation, he has always been willing to experiment with new methods and approaches. He is credited with introducing the concept of access control units (ACUs) to the U.S. domestic market. An ACU is a stand-alone glass vestibule that attaches to the entrance and exit of a retail branch. It was originally pioneered in Puerto Rico and is an extension on the idea of a conventional mantrap. Its purpose is to thwart takeover robberies involving several armed suspects since only one person can enter the bank at a time. Using metal detectors and weight sensors, the bank teller can control who enters or leaves when an alarm is activated within the mantrap.

Under Foil's direction, the bank has purchased several of these units and is expanding their use. The direct economic advantage to the bank has been its ability to successfully eliminate the need for a security officer at these branches, saving the bank approximately $30,000 per officer per year. Moreover, the retail unit is safer, and the employees have direct control over who enters and leaves the branch. Customers like the devices because they feel safer. The end result is a three-way win: the customers, the branch employees, and the bank win through an improved level of security and a lower operating expense.

Was a nonsecurity manager required to bring about this success? Obviously not. However, this type of nontraditional thinking is commonly brought out by assigning individuals with a broader business experience to the security manager's post. And this is not to say that those brought up through the traditional security ranks could not, or do not, have similar critical thinking capabilities. But given the individual biases of senior executives and their personal experiences with limited thinkers in the ranks of security, it is easy to understand why they believe that nonsecurity security managers are their managers of choice.

Upside 2: Broader Business Orientation. Foil's truer contribution to the bank is his track record of addressing the daily operational challenges associated with running the security program at Mellon Bank. The bank, like most other organizations, is continuously looking for ways to hold even or lower its operating costs. As a result there is constant pressure on unit heads to seek alternative strategies. Given Foil's background and business orientation, he is willing to experiment with the window of risk to determine the optimal degree of opening. By adopting this overall strategy, he can then adjust his allocated resources to reflect current emphases without abrogating his department's commitment to comprehensive asset protection.

Upside 3: Assumption of a Broader Organizational Role. Another advantage to the organization of drawing on the services of nonsecurity personnel is the company's ability to leverage on the personnel's experience to assume greater organizational roles. Nonsecurity managers are found assuming unit head responsibilities for a variety of support operations, including food services, transportation, shipping and receiving, facilities management, to name but a few.

Upside 4: No Vested Interest. The security profession has long been characterized as one of those industries largely driven by a strong internal network. Phrases such as "good ol' boys," "the fraternity," "closed shop," have been commonly used in the past. They reflect a time when security directors were a small group, tightly controlled by a previous culture that promoted selected inclusivity and general exclusivity. As we have seen already, security professionals were largely drawn from the ranks of law enforcement, and being an ex-policeman gave you a certain degree of instant credibility and trust. A number of excellent books and papers have been written over the years analyzing this we-they syndrome, which is as much alive today as it was at the turn of the century.

Given their background, it is not surprising that security directors of yesteryear reflected a value system, and therefore a decision-making process, that favored "one of their own" over someone else. Whether or not this culture truly exists today as a predominant influence has also been the topic of some debate. Suffice it to say, it exists to the extent that many corporate executives believe that security directors are still largely a closed group. It is not uncommon to see senior managers seeking out individuals with no prior security history to avoid the inbred favoritism or being forced into preselected purchasing choices. Further, it is assumed that an individual with no particular ties to the industry can make more objective operational decisions vis-à-vis company policies, practices, staffing, and other resource allocations because they hold no preset group of assumptions.

Downside 1: Lack of Advocacy.   By going outside the profession the company always faces the risk that the security manager may not be a strong advocate of security. If the security manager lacks an internal commitment, the function of protecting assets will suffer. Over the past two years, I have come to know firsthand four current senior-level security managers of Fortune 200 companies who are openly indifferent to asset protection. When asked how they came to assume the added responsibility of security, they confided that their boss thought it was a positive move. In short, the organization wanted to recognize their efforts and contributions and decided to "reward" them by giving them the added duty of security.

As companies resize, they will commonly look for managers they believe have stretch capabilities. These managers are commonly "asked" to assume added duties. Not wanting to appear as though they are not team players, they accept, at the same time knowing that this new accountability is not something they would naturally pursue. The end result is a lack of strongly advocacy for a responsible security program. Stated another way, security simply becomes another area of direct reporting—an added burden. Or, as one of the four managers I spoke with candidly characterized it, "For me, being accountable for security means I have another opportunity to fail."

Downside 2: The Intimidation Factor.   For the uninitiated, the business of asset protection can be intimidating. Bound by constantly shifting legal opinions regarding liabilities, lacking defined regulations to serve as a guideline, and considered by many more a necessary evil than a value-added benefit, the security business can be frustrating for even the most ardent enthusiast.

Private security is a growing business in and of itself. Estimates for yearly expenditures range from a low of $35 billion to a high of $45 billion. Regardless of the exact value, the amount of money spent on security is considerably higher today than it was ten years ago when estimates ranged from $10 to $15 billion annually. With this explosive growth, the business of protecting assets and people has become very sophisticated, and figuring out the proper resource allocation for an organization can be a very complex process.

Downside 3: Loss of Credibility.   Whether it is a case of indifference, lack of proper prioritization, or the desire to be effective yet the lack of adequate resources, it is easy for the nonsecurity manager to lose credibility as a result of a classic organizational Catch-22. Regardless of executive management's reasons for assigning security to the generalist, if daily operational needs can not be effectively met, or if a more serious event occurs and it is not handled properly, the generalist loses credibility. Oftentimes the manager's loss can be even greater (for example, demotion or termination).

Once the generalist has accepted the security position, the senior management team is ready to move on to the next issue and assumes that their security needs are well in hand. "After all," they rationalize, "we have Joe in charge of security now, and everyone knows that Joe is a great manager." If Joe can handle the nuances of the position, executive management will have demonstrated their brilliant business acumen. Unfortunately, there is no guarantee that Joe will be a success.

Downside 4: The Need for External Support.   Given the complexity of providing security at some organizations, generalist managers are apt to seek the technical expertise of vendors and niche consultants. When vendors are sought out, their advice and recommendations are typically provided at no cost. But the cost of the time and expertise of these vendors is reflected in the purchase and/or installation cost of the systems they sell. Unless the generalist manager is a shrewd negotiator or has some knowledge of the marketplace, he or she can easily be duped or can take the most conservative route and over-spend. After all, the security manager cannot afford to be criticized for making decisions that could put employees, customers, and visitors in harm's way. Nonetheless, the end result is that the company spends more than it would have if the security management was left to a specialist.

Moreover, seeking out vendors is not always the wisest course of action because there is the inherent risk of a conflict of interest. Vendors

want to sell their service and/or product. While they may be well inten-
tioned, they are not necessarily objective since their "square box" may
not be the most appropriate solution for a security manager with a
"round-hole" problem. So, too, there is always the issue of whether or not
you can trust a vendor to be honest. Even though the vendor may be selling security services and products, this is no assurance that the vendor is
necessarily honest in assessing the company's needs and offering the most
appropriate and cost-effective solution.

Few companies actually budget for technical or niche consultants.
Consequently, authorization to use their expertise may be difficult to
obtain. If the consulting costs are okayed, the expectation is that the manager will recoup such an investment as quickly as possible. The manager
needs to make a strong business case for employing such services, which
in and of itself can consume precious time.

Ron Fischer and Mary Rabaut suggest that there are five critical
steps in selecting the right consultant:

1. *Do some research.* Network with professional and industry contacts,
   review trade journals and identify other companies, or areas within
   your own company, that have successfully tackled similar problems.
2. *Evaluate the consultant's style and expertise.* A proven track record for
   resolving similar issues for other firms is a key requirement when
   you're choosing a consultant. But so are the interpersonal and communication skills that create the right "chemistry."
3. *Compare the consultant's strengths against your needs.* Ask each firm
   to describe its ideal consulting assignment based on its expertise.
   Then design the engagement that best addresses your issues. Map
   the strengths of each consulting firm against your requirements—
   and determine the best fit.
4. *Analyze each firm's approach.* Is the firm open-minded enough to
   spot new opportunities that might arise when you are unraveling an
   issue? Is it flexible enough to shift gears and capitalize on such
   opportunities? Does it create a tailored solution or force fit a pre-
   defined one? Does the firm have a clear, sound view of the future so
   as to create long-term value? Is it sufficiently broad-based to link
   functional symptoms to cross-functional problems?
5. *Recognize that less is more.* To develop a meaningful proposal
   addressing your issues, members of your staff will need to spend
   time with each consulting firm you're considering. Therefore, hand-
   pick one or two firms to evaluate. This will be far more productive
   than staging a "consult-off" involving dozens of unknown firms.[2]

You can readily see that selecting a qualified consultant takes time and money. If a firm can demonstrate that they can give you a significant return on your investment, the effort may well be worth it. Conversely, you need to ask yourself if the organization wouldn't be better off in the long run employing a specialist who might have the same or a similar skill set.

SUMMARY

In this chapter we introduced the notion of the eclectic manager, reflecting the changing profile of today's security executive. Unlike previous times when the typical security manager had a background in the public sector, asset protection managers today are of fairly diverse experience. We saw that those who have migrated to the world of private security from law enforcement or the military, including both security professionals and the executive managers to whom they report, have a number of inherent biases that need to be overcome. Jeremy Tarcher suggests that a new perspective is needed, involving changing from the traditional orientation of viewing organizations as a hierarchy to adopting a willingness to embrace a flatter, more interactive role with subordinates and end users.

In addition to reflecting more business orientation, today's security managers are just as likely to emerge from other business segments altogether. Moreover, it is not unusual to find that a security director is not even an employee of the corporation. For as companies resize they are asking third-party providers to be their external business partners. The reliance on external resources in selected business arenas has broken wide open and even spilled over into the public sector.

We also looked at two emerging models. The first is a transitional model, which demonstrates a move away from operational management and toward internal consulting. The second model reflects a company that has completed the transition.

We explored in depth the three classic security manager models. These are the resident manager, the contract security manager, and the nonsecurity security manager, or generalist manager. Regardless of which model an organization opts to use, the duties and responsibilities of the security manager remain fairly consistent and fall into one or more of the following categories:

♦ corporate policy setting
♦ program management

- daily operations
- employee protection
- proprietary property protection
- investigations
- loss prevention
- human resources

We explored the challenges facing the contract security manager who is more frequently being asked to serve as the de facto security head. It is particularly critical for such managers to break away from their traditional roles of being receptors and assume a more proactive stance. Unlike days gone by, today's corporate executive is deferring to external partners and asking them to be true contributors to the management team. It is up to the security provider to rise to the challenge or be passed by.

Finally we examined the use of generalist managers as security decision makers. Even though generalist managers are a viable alternative, it is an option not without inherent risks that need to be calculated up front, with contingencies developed accordingly. On the positive side we found that generalists can bring new insights to the security post. They usually have a broad business orientation that sensitizes them to bottom-line performance and allows them to assume a broader organizational role. Further, they are less likely to be influenced by potential vested interests and conflicts.

On the downside, we found that generalist managers can be their own worst enemy if they do not have the level of commitment to security or if they can't be advocates for a strong security program. Some can be intimidated by the added responsibility and can therefore experience of loss of credibility. Also we found that companies that rely on a generalist can open the door to inefficiencies and a reliance on other external sources that may actually cost the company more, for example, by contracting for inappropriate systems or consulting services.

Having examined the eclectic character of today's asset protection managers, we turn our attention to one of the most difficult challenges facing today's third-party suppliers.

5

Busting the Commodity Syndrome

> I now realize one immense omission in my Psychology—the deepest
> principle of human nature is the craving to be appreciated.
>
> ...WILLIAM JAMES

Recently management experts have taken to describing support services in one of two ways: essential services or commodity services. Essential services are regarded as those activities that an organization needs to have to generate revenue and remain profitable. All other activities, they contend, are commodities and can be competitively bid out. The suggestion is that there is little difference between one commodity supplier and another. Thus, the smart business person is the one who can select the "best" based, in large part, on the lowest cost. Unfortunately security services have fallen into the commodity category.

Isn't it ironic then, that in this era of outsourcing, in a time when American businesses have decidedly turned to a reliance on external sources to address their internal support needs, contract security services are bleeding red ink?

As businesses turn to outside security providers to meet their asset protection needs, the relationship seems to be characterized as more of a tug-of-war than a partnership. For the past several years security industry giants, such as the big three—Borg-Warner, Pinkerton, and Wackenhut—

have published annual reports showing a steady erosion of profits in traditional guard operations. Because they are publicly traded, these companies are required to openly disclose earnings. Their counterparts are spared this rule because they are privately held. Nonetheless, in the hallways of conferences and association meetings the privately held companies, too, confide that their margins are diminishing at alarming rates— no pun intended.

Why the decline? The issue is multilayered and somewhat complex. It is important that we address the diminishing returns of security providers and seek remedies, since both the private and the public sector are relying more and more on these providers to protect their asset base and employee groups. When all is considered, at the core there is a perception on the part of client organizations that security is an organizational commodity. Senior managers, even at some of the more enlightened businesses, typically look upon the procurement of security services much as they would the purchase of an automobile. In other words, "best value for best price," which really means "adequate coverage for the cheapest price."

Here's an example of what I mean. I was recently asked to be part of the process of selecting a national provider for one of the country's largest financial institutions. The president of one of the prospective providers spent a considerable amount of time addressing the group about the issue of security being perceived as a commodity. When he left, the group agreed that to build a successful relationship with clients we need to begin by breaking down this perspective.

Feeling satisfied about the group's newly gained insight, the selection committee's chairman and I stepped out into the hallway to discuss the day's events. Soon afterward we were approached by the bank's most senior manager, who had ultimate responsibility for security. Since he had not been present at the presentations, we began to discuss what we had heard. Without warning he cut us short by asking, "What do you think the bottom line will be? After all, this is a commodity issue. Let's get the best guy for the best price [he meant lowest] and move on."

What do you think the outcome was? If you answered a quick "The lowest price provider won the contract," I wouldn't blame you. Typically that should have been the outcome. Much to the credit of the committee chairman (who coincidentally enough was an external property management provider), he turned and told the bank's senior manager that we needed to talk further. At that moment he must have quickly realized that two responses were possible: let the comment and underlying perspective go unchallenged and allow the process to be driven by dollars; or begin educating the executive vice president on why security is not a commodity and needs to be viewed differently.

The outcome was mixed. On the one hand, the final selection was not price driven. The client allowed the selection process to be focused on service capability. On the other hand, once the service provider was selected, the client began to hammer away at the provider's proposed pricing with a goal of reducing the original quote by 15 percent. We'll have more to say about this state of affairs a little later on. For now, however, it's important to point out that managers at client organizations cannot talk of quality customer service, added value contributions, and so forth at the same time as they are viewing security as a commodity to be purchased from the lowest bidder.

Service providers and resident security managers need to "revolt" against such a perspective or be content working in a profession that suffers from poorly paid workers, poor public image, and the image that they are profiteers. A few months ago I was asked to telephone the CEO of one of the top ten security companies. He wanted to complain about the unfair treatment he felt his company was receiving with regards to its policy toward employee retention and the impact of that policy on the company's pricing. In discussing the issue I pointed out that there are many different pricing strategies. His retort was, "Listen, I've been in this business for a long time. I don't care what the so-called experts have to say. Ours is a profession driven by dollars. High bid loses, low bid wins. That's all there is to it."

To underscore this perspective, recall that previously I mentioned that I received a letter from Tom Marano, CEO of Argenbright. In that letter he also wrote, "In an industry that is non-differentiated, the ultimate product is a commodity. With limited barriers to entry and no regulated standard of quality, competition is driven by pricing. As a result, little value is created for the client. Within the client's structure, the security function is a cost center that is not understood by the broader organization it serves. Consequently, a new paradigm is needed."

Both of these CEOs voice the predominant challenge facing their industry: getting over the hurdle of being judged based primarily on price. The first CEO is more fatalistic and will fail in the long run because he has resigned his company to the insidious trap of being measured primarily in dollars and cents. His company may continue to grow, and its revenues many increase, but his company will contribute little to enhancing true professionalism. Marano, while equally concerned, hasn't given up the fight. Instead, he goes on in his letter to say: "I'm not down on the industry. New thinking is required to build the future. If we do not change, our success will be limited. Let me know how I can help." Clearly he sees the need for a radical new approach. That new approach is the focus of this chapter.

THE COMMODITY SYNDROME

One of the unfortunate outcomes of the total quality management (TQM) movement has been the application of the term *commodity* to a service. Total quality management specialists have sold executives across the country on the notion that support services are little more than commodities that can be bought on the open market, largely through a bidding process. Given their attempts to lower expenses and control costs, this perception of services makes a great deal of sense. The rationalization is that janitors are janitors, landscapers are landscapers, and guards are guards. And the thinking is that there is very little difference between one service provider and another, so why not bid their services and let the "best price" be the determining factor?

Best price. What exactly does this mean? As noted above, in today's corporate parlance, best price almost always means lowest price; moreover, it rarely—if ever—means "best value." Best pricing means what it says—that is, the one with the lowest price, ergo the "best" or most advantageous price for the customer. In contrast going after *best value* connotes a willingness to pay a higher price if the return on the investment is higher. This critical distinction gets to the very core of the issue. Convincing executives to look for the best value is key to breaking executives away from perceiving critical support services such as asset protection as commodities.

Services cost. The consideration of being willing to pay for services must then be set within the context of "getting the best result for the dollars spent." If the service is defined primarily in terms of money spent, then quality is secondary, and the services received can never be maximized. Consider the following: An executive receives proposals from two security companies. The first offers a rate of $10 per hour. It's a good offer, and the company will likely provide a solid security service. The second proposes $11 per hour, but this company has demonstrated a willingness to work with the executive to generate revenue of $50,000 per year, or the company has indicated that it can redefine the company's approach to asset protection and reduce insurance premiums, lower litigative expense, and so forth. Which is the best price? The first one. Which is the best value? Obviously, the latter. Perceiving security as a commodity encourages going for the best price and completely misses the opportunity for securing the best value.

On one level there is actually nothing wrong with the concept of best price, because it assumes that there is really no difference in the service offerings from one provider to provider. On another level, such a perspective is riddled with misconceptions and errors. Best-price/low-price thinking is very dangerous thinking, because it makes the issue of quality of no consequence. False corporate heroes are born as executives profess to have saved the company "big money," only to have the resulting lack of quality create significant losses further down the road. At this point you might ask if it isn't possible to have both quality and the lowest price. I contend that this is not possible if the prevailing perspective is to define service as a commodity. Let me explain.

Commodities refer to tangible products. Calling a service a commodity misses the distinction entirely. An alarm is a commodity and has value, but its value is only as good as the service that supports it—the monitoring, the response, the repair, and so forth. Services should bring *added* value. Service is something that the customer needs and is, therefore, an added value. Why? Because without it the customer is not able to meet a particular need.

Service organizations, as a group, have rolled over and accepted an unnecessary fate. They should be fighting back by refusing to be categorized as commodities. Corporate managers should be astute enough to see the error in such a concept. Unfortunately, neither is happening. Caught up in the desire to be a part of the latest management "enlightenment," senior executives have actually fallen victim to the latest management "absurdity." If service providers cannot be differentiated from one another, that is not proof that they are commodities. Rather, it is proof that they have not defined their unique selling proposition (USP). (I will have a great deal more to say about USPs later in this chapter.)

Breakfast cereals are commodities. So is crude oil. Security services, whether pursued properly or not, are not commodities. Security providers intend to deliver customer service and meet expectations and needs—all under the umbrella of asset protection and employee/customer safety. In working with some managers of a corporate security client, I saw that the client differentiated between investigative services and "commodity services." I asked them what they meant. The director looked surprised and said, "Well, guards, of course." I asked him to spell out how investigative services could be a noncommodity whereas guard services were a commodity. At first he laughed as though I should know the difference. After a long moment of silence, he began thinking about the question in more depth. Finally he looked at me and said, "You're right. You can't define one over the other." He got it.

On another occasion a senior manager for a property management company described the need to develop a career development program for his building engineers. Absent a program, he feared he would lose many of his engineers to other opportunities. When I asked if he was thinking along the same lines for his security officers, he commented that there was no need because they provided a commodity service. I asked him if he could differentiate between his engineers and security personnel with regards to "commodity services." Like the security director who originally thought that there was a difference between investigative services and guard services, the property manager also laughed and said that the difference was obvious. Yet, when pressed, he, too, realized that he could not state the difference.

Ask a corporate executive how he or she would rate the services provided by auditors, lawyers, human resource specialists, and marketing specialists. They would most likely talk about the contributions of these professionals to bottom-line performance, revenue generation, and so forth. Ask them what they think of security's services and they will likely describe them as a commodity. Why? Press them on the point and they will just as likely not be able to answer. Sadly, they cannot see security differently because of what they have read or heard from many management consultants.

The notion of defining security services as a commodity is reinforced further by asset protection companies themselves. Instead of defining themselves as service providers, many have "thrown in the towel" and are willing to accept commodification as though it were a fait accompli. I was recently benchmarking several high-powered investigative service firms, among whom were a number of the most recognized, world-class organizations. As a standard question I asked members of each firm how they perceived themselves in relation to their clients. To my surprise, three of the firms described their services as commodities. When I asked why, each paused and reflected. They had become so accustomed to bearing the commodity label that they had unconsciously adopted it as well.

Some might ask if the issue of being defined as a commodity is really much ado about nothing. I don't think so. I am staunchly opposed to the label for three reasons:

1. *The term commodity connotes a buyer-seller relationship.* Those familiar with Chapter 7 of my previous book know well that the buyer-seller relationship is the lowest form of client-provider relationship. It subjugates the provider to a forced "welfare" relationship with the client. It is a one-way street wherein the client dictates terms and conditions and the supplier is expected to roll over and comply.
2. *Commodities are price driven.* To equate your identity with a commodity is to show your willingness to let price be the primary driver in your business relationships.
3. *Most people assume that commodities are more price driven and less sensitive to the issue of quality.* As we have been discussing, the

underlying perception is that commodity pricing is driven more by volume and prevailing conditions than by anything else. In reality, this is not true for all commodities. Yet, the norm is to associate commodities more with price than with quality. The end result is that quality suffers.

DEMAND-SIDE/SUPPLY-SIDE COST CONTROL

Another concept that has surfaced among management theorists and practitioners is that it is beneficial to control the variables that drive up the cost of delivering services. The associated term is *demand-side/supply-side cost control*. Unfortunately this term is often confused with the concepts of supply and demand as applied to economic theory. Here the term *demand-side/supply-side cost control* means that cost control is dependent on internal user demands and supplier costs. In other words, the more services that are demanded, the higher the cost, and the less services required, the lower the cost. Further, the lower the supplier's costs and profit, the less the supplier will charge. Although the principle may be valid, corporate managers don't act on it. Here's what I mean.

Trying to reduce or redefine internal user demand is a process that can be fraught with frustration and danger. With regard to security, corporate politics, unrealistic demands, and fears of personal safety all fuel the emotionalism associated with cutting services to a more realistic budget level. Since they can't cut back on the demand for services it is easier for corporate managers to apply pressure on their suppliers to lower their charges. After all, suppliers are frequently reluctant to fully disclose their actual costs: consequently, it is assumed that they are inflating their costs as a way of generating higher profit margins. To bust the commodity syndrome, it is important to understand the underlying dynamics that feed the demand-side/supply-side phenomenon.

The Demand Side

Beginning with the demand side, the larger the company, the greater the internal vested interests. For example, consider the retail side of a company's business. As revenue generators, retailers are highly influential within the organization. Executive management will listen closely to what they want or expect, especially if it involves the safety of employees and customers. If the retailers' expectations are unrealistic but are supported by risk managers and attorneys reacting to owner liability issues, it is difficult to separate emotions from facts.

Recently several corporate managers assembled to discuss how the company could reduce its security costs without affecting the quality of service. Since the meeting was billed as a brainstorming session, managers representing various segments of the company were invited. Since security was a current "hot topic," the majority of those managers who showed up came to voice their input on security. As the meeting started, the manager for the largest retail segment began voicing her opinion, which centered on the need for more security.

This manager was quickly joined by a corporate attorney who talked about the dangers of reducing protection in view of recent court decisions on premises liability. The lawyer discussed the issue in general terms, spending a great deal of time on the issue of workplace violence. The lawyer failed to cite any of the six recent pro-owner court decisions in which owners' duties and responsibilities regarding the foreseeability of third-party injuries were limited.

The attorney's remarks were supported by the company's risk manager who also monopolized the discussion with anecdotes about increased losses and rising premiums. Finally the security manager joined the discussion and reinforced the call for increased security based on "history trends and rising crimes rates," even though that very morning's newspaper had run a feature article about the three-year downward trend in crime, especially in this company's industry.

After these "impromptu" presentations, the facility manager asked to have the floor to offer his observations. He was an external property manager and, coincidentally, a lawyer. He began by informing the group of the recent pro-owner court decisions and reminded them about the decreasing crime rate. He went on to ask for specifics from the risk manager only to be told that she would "have to research her sources." He explained that the meeting's purpose was to discuss possible ways to lower demand in light of recent trends. When he finished, the retail manager pushed her chair back, stood up, and announced that she was leaving. She stated that she felt she had a "moral obligation" to increase security and would do so—with or without the group's approval. Stating that she had no intentions of lessening security, she left the room.

Set against the current concerns regarding workplace violence, internal customers want more, not less, security. This demand is often in direct conflict with executive management's mandate to reduce operating expenses as part of their restructuring plan. User demand remains high until unit managers are asked to pay for it out of their own budget, only escalating feelings of bitterness between the opposing parties. Since most unit managers either don't budget for security as a direct charge or are working as a cost center and therefore cannot offset the expense against revenues, they will balk and point accusing fingers at anyone who suggests a reduction in coverage, warning that resulting injuries and deaths will be their burden to carry.

During such battles what should be the role of the security director or third-party provider serving as the security manager? You might be quick to recall one of Murphy's maxims: Seize the Moment. After all, such battles might be the opportunity the security director has been looking for to promote overdue support for more resources. Again, wrong! The security manager should definitely attempt to bring balance to such a situation. Even Murphy would agree. As you will recall, seizing the moment must be done against a backdrop of ethical principles and factually correct data. The underlying point is that internal customer demands are very difficult to break down, because much of what is believed to be required is mixed with perceptions, emotions, and oftentimes an *entitlement philosophy*—they simply believe it is due them. There are several other factors at work, including:

> *The greed factor.* One manager, not wanting to be outdone by another, will demand something the other has in order to maintain parity.

> *The mislead factor.* Not knowing the real facts, but wanting to see circumstances in one way instead of another, the internal customer is easily swayed—innocently or deliberately.

> *The payback factor.* Managers collect and pay corporate debts as a way of conducting business. Depending on the issue at hand and the perceived long-term gain, managers will support one another and demand more than is really needed.

> *The indifference factor.* If they are not required to pay for it, it is easier for managers to demand it. Being indifferent to the cost, since they are not accountable, they will demand goods and services and leave the expense issue to someone else.

Demand-side requirements need to be worked out rationally. A company rarely profits from attacking the issue from strictly a cost approach. Security is seen as a cost center, and cost centers, by their very definition, are not revenue generators. While many business units have experimented with the concept of making cost centers into revenue generators, few have been successful. (Frankly, I am a strong advocate of this approach. However, the time is a long ways off when cost center managers will be effective revenue generators. The skill set necessary to manage both is not easy to master, and managing a cost center requires a radically different approach than managing a business unit.) The end result is that to offer the development of new sources of revenue as an alternative means of funding increased security coverage is fairly unrealistic for most of corporate America today.

As a part of a rational approach to demand-side requirements, internal users need to break away from the traditional perspective of the haves and have-nots, although this way of thinking is rooted in our society. Unfortunately this perspective drives how operating units function on a daily basis. One of the most important tools for achieving success under these circumstances is to recognize the role competition plays in this dynamic. As a psychiatrist friend of mine notes, "We are a society built on the warrior metaphor. To us everything—religion, education, business, government, even personal relationships—revolves around one side winning, the other losing."

When it comes to sharing resources, business managers are quick to agree that sharing makes sense because there is also a strong core value that says, Life ought to be fair. We want what's ours, and we believe that others are entitled to their share. Unfortunately, there is no simple way to define the limits when it comes to the issue of sharing. It is not as simple as saying "I get half, you get half." One group's perceptions or needs might lead it to conclude that it should receive more because its need is greater.

Clearly we need to find ways to define what is essential to operating the business versus what would be nice to have. We can begin by developing a strong and pragmatic sense of ownership. Here's a simple question business unit managers need to ask themselves when seeking allocations: "If I owned this company, would I spend the money?" Let's look at a quick illustration.

Assume you are building a home in a nice neighborhood. As a security specialist you believe that an alarm system is an important feature. But as you are renewing your budget, you discover that the flooring is going to cost a little more than anticipated. You also realize that you prefer brand A window coverings over brand B, even though brand A costs more. Eventually, it's decision time. To keep all the other "I wants," you have to choose. If retaining the security system is important, something else has to go.

Perhaps you elect to go forward with a less impressive security system, or maybe you decide to defer final installation until a later time. After all, you rationalize, this is a nice neighborhood, and crime isn't that bad. In short, what you initially demanded (your perceived need) eventually found itself lower on the priority list. This simple illustration is very powerful, especially for security managers and end users who demand more security in a business world built on competing/conflicting demands and limited resources. It's a beginning point for establishing a rational approach to the demand side. Other shared perspectives are required; these are addressed in Part III in our discussion of the *Envisioned Leader*.

The need to redefine internal user demand is critical because it is possible to achieve significant savings without affecting the supplier-side costs. It has been my experience that reductions in services requested on the demand side can far outpace possible supply-side cuts. In a recent analysis I participated in for a retail bank with branches in a number of states, we discovered that 57 branches out of 350 did not need their security officer. Similar studies have found that there is overstaffing in retail chain stores, that officers are unnecessary at certain sites because technology could have been just as effective, and that fewer officers are required in certain areas as a result of revised deployment plans.

To quickly recap our discussion thus far, properly allocating what limited resources are available requires rationally defining what internal users really need as opposed to what they emotionally perceive that they need. The other side of this formula, the supplier side, also needs to be addressed.

The Supply Side

The Hired Gunslinger

When we consider the supply side, the commodity syndrome takes on an added complexity. I have found that most large consulting houses operate on a host of false assumptions regarding the security service industry's pricing policies. Desiring to reduce operating expenses across the board, corporate executives are quick to pay as much as seven-figure sums to national consulting firms purporting to know all about downsizing and cutting costs in specialty support services. Advising their clients that security providers typically realize profit margins in excess of 12 percent to 15 percent, these so-called experts rely on anecdotal data, "what's heard in the market," and guesstimates derived from one service sector or another rather than basing their judgments on empirical information gleaned from an analysis of profiles of actual billing rates.

The end result is troubling at best. Who would you be more inclined to believe if you were a corporate executive—the independent consulting house that is charging you a very large fee and advising you to be suspicious of a provider's vested interest? or a third-party contractor wanting your business and telling you that such profit margins are simply untrue?

It is very difficult for a corporate manager not to believe the independent consultant—his hired gun. Therefore, it takes a courageous senior manager to ask the high-priced consultant to prove his or her statements. If consultants don't have to prove their assertions, the end result is that the client has false expectations, and the supplier is forced to be defensive at the very outset. Is this a sound basis for building a trusting partnership?

Before moving on, it is important to note that the supplier's projected costs *can* typically be reduced from the original proposal. The supplier's initial bid is almost always based on some assumptions that are subject to negotiation, mostly because clients are rarely thorough in defining their expectations and requirements in the proposal process. Consequently, suppliers will commonly bid based on the expectation that some price negotiation will follow. This is not to suggest, however, that the suppliers are deliberately padding their estimate or inflating their costs. Clearly, some security companies pad their prices as a way of doing business. Outright padding with the intent to make inordinately high profits is unusual, however. The problem for the industry, as a whole, surfaces when smaller accounts yield much higher profit margin due to the lower operating cost, and there is no attempt by suppliers to explain this phenomenon.

The Misassumptions About National
Contracts and the Sea of Penguins
Over the past few years I have been asked to assist several large companies in redefining their security operations. Typically I am asked to come in after one of the larger consulting houses has convinced the client that there are significant cost savings to be achieved by decreasing the fee paid to the supplier, based on formulas derived from the consultant's own assumptions. The primary misconception I have seen consultants putting forth is the notion that by seeking "national" contracts the supplier can bundle its costs and pass along the savings to the client.

Geographic bundling for the security industry doesn't work under current configurations. Security suppliers with national or large regional operations have historically established themselves via a branch network. For every given number of square miles or concentration of accounts within an area, the security company typically establishes some sort of administrative support facility. Depending on the size of the office, it is considered either a branch or a regional office. The result of increased geographic distribution is compounding of overhead costs. Business executives believe, or they are told by their hired guns, that if a security company can bid on a big contract that represents thousands of hours annually, they should be able to reduce overhead and pass the savings on to the client. In fact no such savings can occur because there is still overhead at the local level. From a cost perspective, for most security firms it doesn't matter whether the client is national or not, the supplier needs to support the client at the local level; consequently the overhead remains constant.

The net effect of these conflicting statements by consultants and suppliers is disbelief and conflict. The consultants contend that the security companies "don't get the concept of strategic partnering"; the security companies argue that the consultants don't understand the security business and how it is structured. While the finger-pointing goes on, the client is literally caught in the middle, finally to come to the realization that both promises made and expectations generated will most likely fall considerably short.

Until security companies are willing to reorganize, few true national contracts will be awarded. Setting price aside for a moment, another major obstacle to suppliers gaining national contracts is the usual inconsistency that exists among offices. I once told a news writer for *Time* magazine that there isn't a large security company in America that I haven't praised for some aspect of its business. And there isn't one large security company in America that I haven't damned because of some aspect of its business. I was responding to an article by the writer giving, what I believed was, disproportionate praise to one supplier while brutally attacking others. The truth of the matter is that no security company with a national or large regional office network has yet found the formula for assuring continuity in delivering consistently high performance from one office to the next.

From their local branches, large suppliers commonly service a wide variety of clients. Very few security companies specialize in market niches; instead they offer their services to anyone on the premise that the fundamentals of security are the same, regardless of the nature of the client. I believe that this traditional approach is the core reason why most security companies are mediocre at best. Moreover, this way of doing business contributes to what I refer to as the phenomenon of being "in a sea of penguins." In other words, in such an environment, there is little to distinguish one security firm from another.

Security providers are undoubtedly their own worst enemy when it comes to promoting the commodity syndrome. By organizing themselves geographically as opposed to functionally, they can't help but look alike. If there is any solace in the adage Misery loves company, then security providers should take heart in knowing that theirs is not a unique problem. Over the past year the senior vice presidents of three of the largest property management companies have confided to me that they also see themselves no differently from their competition. The same can be said for many other service organizations as well as suppliers and mass retailers. When price is the only factor, it should not be surprising that customers begin to define both tangible products and intangible services as commodities.

Look-Alike Pricing

Even pricing among security suppliers is becoming fairly vague, and this phenomenon adds to my "sea of penguins" comparison. Over the past several years I have assisted dozens of companies in the selection of a security provider. Since 1979 I estimate that I have had the opportunity to review more than a thousand security operations. A typical selection process will entail checking out more than twenty suppliers and as few as three. These opportunities have taken me to nearly every major metropolitan area in the United States and into a very wide array of businesses.

From January 1, 1995, through July of 1996 I gathered data on seventeen major metropolitan areas across the country and twenty-one security providers. Each supplier company offered proposals or signed agreements in at least one of these markets. Most supplier companies made presentations or signed contracts in at least six or more of the areas. In each case the suppliers were asked to submit their costs based on a billing rate format I developed several years ago.

The security industry is one of the very few industries that is routinely required to submit very detailed cost breakdowns. Sadly, mean-spirited clients can use the billing rate format to hammer away at supplier's expenses, trying to prove a personal point, or inexperienced managers may simply ignore the information since they don't know enough to discern what it is they are analyzing.

The matrix in Table 5–1 represents billing rates for the twenty-one security companies and the seventeen metropolitan areas. As you review the matrix, that was compiled by my company in 1996, you will note a great deal of consistency between the composite scores offered by the twenty-one security companies. The only exception is in area 12—Reno/Las Vegas. You will note that the costs there are higher for such categories as insurance, hiring and testing, and training because many of the company's accounts were with casinos requiring armed guards because of the customer mix. The costs for each category are averages derived by each participating company in any given locale. For example, in area 4, Boston, the costs are the average of the identified or agreed-to costs between one or more clients involving eight of the twenty-one companies. Similarly, in area 13, San Francisco, I present the averages for five clients and nine of the companies. For the sake of consistency, only proposals or agreements that were based on the

Table 5-1 Price Comparisons

	Area #1	Area #2	Area #3	Area #4	Area #5	Area #6	Area #7	Area #8	Area #9	Area #10	Area #11	Area #12	Area #13	Area #14	Area #15	Area #16	Area #17	Group Average
Wage	$8.00	$8.00	$7.75	$8.00	$7.75	$7.75	$7.75	$8.00	$7.50	$7.75	$8.00	$7.75	$8.00	$7.50	$8.00	$8.00	$8.00	$7.85
Tx & Ben	$1.68	$1.68	$1.63	$1.68	$1.63	$1.63	$1.63	$1.68	$1.56	$1.63	$1.68	$1.63	$1.68	$1.56	$1.68	$1.68	$1.68	$1.65
Ins. Other	$0.27	$0.23	$0.20	$0.24	$0.26	$0.24	$0.25	$0.24	$0.18	$0.21	$0.27	$0.46	$0.23	$0.23	$0.27	$0.21	$0.21	$0.25
Equip	$0.03	$0.02	$0.03	$0.02	$0.04	$0.03	$0.03	$0.02	$0.02	$0.02	$0.03	$0.04	$0.02	$0.02	$0.03	$0.03	$0.02	$0.03
Uniform	$0.24	$0.25	$0.19	$0.21	$0.25	$0.22	$0.23	$0.21	$0.21	$0.25	$0.22	$0.26	$0.23	$0.23	$0.22	$0.23	$0.21	$0.23
Procure Clean	$0.12	$0.13	$0.13	$0.14	$0.12	$0.13	$0.13	$0.13	$0.12	$0.11	$0.12	$0.14	$0.12	$0.13	$0.14	$0.15	$0.13	$0.13
Advert.	$0.02	$0.01	$0.02	$0.02	$0.01	$0.01	$0.01	$0.02	$0.01	$0.01	$0.02	$0.02	$0.01	$0.02	$0.02	$0.02	$0.02	$0.02
Hire/Test	$0.05	$0.04	$0.07	$0.06	$0.04	$0.04	$0.04	$0.06	$0.06	$0.04	$0.04	$0.11	$0.04	$0.04	$0.04	$0.05	$0.06	$0.05
Train.	$0.06	$0.07	$0.07	$0.07	$0.08	$0.06	$0.06	$0.06	$0.07	$0.06	$0.07	$0.14	$0.05	$0.05	$0.06	$0.07	$0.08	$0.07
IOT OJT	$0.18	$0.19	$0.14	$0.19	$0.19	$0.18	$0.18	$0.12	$0.14	$0.18	$0.17	$0.21	$0.19	$0.18	$0.14	$0.17	$0.15	$0.17
AOT	$0.04	$0.02	$0.06	$0.07	$0.02	$0.06	$0.07	$0.05	$0.06	$0.07	$0.06	$0.07	$0.05	$0.05	$0.06	$0.04	$0.05	$0.05
Br. & Reg OH	$0.61	$0.43	$0.57	$0.55	$0.53	$0.47	$0.60	$0.51	$0.38	$0.63	$0.61	$0.54	$0.58	$0.58	$0.50	$0.60	$0.52	$0.54
Profit	$0.32	$0.56	$0.39	$0.37	$0.52	$0.65	$0.55	$0.55	$0.31	$0.65	$0.38	$0.49	$0.53	$0.65	$0.36	$0.39	$0.43	$0.48
Bill Rate	$11.62	$11.63	$11.25	$11.62	$11.44	$11.47	$11.53	$11.65	$11.64	$11.61	$11.67	$11.86	$11.73	$11.26	$11.52	$11.64	$11.56	$11.52

AREAS

#1 Alburquerque
#2 Arizona
#3 Atlanta
#4 Boston
#5 Chicago
#6 Cleveland/Cinn
#7 Dallas/Houston
#8 Denver
#9 Indiana
#10 Minneapolis
#11 Portland
#12 Reno/Las Vegas
#13 San Francisco
#14 Salt Lake City
#15 Seattle
#16 Tampa/Miami
#17 Washington D.C.

SECURITY COMPANIES

#1 Aargus
#2 ABM/ACSS
#3 APS
#4 Argenbright
#5 Arko
#6 Barton
#7 Borg-Warner
#8 Curtis
#9 Celedon
#10 First Security
#11 Guardsmark
#12 InterCon-Toronto
#13 InterCon-Los Angeles
#14 IPC
#15 Northeast
#16 Northwest
#17 Ogden
#18 Pinkerton
#19 Stanley Smith
#20 State Security
#21 Wackenhut

prevailing area's labor rates were used, the wage spread being between $7.50 and $8.00 per hour. The clients represented high-tech and corporate campuses, commercial class A high-rises, residential complexes, health care facilities, hotels and casinos, retail malls, and light industrial complexes.

Before moving along, I want to share with you a more recent study I completed for two of my clients in the San Francisco Bay Area. Conducted in early 1997, this salary study shows that an interesting phenomenon appears to be emerging. The net effect is the establishment of average salaries significantly above what has heretofore been commonly believed.

As our current business cycle reflects a condition of full employment, salaries for blue collar workers in the Bay Area have risen dramatically. There are a number of reasons for this, not the least of which is competition among employers and their suppliers for qualified workers. As companies seek retention of valued employees, they are discovering that compensation packages need to be competitive. To stay ahead, organizations will up the hiring ante; e.g., offering sign-up bonuses and paying what they believe is above-average starting wages. The interesting side of this phenomenon is that as one company increases their base wage package, another matches it or increases it.

The consequence of this scramble for employees among service sector firms is very positive for the individual worker. Security companies who have traditionally fought among themselves and their respective clients to increase officers' salaries are now finding it difficult to retain their officers because other non-security companies or non-security divisions within their clients are actively recruiting quality people. As companies such as those in California's Silicon Valley compete for best in-class security operations, they recognize the need to address the issue of competitive pricing.

For this study let me begin by identifying my sources:

♦ U.S. Department of Labor
♦ State of California Labor Department
♦ The Abbott-Langer Annual Report of Security Wages
♦ Comparative rates quoted by selected security firms
♦ Benchmarking data provided by several local chambers of commerce
♦ Labor rates extracted from my other client work
♦ Benchmarking data received directly from corporations representing the following business sectors:
  ♦ 4 financial institutions
  ♦ 4 health care organizations

- 9 property management companies
- 7 retail organizations
- 2 public utilities
- 4 manufacturing firms
- 3 energy companies
- 9 high-tech firms in the silicon valley

♦ In the Silicon Valley starting wages vary from a low of $7.50/hr to more than $15.50/hr. This is for a uniformed unarmed security officer.

One of the best examples is a quick review of the Want Ads in the local papers. Guardsmark advertises starting positions for $8.00/hr to $9.50/hr. A major competitor has a similar ad, however their wages begin at $10.50/hr to $11.50/hr. Other security companies are offering similar wage ranges.

♦ Corporations and security service companies consistently report that the lower the wage the higher the turnover.

♦ The average starting wage is $8.50/hr. This is only $3,180 above the national poverty wage and approximately $1,700 above the Bay Area poverty wage according to the U.S. Department of Labor.

♦ The average non-security blue collar wage is in excess of $20,000 annually. For example, the average secretary's wage in the Silicon Valley is in excess of $23,000. (Isn't it interesting that security officers are charged with protecting a corporation's assets estimate well in excess of $1 billion, yet they are compensated less than that of a clerk?)

♦ Silicon companies committed to strategic partnering with their third-party security supplier average a starting wage in excess of $9.00/hr, e.g., $9.17/hr. This is accompanied by an escalator schedule that is performance based. Such schedules are usually set at 180 days after initial employment and after one year. The escalator will range from a low of .50/hr increase to $1.00. After one year an officer base wage will range from $9.67/hr to $10.17/hr.

♦ Any additional certifications generally translates to $1.00/hr more. In other words, if the officer is expected to be ER (Emergency Response) certified they are paid a minimum of $10.17/hr. After or during their first year they receive an escalator increase that takes them to more than $11.75/hr., as a minimum.

♦ Escalators have consistently been held at 3 percent per year over the past several years. This means that after the first year an officer will receive a minimum of 3 percent over his/her starting wage from the previous 12 months, provided they have satisfactorily met established

performance criteria. This, of course, assumes that we are not dealing with a unionized situation or an armed position.

♦ Supervisors are almost universally paid $1.75/hr to $2.50/hr over
   the security officer's base wage. It is not uncommon for them to
   earn more than $3.00/hr over the security officer's base. This is par-
   ticularly true when there are console operators resident on the
   account.

♦ Console operators typically receive $1.50/hr to $2.00/hr more than
   regular officers.

♦ Lobby receptionist positions are commonly staffed by security officers. When they are not, the individual usually receives .50/hr to
   $1.00 less than security officers, unless the console serves as the
   central console and is equipped with security devices and systems.
   In these cases, the receptionist is paid the same as an officer or is
   staffed by a senior officer or supervisor.

In summary, salary averages for the Silicon Valley as of the beginning of 1997 are as follows.

♦ Starting average wage: $ 8.50/hr to $ 9.00/hr
♦ Median wage after Year 1: $10.25/hr to $10.75/hr
♦ Senior Officers (2 years +): $12.25/hr to $13.50/hr
♦ Average Supervisor Wage: $14.50/hr to $15.50/hr

Remember, these are averages, while there are salaries below these
averages, there are an equal number above. Further, it must be remembered that the lower the wage scales, the higher the turnover. A final critical variable needs to be noted:

♦ Those companies demanding value added services and strategic
   relationships with the external partners are consistently well above
   these averages; e.g., anywhere from $1.00 to $2.00/hr higher.

Most providers are reluctant to submit cost breakdowns like those
we have seen in Table 5–1. On one plane, this is understandable, but if
partnering is to occur, the associated supply-side costs need to be shared.
My purpose in publishing this information is to demonstrate that there
are not hidden pockets of excessive profiteering in security billing. In
reality, there is likely to be some room for negotiating away some overhead costs. Whether one calculates overhead based on the proposed wage
or as a part of the total bill rate, the components remain the same. Over-

head includes staff support, equipment, facility and vehicle leases, marketing commissions, and corporate charge-backs.

The Want-To—Can't-Do Suppliers

In the economic climate of the 1990s, corporate America understands the need for suppliers to make a reasonable profit. What is a reasonable profit? This is what lies at the core of the tug-of-war between client and supplier regarding price. Today businesses and organizations believe that a profit margin of 5 percent to 8 percent is not unreasonable for security providers. The problem is that most organizations believe that security companies are making considerably more. More troubling is the fact that when providers try to convince potential clients that their profit margin is less than 3 percent, they only weaken their credibility. As one investor noted, "Why would a company seek to stay in business achieving a 1 percent to 3 percent margin of profit when the same money spent to run their operation could be deposited in a commercial bank account and draw more interest?" This is a very valid question. The matrix in Table 5–1 seems to validate that a 4 percent to 6 percent margin is a more realistic number, and these figures appear to be more in keeping with client expectations.

In October of 1995 I hosted an executive symposium for the top fifty security companies. As part of this two-day event, we discussed profit margins. Among those in attendance were the security contract decision makers for ten companies representing more than $200 million in annual contract services. When asked if they believed that a profit margin of 5 percent to 8 percent was reasonable for security providers, they all agreed. The only caveat they gave was that they would ask for full disclosure to assure that security providers were reporting their actual profit margin.

One of the biggest skeptics in the room was an executive from one of the top five security companies. A couple of months after the symposium we had an opportunity to meet again. At that time he informed me that his company had candidly canvassed more than two thousand of its clients, asking if they, too, were comfortable with a profit margin of 5 percent. He smiled and said that he would have bet otherwise, but to his amazement the overwhelming majority of these clients confirmed that this range, as a minimum, was reasonable. Why then is there a general belief that a range of 1 percent to 3 percent represents the level of tolerance, as opposed to something higher?

Many answers have been advanced from both sides. While each has degrees of validity, it is my belief that the question of profit margins revolves around two issues. First, as we addressed above, security providers have historically been reluctant to "open their billing rates" even though they are frequently asked to do so. When they fail to do so, they only perpetuate the myth that they have something to hide.

As strategic alliance specialist John Eglert notes, it is only when the client is aware and comfortable with the supplier's costs that the stage can be set for developing a true partnership. He adds that after the first contract is signed and the partnership begins to take hold, it is rare for the supplier to be asked to disclose costs anymore. Trust is developed, and confidence is established that one partner would not take undue advantage of the other.[1]

Second, security companies do make a considerably higher profit on the staple of their business. Here I am referring to what is known as the 168s/336s in security provider parlance. These are accounts that require only 168 hours or 336 hours of coverage per week. They are the "mom and pop" accounts. The clients are small, require little by way of resourcing, and are usually interested in low-wage employees and rarely question the billing rate. These clients assume that the rate they are quoted is competitive. Generally it is. Yet the cost associated with servicing this type of account is the lowest for the provider, thereby allowing the provider to reap sometimes very high profit margins. This information has made its way to "the street," and large clients or their consultants assume that the same holds true for them. In such an environment the supplier is put on the defensive and the pricing tug-of-war begins. Even if the prices and profit margins are fully legitimate and the differences between large and smaller clients can be fully explained, the perception is perpetuated that security companies make very large profits.

Before turning our attention to ways in which a supplier can bust the commodity syndrome, a final point regarding supply and demand is in order. Even though I do not have the scientific data to support my hypothesis at this time, my experience with large organizations over the past few years has lead me to an interesting conclusion. Greater savings are achieved over the near and longer terms as a result of reducing demand rather than by forcing concessions by suppliers. This is not to suggest that reductions on the supply side cannot be realized; rather I have found that the typical ratio of reduced operational expense approaches 2 to 1 for demand over supply. In other words, if a reduction goal of 15 percent is established, 10 percent can be realistically achieved on the demand side and 5 percent on the supply side. Ironically, in every case, the initial expectation is exactly the reverse. This is something that merits further research.

STRATEGIES FOR COMMODITY BUSTING

Breaking away from the deeply entrenched perception that security services are a commodity is not easy. It requires a strategic plan. To bust the commodity syndrome will require a radical paradigm shift for most business executives since most have come to view nearly all support services as commodities. The same shift will be required of students and teachers at business colleges and universities, as well as among management consultants. In the interim, here are some suggested strategies.

Being Willing to Say No and Walk Away

Security companies want clients' business. They want to service clients and meet their expectations and demands. Is this always realistic? The simple answer is no, and particularly if the client or prospective client is not willing to work with the supplier on pricing. Security, by its nature, encounters unplanned events. A service provider needs to know that events that are not under its direct control will be met with understanding and cooperation (that is, commitment) from the client. When price points are negotiated at an unacceptable level, the supplier should generally be ready to walk away.

I say generally because there may be legitimate reasons for a supplier to maintain a relationship even though it is below the supplier's accepted margins or even if the supplier will have to operate at a loss. For example, the client may be a long-standing account and may be temporarily in financial trouble. Near-term support during tough times may well prove to be worthwhile over the longer term. Or perhaps the supplier wants to break into a new market, sees the potential client as an excellent referral, and thus will bear the cost as an investment toward future business.

If none of these special circumstances are present, then the supplier needs to walk away. To do otherwise not only creates a bad precedent but also reflects bad business management. After all, one of the primary reasons a for-profit company exists is to make a profit! Walking away is a tough decision for the supplier, and it may not be something that the supplier can do overnight. Legal restrictions such as providing notice, reforecasting, getting bank credits, and other considerations need to be taken into account first. Consequently, the decision may require an action plan extending over the life of the current contract. Backing out is not always a simple process by any means.

Developing Your Unique Selling Proposition

At the outset I introduced you to the concept of your *unique selling proposition* (USP). As we noted, your USP is what differentiates you from your competitors in the marketplace. It is that characteristic or strategy that sets you apart from the sea of penguins that surround you. You may also recall my mentioning Paul Franklin earlier, as well as how successful security management can be likened to fly-fishing. Franklin was the first to introduce me to the concept of USP. By way of introducing the concept he told me the true story of an Australian dentist and what can happen when you begin to think outside the box in search of your own USP.

For most of us, going to the dentist is not an experience we look forward to. But Dr. Charlie in Australia has taken a radically different approach to the business of dentistry. Motivated by the desire to maximize his earning potential while providing high quality service, he realized that he needed to define a niche market and excel within it. As opposed to advertising his services and relying on volume to achieve profitability, he decided to meet the needs of a much smaller marketplace and thereby not only create a stable customer base but also charge a higher price for a perceived specialty.

Realizing that he needed both a unique selling proposition that would distinguish him from other general dentists as well as a track record of successfully meeting his customer expectations, he set out to define a new category of dentistry. Specifically, he opted to position himself as a dentist who would take business based only on personal referrals from other patients, and at the same time he introduced the concept of "happy dentistry." New patients would come only as a result of personal referrals from current patients who were totally satisfied and could therefore personally "guarantee" to their friends and relatives that they would experience the same level of satisfaction with Dr. Charlie.

To accomplish this high level of customer satisfaction, the dentist realized that the patient's experience needed to be both unique and successful. He began a process of reengineering his entire approach to the patient-doctor relationship. As new ideas come to mind or as he gets feedback directly from his patients, Dr. Charlie attempts to integrate the innovations into his practice—all with the aim of continuously improving the services he offers.

Here are some of the techniques he employs that distinguish him from his competitors:

♦ When patients arrives at the office, which is a converted Victorian house located on a residential street, they discover that the door is locked, and to gain entrance they need to ring a doorbell. Patients' first impression is that they are going to visit a friend as opposed to being just a number entering an office building.

◆ Patients are greeted at the front door by the dentist's customer service representative, who invites patients into a small parlor and provides them with a cup of coffee or tea or a soft drink. Since patients are referred by someone known to the dentist's staff, new patients are greeted by name.

◆ The parlor is equipped with a stereo system, and patients are given their choice of music, if desired, drawn from a wide selection of different musical offerings. The customer service representative will offer patients a periodical or newspaper that they prefer to read (remember, since new patients are accepted on a referral basis, this type of information is solicited by the dentist's staff at the time of referral).

◆ When Dr. Charlie arrives, the initial conversation centers on getting to know patients and some of their general lifestyle habits so that not only is a personal relationship initially undertaken, but also the dentist begins to develop a database relative to any potential issues related to patients' dental needs.

◆ Considerable care has been taken with the total environment, including the smells that permeate both the parlor and the examination/dental care area. Dr. Charlie knows that smell has a strong effect on memory, and over time he came to the conclusion that his patients typically associate past visits to dental offices with a certain smell and an unpleasant experience. Consequently, he experimented with several odors designed to divert patients' attention away from being at the dentist and to shift their focus to more soothing thoughts. These include various perfumes, the smell of freshly brewed coffee, and a variety of other aromas. What he discovered was that the most pleasing and long-lasting aroma is the smell of fresh-baked muffins. Therefore, when first introduced to the parlor, patients are also offered their choice of fresh-baked muffins and pastries made in the on-site kitchen.

◆ While in the dentist's chair patients are given their choice of music or videos that can be viewed on monitors mounted overhead.

Each of these amenities has evolved, as noted above, based on feedback directly solicited by way of a customer satisfaction survey, which Dr. Charlie's office mails to patients within one week of their visit and follows up with a personal contact via telephone. In addition, patients receive a second phone call to specifically address any dental concerns that require follow-up. Moreover, approximately two weeks later patients receive in the mail a small token of the doctor's appreciation for selecting him to be their dentist.

This level of personal attention is designed to assure that patients return and that they will be willing to refer new customers to the dentist. This type of out-of-box approach has many lessons for a corporate security director or third-party provider of security services. As radical as it may sound, the security decision maker needs to clearly identify who the primary users of the security services are, and tailor particular services to those users. This is not to suggest that all other clients should be ignored. Rather, it's a process of "target hardening" the primary users of security services to assure that you retain their support. A lesson for the provider is that market differentiation is a critical key to success. In other words, by choosing the right market niche you may make a higher profit, and therefore you may not need to rely on volume as a driver of profitability.

Your USP can be used for more than just attracting specific programs or clients. Since it is a tool for demonstrating your uniqueness, it can also serve to promote your credibility and serve as leverage for attaining greater responsibilities within the organization. This is particularly important for security managers insofar as they are continuously being challenged to demonstrate their added value. Likewise, for external providers this represents an opportunity to integrate yourself further into the fabric of the organization, and potentially you can use your USP as a springboard for suggesting new service offerings and therefore creating the opportunity to enhance revenues.

Developing Your Strength and Continuously Playing to It

There is a biblical saying that you cannot serve two masters well. Security companies that try to be everything to everybody have fallen into this trap. Customers want a feeling of exclusivity. They want to be treated as if their needs are uncommon, even if they aren't. They want to know that they are special and will receive special attention from you.

Paul Franklin suggests that your strength is defined as what your best customers value most about you. It is your highest value in their minds. For example, if they are in the health care business, they want to identify you as being a health care specialist. It should come as a surprise to them that you specialize in other lines of business, for example, banking, retail, high-tech, and so forth. What distinguishes you from others, and therefore defines you as something other than a commodity, is not the uniform, logo or other outward insignia. It is not your most clever achievement or your size. It's what you bring to your client on an ongoing basis.

Remember, commodities can be bought and traded. Relationships cannot. That is why Tom Marano, as mentioned earlier, was so on target when he said that security is all about selling and maintaining relationships, not hours. Hours are commodities; relationships link people to people.

Basch's Hierarchy of Horrors

In Chapter 8 I will introduce you to Michael Basch and his concept of the *Legendary Leader*. For our purposes here, however, Basch offers an approach for defining your level of uniqueness. Coined the *hierarchy of horrors*, it is a simple, low-road approach that builds to a higher level of performance. Basch advises you to spend time with your staff, former clients, even current clients, and identify those times when situations just did not go right. Analyze the factors of such situations by asking the following questions:

♦ What went wrong?
♦ What expectations or needs were missed?
♦ What was the root cause of the problem?

Such questions are part of the process of continuous quality improvement. The hierarchy of horrors forces you to look at experiences gone bad. It is also an opportunity for learning and generating necessary feedback that can lead to new learning and new discoveries. By employing this technique, you can make needed modifications, all of which can be designed to enhance value and create a deeper relationship with your staff and clients. Remember, as the relationship becomes more personal, you become less of a number (and numbers are frequently used in dealing with commodities).

Developing Vertical Markets

Earlier I referred to security companies needing to restructure themselves if they are going to break the commodity syndrome. The traditional strategy of defining themselves as "jacks-of-all-trades," capable of providing security to any business, anywhere, simply isn't making it. This generalist approach not only carries a heavy administrative burden but also works against providers' ability to define their USP.

Vertical structuring means developing a division totally dedicated to a particular niche, with its own marketing plans and its own infrastructure designed to support this function. Vertical market structuring is not a new idea, but this strategy is rarely found within the security industry because the overwhelming number of security companies continue to be fairly traditional in their approach to business. This holds true for even the largest firms. Breaking the commodity syndrome requires suppliers to demonstrate that they are more than just security services. Many nonsecurity managers have confided to me over the years, "My problem is that when I think of security, all I can envision is a bunch of guards either walking or standing around." Sadly there is a great deal of truth to this observation.

Structuring along vertical markets allows security companies to develop specialty programs and, more importantly, a specialty reputation. Even though there is a great deal of transference between industries with regard to basic security functions, business owners and managers look to those suppliers who understand the nuances of their particular business sector. For example, retail mall managers recognize that a walking patrol's duty may be similar to that of any other mobile patrol in another setting. However, the interaction of the walking patrol with mall customers, particularly teenagers, is different from the interaction between the security officer and these same people in other contexts (sporting events, schools, and so forth). A security firm with special experience in this setting will have a decided advantage. It's very difficult to convince a client that you have the client's best interests at heart when a replacement security officer is asked what his or her previous experience is only to discover that he or she has no experience in the client's business arena.

In March of 1996 I had the opportunity to speak before a group of high-tech facility managers. One of the primary concerns voiced by members of the group was the lack of security services companies specializing in their industry. Many of them said that if such a company existed, they would send their business in that direction. I have shared this story with four of the top ten security companies. Six months have passed, and not one of these providers has picked up on this idea. Why? I strongly suspect it's because they simply don't know how to do it.

Developing vertical markets involves more than simply hiring a specialist and then marketing to a particular segment in which you want to develop a specialization. Yet several security companies believe that this is the correct approach to take. Typically, they will hire a person with name recognition in a particular market, integrate that person into the sales force as a "business development" specialist, and ask the specialist to serve as a resident advisor to their human resources and training departments. This is not what I mean by vertical structuring.

In vertical structuring the needs of the new niche will be reflected in the recruitment, training, the deployment, and the systems support necessary to meet the needs of servicing this particular business segment. Once the infrastructure is in place, you can focus on specific programs and initiatives designed to meet the client's particular needs. You will have eliminated the burden of trying to serve multiple masters, which often have competing demands.

Managing Programs for Added Value

To bust the commodity syndrome security companies need to be put in a position of truly managing that aspect of the asset protection program that has been assigned to them. Security companies should not be perceived as only providers. It is only when they are given the opportunity to manage that they can begin to control their own organizational destiny. The managing process forces them to develop value-added contributions.

Successful managers are not looked upon as commodities because they bring a great deal to the business table. They are valued because their vision and contributions make them a part of the team. For instance, such managers look for ways to improve their department's efficiency, and they are willing to try new initiatives and risk individual gains for the greater good of the team. This willingness to contribute defines the value of these managers and elevates both them and those that work for them above the commodity level. Managers are in a position to show executive management the interconnectedness between the protection of assets and employees and the company's profitability. Providers take direction; managers give it. It is in the giving that one can better define added value and implement it.

SUMMARY

We shifted gears in this chapter and focused almost exclusively on third-party suppliers. Even so there have been many important lessons and considerations for the resident security manager here. We turned our attention to one of the most troubling issues plaguing the security industry—the commodity syndrome, an organizational cancer that needs to be rooted out of the entire service sector. It reduces the business of providing valuable services to nothing but a process based on low pricing. By its very essence, the mind-set assumes that cost is the most important determinant.

Our analysis showed that the commodity syndrome is fostered by consultants, educators, executives, and suppliers alike. It is sustained by myths, misassumptions, and a lack of real data. Nonetheless, the idea has appeal because it centers on bargain hunting, or "getting something for less." We also saw how a consultant can sometimes be more of an obstacle than a facilitator. When consultants operate on their own mis-assumptions, they can set up false expectations and pit suppliers against clients. This situation is exacerbated by suppliers' unwillingness to participate fully in the partnering process and openly disclose information about their billing process and profit margin.

Today controlling costs is critical to achieving profitability. But hammering on suppliers to reduce costs is not an effective strategy. Oftentimes more savings and greater expense reductions can be achieved by lowering the internal demand generated by clients. Tackling the customer demand side is not easy. As we saw, it is fraught with many dangers. Yet given the potential savings it can bring to clients, without the need to get significant price concessions from suppliers, it is often the wiser route to take.

Pricing has become so competitive among suppliers that it is no longer a distinguishing characteristic. In the long run, this is a healthy development because it means that suppliers will need to seek alternative strategies for getting new business, based on performance and differentiating themselves from their competitors. Some strategies suppliers can use include being willing to walk away from business relationships, developing their own unique selling proposition, identifying their strengths and playing to them, and learning from past mistakes through the process of establishing a hierarchy of previous snafus.

The challenge for providers is to define reasonable thresholds for profit and to hold firm. Failing to establish acceptable profit margins forces suppliers into the position of being "reluctant warriors." They cannot assure quality when there is no real profit incentive. Yet busting the commodity syndrome requires more. Suppliers need to identify their unique selling proposition, what distinguishes them from other suppliers in the marketplace. They need to look at how their business is structured and seek new strategies for reducing overhead costs while enhancing their value to customers. Sadly many providers have not followed these strategies and have suffered as a result.

6

Establishing Your Collateral Value

Happiness is neither virtue nor pleasure nor this thing nor that, but simple growth. We are happy when we are growing.

... W. B. YEATS

Demonstrating added value is more than an exercise in "what have you done for me lately?" Unfortunately this may not always seem to be the case. Sadly one of today's sacred business icons is the almighty dollar. While there is no doubt that profitability is the central core of business success, it also has its limitations. We'll have a great deal more to say about the threat the almighty dollar poses to envisioned leadership in our last chapter. Suffice to say, many well-intentioned but misinformed corporate executives have come to believe that saving or making money is synonymous with added value.

As we discovered previously, the concept of the value-added contribution is actually rooted just as much in perception as it is in actual performance. This notion may appear to contradict much of the current literature that spells out how to measure your performance above an established baseline; in reality, it is one of the more interesting organizational paradoxes of our time. Let me explain.

Your program has true added value if you can demonstrate that it is an integrated part of the company's overall business plan. Perhaps the following analogy can best demonstrate the point. Recently a major auto company began advertising that its vehicles are self-cleaning. The ads explain that there are parts within the engine that are designed to make the car run more smoothly, perform better, and, thanks to new technology, part of the energy-producing activity of the engine can be converted into a type of self-administering engine maintenance. Great concept. It creates a perception in the consumer's mind that this car has a lower overall maintenance cost. Therefore it is a more attractive choice.

Does the system really work, and, more importantly, does it really lower long-term cost? To listen to this auto manufacturer's competition, the performance of this new model is not as great as the manufacturer would like the public to believe. I'm not a mechanic and couldn't prove the issue one way or another.

With the introduction of the self-cleaning engine, a new paradigm emerges. After all, previously peak performance in an auto engine was defined by the engine's ability to make the car run more smoothly and efficiently; cleaning the parts was thought to be within the purview of an external party (the mechanic). This is what is meant by the term *disruptive technology*. A new technology is introduced that disrupts traditional perceptions, beliefs, and approaches. It's a change agent because it shakes conventional thinking and forces a new, and often-times radical, way of thinking about how we go about the business of doing what it is that we do. Disruptive technology is not new; it's just a new label. Federal Express shook the U.S. Postal Service with the concept of guaranteed overnight delivery. Fax machines and the Internet created even faster and more interactive communication. Each of these, and thousands of other examples, demonstrate that within the context of any given product or service, new ways or added contributions can be achieved without ever leaving the basic framework. The end result is that a manager, even when he or she believes that there is no possibility of bringing added value because he or she has no more money to give, can do so.

A company wants to sell its product or service, make a profit, and hold onto or expand its market share. Security directors need to protect a company's assets and people. Assuming that all of the accumulated organizational fat has been taken out of a particular security program and that the security director is operating on a lean and mean budget, is there anything more that can be done—are there more opportunities (added value contributions) that can be expected? In terms of bottom-line financial performance, if you are ultimately going to be successful, you are going to need to reduce operating costs. This is a three-step process if you are ultimately going to be successful: trimming, consolidating, and synergizing.

1. Trim away excess spending. This step is usually met with resistance and a degree of teeth gnashing, but it is achievable.
2. Consolidate where there are opportunities. This move often involves combining two or more functions into one.
3. Seek synergies among component parts. This strategy often means seeking new alliances with functions not traditionally perceived as being associated with one another.

It's this latter point that leads us to the focus of this chapter. We are going to center on a discussion of what I call your *collateral value*. It involves your ability to demonstrate added value within the context of your primary core competency. In other words, instead of seeking new areas to manage beyond the realm of asset protection (to prove your worth as a generalist manager and therefore enhance your organizational net worth), you seek opportunities under the umbrella of security—even though such opportunities may not be so readily apparent. In short, you create your own "disruptive technology."

Bill Walsh, the former head coach of the San Francisco 49ers was once asked what really excited him about the game of football after forty years of coaching. He responded that he was always looking for something new within the context of the game. He would ask, Is there a new dimension to our playbook, offense or defense, that hasn't been explored? His efforts have had an influence leaguewide, with most coaches adopting parts or all of what is commonly referred to as the West Coast offense. Similarly in defense Walsh's influence was carried forward by his successor, George Seifert, the result being that through the 1997 season, the 49ers were consistently ranked among the best in the National Football League.

Finding new ways to work within the context of your competency is what collateral value is all about. Just as Walsh and Seifert found their "added value" within the game of football, so too similar innovation can be accomplished by the forward-thinking security manager. For you the question ought to be, What new approach can be found within the context of asset protection? Does this imply that security managers ought not look outside their basic skill set of asset protection to demonstrate their ability to make contributions to a company? The answer is an emphatic no.

DEFINING YOUR COLLATERAL VALUE

For me, one of the more interesting examples of someone enhancing his collateral value is the case of Doug Griffin. As of this writing he is with Bank of America. He is one of the survivors of corporate mergers, having been with Continental Illinois National Bank in Chicago, Illinois, when it was acquired by Bank of America. At the time of the acquisition, Griffin was Continental's manager of financial investigations and credit review. His survival is directly tied to his ability to expand his contribution within the framework of his security function. He was so successful that when the merger was first announced, Bank of America saw his value and knew that there was a role for him in the new organization.

His is a story of planned collateral value, and therefore it deserves our attention. As background, Griffin began his corporate career as a protective services manager in a division within the bank's corporate security department. At that time corporate security reported to the executive vice president for administrative affairs and was responsible for physical security, employee safety, and a number of other traditional asset protection functions. Griffin had entered private security after serving as the manager of enforcement with the U.S. Department of Labor.

After two years as protective services manager at the bank, Griffin was given the assignment of managing the department's worldwide investigative unit. Among other duties, this unit was charged with the responsibility of investigating financial frauds perpetrated by both employees and bank customers. As a result of Continental's reengineering initiative, the investigative unit was being transferred to the bank's internal audit group. Instead of spending his time and energy in defining financial fraud investigations as an independent entity within the internal audit, Griffin perceived that the realignment presented a significant opportunity to increase the value of his unit to the bank.

He began by establishing a series of training programs to help internal auditors understand the concepts associated with pursuing financial frauds for criminal prosecution purposes. At the same time a series of similar training programs were established to orient his financial investigators to the ins and outs of internal auditing. By combining both workforces through a shared perspective, the bank was better able to identify vulnerabilities before actual frauds occurred. Further, when an actual crime was detected, the bank also benefited by having a quicker response and the ability to allocate more resources.

Because internal auditors became sensitized to the motivation of criminal opportunists, when they conducted routine reviews they were more alert to the possibility that there were people out there planning to steal or actually engaging in the theft of bank assets. On the other hand, investigative units began to more readily appreciate the value of the internal auditing procedure as a control for protecting bank assets and security.

Based on the successful experience of the shared training program, Griffin began to look for other opportunities for enhancing value. It didn't take long before he realized that his investigators possessed skills that could be put to use assisting business unit managers in identifying creditworthy customers for commercial loans. At that time, the bank had embarked on a strategic plan to position itself as the business bank for companies with annual sales between $150,000,000 and $500,000,000. This meant that Continental, as a national bank, was willing to extend lending opportunities to companies that were primarily privately held and often managed by family members. Information commonly available for publicly traded companies was not so readily available for small private businesses, so the commercial loan department needed to find reliable resources, oftentimes in local markets, to ascertain the financial stability and creditworthiness of their prospective borrowers.

Building on his investigative unit's professional network, Griffin was able to demonstrate that his team could bring significant added value to the due diligence process. Oftentimes his staff had access to criminal record information and law enforcement intelligence that would not have been readily available to traditional credit review sources.

As Continental continued to face pressures to continue downsizing, Griffin was continually challenged to maintain his contribution to the review process in the face of a shrinking staff. With his accustomed far-sightedness, he began to develop a national network of independent investigators in key marketplaces. Often this meant developing personal relationships with private investigators, active and retired police officers, and prosecuting attorneys. By developing this external network, Griffin was able to continue to provide a high level of service without the burden of employing a large in-house staff.

Doug Griffin is one example of a security manager who built on his past experiences to achieve greater organizational value by looking for those collateral opportunities that were synergistic with the basics of asset protection. By taking the broader view, Griffin was able to demonstrate that skills ordinarily limited to specialty areas can have far greater impact within the organization if they are aligned with the organization's main business.

There's an interesting footnote to this story. Griffin's value as a coordinator of an external network allowed him to pursue a personal dream. He and his wife had long wanted to relocate to Denver, Colorado. Their dilemma was that Bank of America was headquartered in San Francisco, and Griffin's office was in Chicago. By leveraging on the concept of the today's virtual office, Griffin was able to convince bank executives that having an office in Denver was actually more cost-effective, since his travel expenses would be cut in half commuting between the two locations. The bank agreed, and today Griffin is a one-person unit supported by a large network of alliance partners working for one of the country's largest financial institutions.

PROTECTING PROPRIETARY PROPERTY AND CONFIDENTIAL INFORMATION

In the context of the information age, the asset protection manager has some very interesting challenges and ample opportunities to demonstrate collateral value. One of the more interesting opportunities lies in security's role in proprietary information protection. Catherine Romano has pointed out: "Information is the currency of the '90s. What you know and what others know about your company can make or break your ability to compete in the future. Yet many managers, accustomed to dealing only with the physical—employees and their surroundings—are not quite sure how to make the leap into the information-based business world. These days, instead of managing the property, plant and equipment, managers are in charge of the company's prime resource—information about the assets."[1]

Since information drives today's businesses, the task of keeping that information proprietary and confidential is redefining the scope of today's security executive. I used to tell aspiring security professionals in college or new to the security world that the future would be in information protection. Today I tell displaced security executives that the future is here. Unless they are content to be associated with physical security only, their here and now lies with contributing more to the protection of information than to the protection of physical assets.

Protecting information from falling legitimately and ethically into the hands of competitors is perhaps even more challenging because of today's electronic interconnectiveness and governmental reporting requirements. Romano adds, "As businesses move toward the paperless office, many are discovering that paper was much easier to safeguard. In the past, people who wanted to keep information from prying eyes locked it in a filing cabinet. Computers were centrally located and the mainframe was housed in a secured office. But the Information Age has made those techniques quaint, if not ineffective, ways to maintain security."[2]

Because the future is now, security executives, proprietary or contract, need to begin thinking about ways to redefine their contribution, lest they become the dispensable Neanderthals of an age gone by. We will spend the next pages focusing on ways to make valued-added contributions to the company's business performance through working into proprietary information protection.

Managing the Alliance

When the term *proprietary information* is used we generally think of either data security or intellectual property protection. In reality, the term refers to both—and considerably more. The link to classical security is achievable because many of the same basic protection strategies are either employed or have direct parallels in data security. From this perspective it is easy to see the potential collateral value in proprietary information protection. By expanding the traditional role of physical security to proprietary information protection, new and exciting value-added opportunities emerge. Equally important, data security is in an arena that is familiar to the security director. But as we shall see, proprietary information is more than computer or data security.

Note, however, that I said that the linking is achievable, but not necessarily *easily achievable*. As with any organizational change, the transition requires careful planning. John O'Leary highlights some of the roadblocks to such integration:

> Computer Security Departments are being folded into the classic security function at an increasing rate. In many companies, managers who once saw computer and physical security as completely different undertakings have come to view asset protection as an integrated assignment.
>
> Merging these responsibilities is not always easy, however. Professionals in both the computer and the physical security departments may resist attempts to bring the two staffs under one umbrella. Both groups feel that their jobs are unique. Computer security personnel may see the physical security staff as part of a "badge, gun, and guard-dog crowd" that does not understand the complexities of the computer. The traditional security staff may see the computer experts as arrogant and unappreciative of core security skills such as interviewing and investigating people."[3]

O'Leary continues by pointing out that initial differences include the contrast in the corporate cultural values of the two groups. He observes that both groups are security related, but that their historical roles and training create vast disparities in the way they view their responsibilities. For example, one of the biggest differences between the two is their approach to crime deterrence:

> Computer security professionals tend to operate in an environment where security controls are invisible, unobtrusive deterrents. They know that company employees will complain if they are required to remember too many passwords or if they have to wait for long while the hard drive is scanned for viruses. Consequently, computer security practitioners are usually well-tuned to the performance implications of their proposed security measures. Their mission is very much a sales job. The opposite is true in the physical security arena, where employees want to see a visible, active staff. A show of force, the presence of obvious security measures and technologies, even rumors of the existence of prevention or detection mechanisms can be effective deterrents.[4]

Another obstacle to overcome is the differences in professional backgrounds. Many people in computer security have migrated from the data processing field. Most people in classical security positions have a background in physical security or law enforcement. Their primary allegiance is to the security function, and they commonly view themselves as *separate from* the operational department to which they might be assigned. Data security specialists more often view themselves as *a part of* the operational unit. This difference in perception is crucial to understanding the disparities between computer security and the traditional security function.

Computer and physical security professionals are also trained differently and develop distinctly different perspectives about their roles. Typically those who enter security through data processing are not taught the interviewing and interrogation techniques that physical and personnel security people learn and perfect. Computer security professionals do, however, understand how technical components of the computer network interact. O'Leary continues, "To them [the computer professionals], troubleshooting a security problem involves trekking through various system security domains, each with divergent architectures, incompatible audit mechanisms, unique product implementation strategies, and different levels of compliance. The traditional security staff has been trained to focus on people and their actions, not technology."[5]

Success in merging computer and physical security to enhance the respective collateral value of the functions depends to a large degree on the person chosen to lead the group. A leader with credibility is often the first criterion. As O'Leary notes, "The most important step a company can take when merging these two departments is to choose a leader respected by both the computer and physical security staffs. To get past this phase, the new leader must show that he understands the complexities of the other discipline or is willing to learn."[6] Fred Tilley of the Bank Boston serves as an excellent example. With a background in data security and auditing, Tilley has made the transition from a single-track specialist to a collateral generalist. Today he is director of corporate security with responsibility for both data security and physical security, including fraud investigations and due diligence collaboration. Although Tilley could have relied on the talents of his protective service group to handle the operational responsibilities of physical security and investigations, instead he brought himself up to speed on the issues, dynamics, and nuances of this new side of his responsibilities.

Embracing classical corporate security duties, Tilley worked closely with physical security to increase his learning curve. He joined professional organizations such as the International Bank Security Association to gain access to a new network, and began attending local and national meetings of other physical security groups. Most important, he listened to and trusted his staff, recognizing their expertise. Once he had established his footing, he turned his attention to the full integration of the department, realizing that the department's full potential as a consolidated asset protection group could only be achieved through cooperation and a team approach. One of his strategies was to create crossover teams when the opportunity presented itself. Investigations of computer security breaches, for example, required a combination of technical knowledge and interviewing skills to get information from the person who reported the problem or who was implicated in the problem. By creating team-building opportunities, Tilley created a spirit of cooperation.

Beyond encouraging his people to work together, he carried the team building into joint staff meetings as a means of allowing differences to be aired and perspectives to be exchanged. These meetings allowed staff from both disciplines to learn more about each other. He arranged specially designed internal training sessions so that representatives of each subgroup could be exposed to each other. Tilley found that creating such forums created a dialogue that helped the two units build trust and respect, and it also allowed him to be exposed to any underlying issues that were getting in the way and thus slowing department's overall productivity and responsiveness to their end users.

Operationalizing Proprietary Information

For our discussion here, proprietary property and proprietary information are used synonymously. Proprietary information can be divided into three main categories: data security, marketplace proprietary property, and confidential information.

Data Security

Professional asset managers are quick to limit data security to electronic datasets. In doing so they neglect several critical areas, such as gained expertise, hard copy media, voice mail, and internal processes. Today, data security needs to incorporate protection in the following areas:

- ◆ *Expertise.* Data security needs to guard information acquired by specialists, for example, researchers, programmers, attorneys, consultants, key administrators, and so forth, that can be carried off by others, in short, knowledge.
- ◆ *Hard copy.* We are far from being a paperless society. Hard copy media includes anything that is not electronic or mental whose loss could be detrimental. This includes everything from manuals, customer receipts, and photographs and drawings to receptacle waste containing items such as letters and memoranda.
- ◆ *Electronic systems.* Today computer systems involve more than what is in the mainframe. We live in an era of LANs and WANs (local area networks and wide area networks). Desktop and laptop PCs are complete processing centers. Faxes and electronic and voice mail systems are equally a part of the electronic data world.

Marketplace Proprietary Property

Marketplace property involves those aspects of your business that are critical to maintaining your position or enhancing it in the marketplace. It is an area few traditional security managers have ventured into to any significant degree. Commonly referred to as *intellectual property,* it consists of the following items:

- ◆ trade secrets and patents
- ◆ formulas and processes
- ◆ machines and components
- ◆ pricing strategies
- ◆ industry sources
- ◆ customer/client information

The latter two items are oftentimes not included in the list of intellectual property (IP) variables, but they are critical to the very nature of maintaining competitive market positioning. Including them is most appropriate when the definition of IP is articulated; for example, the definition includes those assets, tangible or intangible, that contribute to allowing one company to maintain its advantage in the open market over another company. Therefore protecting industry sources and specific client information is as critical as protecting internal resources such as classified processes and formulas for manufacturing, a patent on a specific piece of equipment, or a preferred pricing plan for valued customers.

Confidential Information

This component incorporates property that is crucial to the main workings of the business—personnel records, internal communications, agreements, and so forth. Confidential information concerns the infrastructure that supports the overall organization. Information that might otherwise appear to be routine is often highly sensitive, and if it is not protected, the consequences can be disastrous. Profit margins can be affected, customer confidence shaken, and employee morale eroded if certain protections are not in place or adhered to by everyone. Confidential information consists of:

♦ human resource records, including performance reviews
♦ internal communications among business units
♦ research and development reports and updates
♦ pending and past litigation
♦ supplier and strategic partner agreements
♦ reports and work products

Personnel Records.   Your collateral value can be measured by your ability to provide security awareness training and installation of protective measures for each area of the business, including internal communications, research and development, litigation, supplier agreements, and more. As Leonard Fuld notes, "Employees in their workday world consider most pieces of information they handle harmless. They do not worry about what they consider harmless information. What they don't worry about, they don't watch. The information they do not watch can leave unquestioned and unchecked."[7] One scenario that illustrates the importance of protecting confidential information, especially when several different types of information are combined, occurred a few years ago.

A major European bank was interested in expanding its customer service offering to selected companies with a high net worth that were operating throughout Western Europe. They found an American bank—ranked among the top ten—that was interested in selling their European commercial banking business. It appeared that there was a mutual interest, and negotiations proceeded rapidly. Approximately a month before the deal was consummated, a major change occurred within the board of directors at the American bank. A new CEO was named. He immediately halted negotiations with the European bank and announced that the deal was off. He intended to retain the business.

Undaunted, the European bank proceeded to infiltrate the American bank's Western European offices and identify the bank's top performers by accessing personnel records. How? Their people knew that most American businesses bought office furniture, including filing cabinets, from one of three suppliers. Each supplier used its own generic keying system. By buying standard filing cabinets from each supplier, they "procured" a master key for each type of conventional file drawer. Armed with this tool, they systematically tested the integrity of security in each country and soon discovered how to breach each.

The European bank's plan was to identify the American bank's key performers and recruit them away with high compensation packages. Within five months they were able to recruit nineteen executives away from the American bank. As one executive put it bluntly, "If they [referring to the American bank] won't sell their business to us, we'll simply recruit it away. By the time they sue us in all seven countries, we'll be pretty well established. Sure we'll lose some business, but overall it's worth the investment."

Adding to the misery of the American bank, each recruited bank manager was expected to bring to the new bank his or her customer list, product pricing sheets, and operating manuals. Before the Americans could react and secure injunctions, let alone establish the necessary legal proofs regarding the loss of their valued assets, the European bank was up and operating.

Had the American bank begun by involving the security manager in the early phase when the decision was made to withdraw from the negotiations, would the security executive have been in a position to consider potential loss scenarios and plan accordingly? At the very least, look at the opportunity security missed to put the local security forces on heightened alert to try to prevent an unfortunate set of circumstances.

Internal Communications. Leonard Fuld observes, "Most members of management recognize the importance of protecting the results of research, but this recognition often does not extend to the many small increments of information scattered throughout the organization. In actual practice, when a new product reaches the manufacturing stage, almost all attempts to control the flow of information are abandoned."[8] American businesses are keenly aware of the sensitivity associated with new research. Yet there is a general failure to follow through in controlling the internal correspondence regarding research after a new product has gone to market. It's as though once the baby is born, there is no need to care for it.

In today's litigious society even the most seemingly innocuous memo can be used against well-intentioned employees. Does this mean we should stop corresponding? Obviously not. Yet common sense, coupled with awareness of potential outcomes, should rule. Security managers can establish collateral value by helping to secure internal communications and by making employees aware of the potential misuses of internal communications.

Research and Development.   In much the same way, a parallel can be drawn with consequential research, which results from original R&D projects. It is common for research, when shared, to generate additional research. There can be a potential for serious losses if the protections applied to the original are not in place for subsequent efforts. Here's a quick example.

A major West Coast medical research firm had affiliated itself with a major university. The university's main computers were accessible on the Internet so that research could be shared with other students, faculty, and R&D specialists. The medical research facility prided itself on the number of Nobel Prize recipients on its staff. Because of the firm's academic ties, the general belief was that their studies were safe out on the internet because of the "common bond" enjoyed among the worldwide community of medical researchers. It wasn't until members of the firm began to suspect that some of their original research had been corrupted that they grasped the idea that not all scientists necessarily subscribe to the same code of ethical behavior. Like anyone else, researchers can be influenced by factors such as financial rewards and worldwide recognition. Moreover, without true protection (for example, software firewalls), research is vulnerable to the threat of college pranksters hacking their way through original research, with the potential for significant loss—both in terms of the credibility of the researchers within the scientific community and the revenues derived from research grants.

Intellectually people understood the potential, but emotionally they do not want to accept the reality. Although the data security specialist at the medical research firm offered warnings, the researchers viewed her primarily as a systems analyst, and for years they created roadblocks to her proposed security measures claiming that protective devices and security data architecture were too restrictive and costly. Lacking the business acumen to counteract these arguments, the data security specialist languished. It wasn't until the inevitable occurred that the lesson of protecting research came home. Luckily for the firm, the loss it sustained was less than that experienced by many others. Yet the loss could have been avoided altogether had there been a collaborative approach between the security director and the data specialist.

Litigation—Past and Pending. Pending and past litigation can be particularly sensitive, especially in today's highly litigious society. Some would argue that confidential settlements need to be protected more than most other assets because of the high costs associated with potential future exposure. Working with legal counsel to develop policies and practices designed to protect the written and spoken word is both a critical and an excellent collateral value contribution that security can make.

It's surprising how few companies have developed guidelines for employees, especially managers, concerning the protection of information associated with past or current litigation. Since many actions end in settlements, part of the resolution is usually an agreement to keep the terms and the issues of the settlement confidential. Today's out-of-court settlements for premises liability cases exceed, on average, $600,000 according to noted forensic expert Norman Bates.

Attorneys are quick to advise employees not to discuss aspects of a case, yet they give little attention to records retention, document destruction, duplication of material, security of exhibits, and so on. The security decision maker has an opportunity in these circumstances to set forth instructional material and work with business unit managers to keep developed and/or collected materials confidential and secure. Keeping abreast of litigation, especially in the areas of intellectual property and trade secret protection puts the security manager in a position of being able to offer asset protection strategies that are consistent with the end users' requirements.

Supplier Agreements. Procurement personnel and department heads will go to significant lengths to negotiate exclusive contracts with their suppliers. This is especially true with preferred providers, national suppliers, and strategic partners. As part of developing their relationships, staff will offer price concessions, delivery preferences, response times, and special guarantees. On their own, any one of these terms and conditions can give the company an advantage in the marketplace. Collectively, they can create a significant shift in market position. Once in place, these agreements need to be protected. As we'll discuss below, contracts are particularly vulnerable to breach of confidentiality. Human nature drives many to boast about their accomplishments. After all, people want to be recognized for their hard work, tough negotiating skills, and so forth. Unfortunately by openly discussing the terms of business agreements, staff can give away the company's market advantage.

As a management consultant, I encounter this problem routinely. It is not uncommon for security directors, in an attempt to demonstrate their managerial prowess, to confide in me what they have accomplished in vendor negotiations. They will often talk openly about "their good deal." When asked if they have shared this information with their professional colleagues, it is not unusual for them to admit that they have. In doing so, they jeopardize their efforts, or those of others. Collateral value in security extends beyond the world of physical protections. Security can play a part in the development of confidentiality agreements and terms for compliance, as well as a program of business unit ownership for protecting agreements (including corporate security and their external partners).

Reports and Work Products.   "If it's out of your organization, it's out of your control." This is a simple concept but a deadly one for most companies—and often missed by employees. Organizations generate reports and a variety of other work products. Some are intended for the public; most would gain the company little advantage if they were to be made public. Although it is true that the majority of such documents may not necessarily hurt, complacency about what happens to reports and completed work products can be injurious.

Many states protect work products generated for or through legal counsel. These provisions can be particularly helpful when a company is dealing with consultant studies, supplier reports, and internal analyses. By directing such reports through a lawyer, an attorney relationship is established that adds an additional—though not insurmountable—layer of protection. Conversely, companies intent on protecting internal information often become victims of their own assumptions. Classification schemes are developed, documents stamped accordingly, and warnings boldly printed on front covers: FOR BEARER'S EYES ONLY.

Despite years of warnings from security experts not to do this, it remains a common practice. What an invitation for the person desiring access to such information! We would think it crazy for someone to leave his or her car parked at a busy location, unlocked, with the keys in the ignition and a large sign reading THIS CAR IS UNLOCKED WITH THE KEY INSIDE, yet the branding of documents is tantamount to boldly printing on the front cover, TAKE ME, I HAVE GREAT INFORMATION INSIDE.

When combined, data security, marketplace property protection, and confidential information are critical for any company. As I have told my corporate clients, when the issue of asset protection arises, securing your assets, and by that I mean all of them, is as critical to profitability as are increased sales and expense management. As we have seen, each of these factors on their own presents opportunities for security profession- als with the desire to increase collateral value. Taken in totality, they present security managers even greater opportunities for increasing their contributions.

ASSESSING AND COUNTERING THREATS TO PROPRIETARY INFORMATION

Threat Analysis

Thus far we've examined the three types of proprietary information. Within this context we've also briefly reviewed the many faces of this information. At any given time, under any number of probable situations, proprietary property can be subject to a wide assortment of threats. When security is breached in these areas, as we have seen in a few examples already, the consequences and/or potential exposures are significant. In pursuing how you can demonstrate added value, we need to begin by cre- ating a context. This is best achieved through an examination of potential threats to each type of proprietary information. For the most part, the threats can be outlined as follows:

- ◆ loose lips
- ◆ discarded media
- ◆ trade shows
- ◆ the press
- ◆ planned invasions—physical and electronic
- ◆ opportunists and the disenfranchised

The probability of these incidents occurring on a day-to-day basis is far greater than other types of threats, and typically organizations have been lax in addressing these threats. It is for this reason alone that today's security director should capitalize on the opportunities for making value- added contributions in these areas by assuming responsibility and devel- oping responsive strategies. After analyzing each threat we will then focus on strategies specifically designed to demonstrate your collateral value.

Loose Lips

In the current *Protection of Assets Management Manual*, the authors of "Designing a Proprietary Information Protection Program," point out, "Proprietary information is lost *primarily* because of the deliberate attempts of others to gain access, whether by legal or illegal means."[9] I would take issue with this conclusion. A review of the literature and my thirty years of experience suggest that the primary cause is plain old carelessness. Following are some classic examples.

Employee's Off the Job.   Cocktail parties, golf games, backyard barbecues, and your spouse's company picnic are among the top "leak opportunities." Just as we noted earlier, people want other people to know how much they know. Bragging kills—if not people, certainly potentially important confidential information. Sadly some of the leading practitioners of party boasting are corporate executives. Wanting to impress other corporate executives, they make inadvertent slips. Take the case of the security services president (someone you would think would be particularly sensitive to this issue). His company had just landed a very large account in a new market, and he was attending a local security conference. He commented to a trusted confidant that part of his company's strategic plan was to make this new market a cornerstone of the company's business. To accomplish this, the company had targeted a major competitor already entrenched in the market, and was developing plans to undercut the other company.

The security services president made the comment at a cocktail party hosted by the security group after the first day's meetings. Standing next to the president at the time was a regional manager for his competitor. The president was unaware of the other gentleman's identity and continued to talk. When his colleague asked how he intended to take over the market, the executive laid out several key details of the company's a new marketing plan. Afterward the president excused himself and left to mix with the other guests. As he walked away, he felt good about his brief conversation with his confidant. So did the confidant, so did the regional manager.

I include spouses' company picnics because they are a growing source for inadvertent leaks. Given the great number of professional working couples today, the adage It's a small world, takes on greater significance. For example, a data analyst for a high-tech firm attended his company's annual Christmas party and sat at the same table with one of his associates. Their respective wives were with them. After a short time the analyst commented that his wife was the vice president of a large bank and that she was negotiating the final financing for a merger between two companies, and he named them both. She, in turn, said that the merger had a few obstacles to overcome, but within three or four months the deal would be announced.

Since the companies involved were headquartered on the opposite coast, she thought there would be no harm in mentioning them in conversation, but then she asked if they could change the subject. The wife of the second analyst thanked her, saying that she was very uncomfortable since she was a corporate officer of a major competitor to one of the involved companies. She added that she was sure that her senior management staff was unaware of the impending merger and how it would affect her company's market position.

Friendships.   Just as it is not unusual for work colleagues to develop friendships, the same can often be said for professional relationships that crop up between counterparts of competing companies. As a former security director of a major bank, I knew many bank security directors. Over time some of these relationships progressed from a professional association to a true friendship, and some of these friendships continue today. The same principle applies to R&D specialists, marketers, heads of new product groups, and other professionals.

Perhaps another way of viewing this is to note that people tend to run in the same circles as their professional counterparts. In turn, it can become very difficult to separate professional talk from unrelated discussions. I believe we would all agree that common to most of us is the desire to be recognized by those closest to us for our knowledge and expertise. When we're mixed up in friendships involving people who work for competing companies, we tread a very dangerous and thin line. Professional peers often try to impress one another with the importance of what they are working on and what they know. The threat becomes even greater when peer relationships slip from a casual friendship into very personal or romantic relationships. The director of public relations for a large mid-West multinational company was introduced to an executive from one of the organization's primary competing companies. The two executives began dating almost immediately, but their relationship ended within a few months because they found it difficult to separate shop talk from their personal lives. While this particular relationship ended without disclosure of proprietary information, very often pillow talk is found to be at the root of the unintended release of confidential information. Although it is both unfair and nearly impossible to discourage the forming of such relationships, it is paramount that the respective parties clearly understand the dangers involved both for their respective companies and for them—that they could lose their job as a consequence of such slipups.

Suppliers and Vendors. External providers can present a real problem. Often companies have no choice but to give their providers confidential information. To fulfill orders and meet production requirements, you have to expose part of what you are doing. Consequently, your risk is magnified because the information is now out of your control. In some cases the provider may be totally unaware that he or she is exposing your proprietary information. For example, I was at my printer's office one day working with material for a slide presentation that I was preparing. I happened to flip over a sheet of scrap paper the printer had provided. Being an environmentally conscientious business owner, he was printing my project on rejected print runs from other customers. On the back side of this sheet I discovered the purchasing agreement between one of the San Francisco Bay area's largest software houses and its largest supplier. Everything, including pricing, sample product, and the terms and conditions of the two parties was there. Had someone with an eye for a quick and unscrupulous profit found the same paper, that person could have gone to the software company's competitor and offered to sell the material. As it was, I handed the paper back to the printer and cautioned him about the potential risks.

The same inadvertent but real threat is possible when your suppliers subcontract your work out. Take the case of a large specialty catalog retailer who had worked very hard to build a selective mailing list of prospective customers. The company's competitor was constantly beating them in direct mail promotions and undercutting them on price. The company suspected espionage and undertook an investigation. The conclusion was that one of their contractors was subcontracting out much of the work. This subcontractor, not having any contractual obligation or ethical squeamishness, surmised that the catalog retailer's chief competitor might be interested in the promotional material. He contacted the competitor who gladly procured the information. Because of their streamlined operations, the competing company was able to get their advertising to the marketplace quicker, thus undercutting the larger catalog house.

Equally troubling is the emergence of certain industries that cut across the business spectrum, thus potentially exposing one company's proprietary property to several competitors. Multimedia production companies serve as an excellent example. According to Mark Radcliff, absent any written restriction, multimedia companies will take a product developed for one company and incorporate it into their own marketing plans as a means of demonstrating the type of product they are capable of producing.[10] In other words, a product developed for General Motors by a multimedia company could easily be shown to Ford Motor Company by the marketing force of the multimedia firm as part of its portfolio when the firm was soliciting new business for themselves.

How often is this done? I was recently introduced to the senior programmer for a large multimedia company. Having just recently completed reading Radcliffe's article, I commented to the programmer about the article. He responded that he was not aware of the article, yet he exclaimed without hesitation that this is commonly done. He went on to add, "It's a great way for us to get new business. When one company sees what we can do for their competitors they are oftentimes interested in us." When I asked him if his company had ever inadvertently shown one company's proprietary information (material under development and not yet ready for public release) to another company, the programmer stopped and thought for a minute. He replied, "I guess we have. It's just something we never think about."

I am a strong believer in the concept of sharing information, provided that the information is controlled and managed properly. In giving, one receives. Unfortunately, many people cannot differentiate what they should or should not give away unless they are made aware of potential threats and the associated potential loss. American business executives typically fail to understand this concept. As we shall see shortly, this is where another of your collateral value opportunities emerges.

Discarded Media

I was flying home one evening from Chicago, working on my laptop computer. The gentleman next to me was equally engaged, reading a series of documents extracted from his briefcase. At one point he stood up, dropped the file he was reading on his seat, and went to the restroom. I looked down and noted that the cover bore the logo of the airline I was flying on. Across the front was stamped in large bold letters: CONFIDENTIAL: FOR ADDRESSEE'S EYES ONLY. Under this warning was the document's title in nearly equally large printing: STRATEGIC MARKETING PLAN—FINAL VERSION. Also included was the name of the division.

Several thoughts raced through my mind, among them:

♦ Say or do nothing. Write it off as one more example of executive sloppiness.
♦ Pick the report up and drop it into my briefcase and then mail it back to the company with a note explaining how I came into possession of it. As I gave this option a second thought I reasoned that if properly presented, this could be a great introduction for my consulting services. Or it could really make the airline mad, and I might run the risk of being charged with theft.

♦ Identify myself to him upon his return, explain my background, and advise him of the dangers associated with leaving such a document unattended.

As other scenarios raced through my mind, I noticed he had exited the restroom and was chatting with one of the flight attendants. In all, nearly twenty minutes passed before he returned. When he finally came back, he looked at me, and we smiled an acknowledgment of each other. After he picked up the report I leaned over and said: "I couldn't help but see that report on your seat. Hi, I'm Dennis Dalton, and I am a marketing manager for ABC Airlines [using the name of his chief competitor]. That's a great report you're reading."

I could see the blood begin to drain from his face. Before he had a stroke, I told him who I really was. At first he was understandably upset about my not so funny joke. Then he laughed a little and acknowledged that leaving the report exposed was truly a dumb thing to do—especially when it could have been so readily taken.

We began to talk. I started off by telling him not to feel totally foolish. After all, the person who stamped CONFIDENTIAL: FOR ADDRESSEE'S EYES ONLY and STRATEGIC MARKETING PLAN—FINAL VERSION was equally at fault. Why advertise what this document is? I asked. When he and the other executives received it, didn't they know what it was? Of course they did. Why advertise that it's confidential? The answer, more often than not, is quite simple. People who write such reports need to advertise the report's importance. For in doing so, they believe that it enhances their own importance.

Allow me to hasten to add that this is not to suggest that all documents should not be marked confidential. Failure to do so could be seen as evidence that the document is not intended to be confidential. The point is that a deliberate and reasoned approach should be used when marking certain documents as being either proprietary or confidential. Hence most experts recommend the development of a classification scheme. Such schemes can be represented by alphanumeric codes, by color, and so forth. The point is that the covers of such documents should not be so blatant. Nor should employees, regardless of their position in the organization, be cavalier with confidential information.

Other not so obvious threats to proprietary information can be just as potentially serious. Chief among them is the practice of searching through someone's garbage for discarded media and other incriminating evidence. Most security experts would agree that the practice doesn't generally yield the intended result, but when a hit occurs, it's usually a big one. In February 1995, *Security Management Magazine* published an article entitled "Talking Trash." In this article the authors noted, "It is foolish to spend thousands of dollars on perimeter security guards and equipment just to hand over sensitive information to a waste paper or trash removal company."[11]

To illustrate their point, the authors cited the example of *Northwest Reports*, a television news magazine airing a story about several Portland, Oregon, banks that failed to protect customer information. The news story focused on one private investigator's search for information in the bank's outdoor trash containers. The private investigator's efforts yielded valuable customer and bank information including credit applications, credit card account numbers and balances, copies of customers' tax returns, safe deposit box information, and bank building information including floor plans and combinations to locks and alarms.

In the early 1990s the *Wall Street Journal* covered the unfolding story of how General Electric's recipe for making diamonds may have been stolen by one of their scientists and sold to rivals outside of the United States. The break in the investigation centered on G.E.'s corporate security department purchasing three garbage bags at $5 each from the neighborhood garbage collectors who had collected the bags from G.E.'s suspected scientist.

As the *Wall Street Journal* noted, "Like any good dime store novel detective, security officials started with Mr. Sung's garbage. Investigators had to separate cut up and foreign documents from scraps of food and laboriously piece them together with tape. What they found was exciting for the gumshoes, but troublesome to their corporate executives. What they found was a maze of companies he had started. It was a full service operation: He sold technology, bought manufacturing equipment, gave marketing advice, even imported diamonds for sale in the U.S. According to the affidavits filed by G.E."[12]

What these anecdotes underscore is the ease with which people can obtain discarded media from otherwise unsuspecting employees. It has long been acknowledged by those in the credit card business that major fraud rings have thrived for years based on information gleaned from Dumpsters located at retail bank branches. Similar treasure spots can be found in large retail mall Dumpsters belonging to both anchor stores and small boutique shops.

Trade Shows

Each year I wait for Comdex. This is the computer industry's trade show, or, as some pundits characterize it, it's the mother of all trade shows. I don't attend Comdex, I just wait to read about it, usually in the *Wall Street Journal*. Why? Because the media has a field day reporting the shenanigans of high-profile executives such as Michael Dell of Dell Computer, Bill Gates, Compaq executives, and so on. It's open duck season, pure and simple. These corporate leaders and their staff, come and actively work the exhibition floor in search of what the other is offering. Reporters write pages in their respective magazines and newspapers about how an executive is able to fleece unsuspecting marketing representatives out of valuable information. Still, year after year they come. Why? Because like so many other industries, it's expected of them. It is as though not coming sends some signal that a company is in trouble. So companies come and spend inordinate amounts of money giving valuable information away or trying to outwit their competitors by engaging in disinformation.

On a less conspicuous level, the same dirty tricks occur at lesser followed trade shows where research scientists, marketing specialists, and even security executives openly talk about their company's latest efforts to gain or hold market position as a result of the latest product development, operational efficiency, cost management technique, vendor agreement, employee outsourcing program, and so forth.

The Press

Just because the sign outside the trade show exhibition show says NO PRESS, this doesn't mean the press isn't there. The same can be said for seminars and workshops. What is said and how it is reported is left to the discretion of the reporters and their editors. And even though the reporter may not hail from the *Wall Street Journal*, CNN, or one of the other major public media sources, it doesn't make what is reported any less public. Take, for example, the article entitled "You're Not Paranoid: They Really Are Watching You," written by John Whalen for *Wired*, a popular computer-oriented magazine with a circulation of more than 300,000. This article is of particular interest since Whalen is writing about the American Society for Industrial Security's annual conference. Here's an excerpt:

> Turns out it's pretty easy to crash the lunch spread at the American Society for Industrial Security's annual convention. You just walk in, sit down, start munching on salad. I didn't set out to trespass—I only wanted to chat up some corporate dicks, ex G-men, and card-carrying government spooks when their guard was down, beef-tip gravy on their chins. The thing was, when I got busted (halfway through a stale roll), it wasn't by the so-called security specialists with the Efrem Zimbalist Jr. hair-cuts—it was by one of those superannuated babes with a cotton-candy coif who police the floor of the Las Vegas Convention Center.

Oddly, it's the professionals who cover for me when my gate-crashing fails. My table neighbor, a security-fence sales-man from New Jersey (razor wire, barbed wire, electrified wire—your complete line of perimeter defense products), has recovered a wayward ID badge from the floor, and it's stuffed with official meal tickets. Mr. Perimeter Defense peels a cou-pon off the wad and saves me the embarrassment of ejection from the ASIS gathering. "Even though our business is secu-rity," he cracks, "sometimes you gotta break the rules."

I had come to the ASIS conference not to breach lunch-time security, but to feast on the latest technology guaranteed to repel vengeful employees—the nest-feathering, profit-skimming, paper-clip-pilfering, goldbricking, shoplifting, ax-grinding, monkey-wrenching malcontents. But hands down, the favorite statistic traded in the cavernous exhibit hall is this one: "Eighty to ninety percent of your business theft is internal."[13]

As one lecturer puts it, "The so-called American dream—I don't think we have that anymore in most companies." What we have instead are disgruntled ex-employees and soon-to-be-ex-employees who will "steal, vandalize, spread rumors, tamper with products, screw with your computers, and urinate in the coffee pot," he warns.

So how do you discuss promising new horizons and opportunities? By keeping open forums such as trade shows, and professional publica-tions, as generic as possible. Discussing the results of studies or method-ologies is both understandable and acceptable. Detailing strategies or fielding questions regarding specific lessons learned so that any competi-tor can gain valuable insights at your expense is both bad business man-agement and potentially injurious to bottom-line performance.

Planned Invasions—Physical and Electronic

Physical Attacks.   In May of 1995, at closing time, two men entered the storage facilities of IST Incorporated in Santa Clara, California. They pulled out semiautomatic weapons and restrained three employees. Hav-ing secured the facility for themselves, they then proceeded to steal more than $250,000 worth of modems, processors, and money chips.

In October of the same year Oregon's Silicon Forest (Oregon's ver-sion of California's famed Silicon Valley) had a similar experience. Five armed, masked men broke into a computer chip company, Oki Semicon-ductor, on Halloween evening. At first one of the employees thought it was a Halloween prank, but then he was hit across the shoulders by the gunman. The robbers proceeded to steal $2 million dollars' worth of computer memory chips. This theft at Oki Semiconductor was the largest heist of chips of that kind on the West Coast, and it underscores the continuing trend of violent takeover robberies at high-tech companies.

As Mark Moreno, staff writer for the *San Jose Mercury News*, notes, "It's become a pattern familiar to computer distribution firms in the Silicon Valley: A young woman enters the office and asks for a job application. She is given one—just as a group of men follows her into the building, with guns drawn."[14] Moreno uses this as his lead for a story reporting the fifth such robbery invasion to hit the city of Fremont, California, in the first five months of 1995. Despite admonitions from security personnel to keep side doors closed all the time, employees at Alpha Systems, Inc. found themselves victims of a similar heist during which hundreds of thousands of computer chips were stolen.

The underlying motivation for such invasion-style robberies will range from street gangs wanting to underwrite the cost of drug deals to foreign governments and businesses seeking to gain an upper hand in the highly competitive high-tech industry. As detective John Dauzat with the Fremont Police Department notes, "I believe they are all tied together. They are doing it for someone or for some group. In other words, organized criminals find that they can finance drug operations through the sale of stolen computer hardware and software to foreign entities." [15]

In 1993 the American Electronics Association measured high-tech losses at $40 million. In 1994 Santa Clara County's famed Silicon Valley experienced fifty-one burglaries of computer companies. Within the first six months of 1995 this number had doubled. Such thefts are not limited to any one geographic area. One Boston warehouse lost $600,000 in an invasion, and a London-based advertising company reported an $800,000 burglary. Catching such thieves is difficult. The FBI estimates that computer parts can be resold between twelve and eighteen times within the first seventy-two hours after they are stolen. Because of this challenge, the FBI has joined efforts with the Technology Theft Prevention Foundation (TTPF), a nonprofit organization that brings together the insurance industry, electronic companies, and law enforcement to combat invasion-style thefts.

Not all corporate invasions are as open and brazen as the invasions we've described. What would otherwise appear to be routine burglary can just as likely be a ruse for something far more sinister and threatening to a corporation's financial viability. In an article entitled "Bungled Burglary? Don't Be So Sure," Henri Bérubé notes that the disturbing trend of common burglary is that it is a means of concealing the theft of larger corporate secrets. In citing a case of what appeared to be a routine burglary in Ontario, Canada, he reports that the Canada's Security Intelligence Service intervened and linked the burglary to a very serious case of industrial espionage. According to the intelligence agency, 20 percent of the companies consulted have expressed security concerns related to perceived threats or actual incidents of economic espionage.[16] Here in the United States, the White House Office of Science and Technology estimates that corporate espionage is costing U.S. companies $100 billion per year in lost sales.

Stealing proprietary property is not new. Nor are the perpetrators limited to drug lords and street thugs. Jay Peterzell, reporting for *Time* magazine, notes that the practice of corporations spying on other corporations, especially involving foreign entities, can be traced back decades. He writes: "The dangers of Soviet military espionage may be receding, but U.S. security officials are awakening to a spy threat from a different quarter: America's allies. According to U.S. officials, several foreign governments are employing their spy networks to purloin business secrets and give them to private industry." He cites several cases where U.S. agents have found evidence that the French intelligence service, Direction Générale de la Sécurité Extérieure, had recruited spies in the European branches of IBM, Texas Instruments, and other U.S. electronics companies. American officials say DGSE was passing along secrets involving research and marketing to Compagnie des Machines Bull, the struggling computer maker largely owned by the French government. U.S. officials say the spy ring was part of a major espionage program targeting foreign business executives since the late 1960s by Service 7, a branch of French intelligence.[17]

The reporter concludes that while the French efforts can be blatant, they are by no means unique. To quote the FBI's associate deputy director in charge of investigations, "A number of nations friendly to the U.S. have engaged in industrial espionage, collecting information with their intelligence services to support private industry." Those countries include Britain, West Germany, the Netherlands, Belgium, Japan, and Israel.[18]

Electronic Threats   Threats to proprietary information are not limited to just physical invasions and surreptitious burglaries. Much more common and more difficult to detect are the hijinks of electronic hackers, opportunists, and disgruntled employees seeking revenge through a company's electronic networks. As employees become more enamored with the use of wireless technology such as cellular phones and satellite-controlled PCs, both the threat and the actual incidents of loss pose a serious challenge for today's security manager.

As *USA Today* reports, "The lack of privacy on portable cellular phones is a little disgusting blemish on an otherwise happy face of an industry: 3.5 million cellular phones were in use—mostly in cars—by the end of last year, a 67% rise and growing." Cellular eavesdropping is not unlike the monitoring of conversations with radio scanners for years. Unfortunately, cellular telephones have become the communication instrument of choice for employees at all levels within the corporation. Even though efforts to introduce digital transmission—a burst of electronic data, so to speak, rather than voices—are quickly unfolding, as one diehard scanning eavesdropper notes in the *USA Today* article, "As soon as they go digital, someone will start selling a device that will undigitalize it for us scanner owners."[19]

For those in the telecommunications industry, toll fraud—unauthorized users placing calls through a phone system—is at an all-time high. Industrywide, toll fraud is a $2.3 billion business, and 70 percent of all large telecommunication users have reported being a victim of fraud. The aggregate cost per victim is estimated at about $125,000. Even though toll fraud happens nearly everywhere, by being aware of the types of fraud and establishing a security program, your company can limit its exposure.[20]

Ameritech's Michael LeBeau notes that preventing toll fraud requires using a little common sense in addition to establishing procedures and installing the right types of preventive equipment. Such commonsense techniques include never sharing numbers with other employees and using personal identification numbers (PINs) that are not tied to such easily detectable codes as a person's social security number, birth date, employee ID number, and so forth.

LeBeau goes on to say that even though a company may make an honest effort to keep its phones protected at night, there are some hackers who can get into the system in broad daylight. By calling through a PBX system, the caller might get through to the operator and ask for an outside line. That open line is all the caller needs to commit fraud. Misuse of call-forwarding, three-way calling, and voice mail accounts for nearly 20 percent of all toll frauds. The good news is that your phone system can be programmed to block these types of calls. Companies and individuals can handle the programming on-site, thus minimizing service user fees and expediting the process.[21]

Whether you are working for an emerging growth company or an established Fortune 500 company, it is not uncommon to find that considerable attention has been given to data security, but little has been done in the area of telecommunications-related protection. This is particularly true for facsimile transmissions. In my work it is not uncommon for me to find that many of my large multinational clients have made limited efforts to encrypt fax transmissions between domestic U.S. facilities, but more often than not they have neglected to install similar encryption devices for transmissions from either the United States to an overseas operation or between foreign facilities. The result is that sensitive data, although protected within the United States, is often vulnerable during international transmissions.

Opportunists and the Disenfranchised

Today the term "over the hill gang" has taken on two meanings. The first and most common refers to any group of people who are over forty years of age. The second usage is growing; it refers to those opportunists who run from a company, taking with them something of value. Downsizing has taken its toll in many ways, not the least of which is diminished employee morale. As job security becomes an endangered ideal, employees at all levels react in a variety of ways. While some attempt to put a positive spin on events, others become disenfranchised and seize the opportunity to either retaliate or take what they believe is due them.

Much of my postgraduate work concentrated on how people within organizations play out their feelings of being rejected or accepted. When people feel that they are not a part of their environment, it doesn't take long for them to feel a sense of alienation. Depending on their value system, background, and motivation, their behavior can take many forms; it can be directed toward a specific individual or the company as a whole. Regardless, for the attentive observer, disgruntled employees generally telescope their alienation long before their actions have serious consequences. In this respect security managers have an opportunity for contributing collateral value.

Essentially, people will develop and retain loyalty to a company if they feel there is a bond of respect, if they have a sense of recognized worth and a belief that there is a personal relationship—regardless of how limited it may be. This holds true when the company is resizing (for example, eliminating or consolidating job functions and laying people off). In short, people want to be accepted. If they believe they are accepted, and assuming that they are not suffering from some mental abnormality, they can deal with having their input rejected or their contributions limited a great deal of the time. There is a serious caution here, however. I use the term "a great deal of the time" because there is a threshold of tolerance. If employees perceive that their input is continuously rejected, or their contribution is rarely, if ever, recognized, the seeds of alienation may soon be sown.

When people feel as though they don't belong, one or more of the following states of mind may ensue:

♦ *Co-optation.* Original values are set aside or severely modified to achieve a "buy in." Behavior is characterized by the motto If you can't beat them, join them.

♦ *Separatism.* The attitude "I'm better than they are anyway" sets in. The employee's behavior is characterized by not attempting to join in; focusing on the mechanics of the job and not the people; sarcasm and distrust.

♦ *Retreatism.* The employee develops defensive tactics to avoid confrontation. Arriving late for work or meetings, sitting behind a closed door all day long—day after day, communicating exclusively by E-mail as opposed to over the telephone or by personal encounters are examples of avoidance behavior.

♦ *Retaliation.* An attitude of "Don't get mad, get even" is a predominant behavioral characteristic. Verbal sniping, taking delight in other people's trouble, setting someone up for a fall, and conspiring to "get back" are demonstrations of the retaliator.

While any one of these four primary motivators can drive people to sell out their employer, these motivators represent a continuum of threat. If employees co-opt their original values sufficiently, they may never act out in any negative way. One example is the case of a moderately radical feminist who joined a largely male-dominated company. As a middle manager she suffered the classic experiences of a professional person wanting to be accepted based on the worth of her contributions. Being a female, however, she was rarely taken seriously, and she was subjected to subtle sexual harassment.

After a period of time, she fell in love with a line-level specialist and married him. Wanting to be accepted by his associates, she found it psychologically more settling to relax her values and assume the more traditional role of the subservient female. This translated into her showing more tolerance for the behavior of her own managerial peer group. Within a year not only was she a strong advocate for the organization, but she willingly accepted the fact that her role within the higher ranks would always be limited. When challenged by other aspiring women who had previously looked to her as a role model, she backed off, saying that for her the battle was simply not worth the personal suffering.

Yet co-optation can take on another, more sinister dimension. As opposed to leading employees to accept the values of their own organization, it can lead them to accept another company's value system. Presented with the right motivation (money, acceptance, and so forth), employees can be co-opted into spying for a competitor. Even though their motivation may be significantly different from that of retaliators, the end result is the same—loss of company assets.

Separatists are not as complacent as co-opters. If so inclined and appropriately motivated, separatists would not need much enticement to betray their company because they have mentally distanced themselves. A degree of *organizational anomie* can set in. By this I mean a sense of not sharing the organization's values or culture. Feeling estranged, separatists create their own sense of moral justification. They rationalize that the company always faces the threat that its secrets will be sold, given away, or exposed—this is a risk of doing business. Just as it can happen to your competitor; it can happen to you. Separatists are no more than the agents for such occurrences. Potentially, such personalities can be very explosive.

Like separatists, retreatists are also feeling and acting out alienation. They represent a higher degree of risk since they actively engage in noncompliant behavior. Although they may perceive that they are not doing anything wrong, or acting in an injurious way, they nevertheless cross a fine line. By retreating and avoiding engagements, they transition from a state of mind to the beginnings of actual disruptive behavior; e.g., hacking, sabotage, theft, etc.

Retaliators pose the most serious threat because they display an active willingness to get even with those who have wronged them. While retreatists claim not to be angry, their behavior reveals a deep resentment at perceived injustice. Driven primarily by spite, they reject the organization and seek revenge discreetly. Acting out in a physical way is not their style. Instead, they delight in their deviousness; they pride themselves on what they believe to be subtleness. Sometimes their behavior is subtle, but most times it is not. Regardless, if tolerated, retaliators can be the cancer that can kill an organization.

People who don't feel accepted can be found anywhere in the organization, regardless of the size of the company. The critical threat is when people who want to seek revenge have access to sensitive assets. Take for example the case reported a few years ago in the *Wall Street Journal* of the partner in a software start-up company.[22] After being disillusioned by his partner, the engineer-partner believed that his input was no longer valued. Driven by greed and revenge, he quit and formed a new company to field competing products.

The other partner was the sales manager. It didn't take long for him to see that sales were softening, and initially he wrote off the cause to "tough competition." When the sales manager tried to save the company, he discovered that his partner the software engineer had developed copyright documents filled with loopholes. After spending $500,000 of his own money, the sales manager lost the company.

The important point to underscore is that managers need to be cautioned against jumping too quickly when one of these patterns is manifested. Like any other organizational behavior model, it is just that—a model. People who feel alienated can conduct themselves very legitimately. More often than not, they simply opt to leave. Others will limit their behavior to voicing their displeasure to whoever will listen. Some will be tempted but never succumb to the temptation for a variety of ethical reasons. And then there are those who, if approached, will report the incident to company managers immediately out of a sense of loyalty, perhaps hoping that by doing so they will gain acceptance.

Primary Motivations for Stealing Critical Assets

In May 1992 the Department of Defense Personnel Security Research and Education Center (PERSEREC) published a comprehensive report of past government spies entitled *Americans Who Spied Against Their Country Since World War II*, which gives a profile of both military and civilian spies.[23] Equally important, the PERSEREC study points out several motivations that lead individuals into a life of espionage. Their results bear a striking similarity to research done in the area of white-collar crime and data gathered by the American Institute for Business Research. In 1992 that research institute published a report jointly with the National Security Institute entitled *Protecting Corporate America's Secrets in the Global Economy*. That publication explores in depth the range of challenges facing businesses in the area of proprietary information.[24] Since the research results are so similar, it seems fair to use both reports to review the common motivators among past U.S. spies. The information gleaned from this research can serve as a general guideline for executives who are developing their own plans for protecting proprietary information.

In conducting their analysis, PERSEREC identified over 150 individuals as potential case studies. Upon review of each person, they developed a set of criteria that narrowed their overall database to 117 cases. Through studying each of the spies in detail, they were able to discern six primary motivators for committing espionage: money, ideology, disgruntlement and revenge, ingratiation, coercion, thrills and self-importance.

Table 6–1 summarizes the primary motives of 115 subjects (2 were disregarded because they fall outside the research criteria). For over half of them, money was the primary motive (they were retaliators). This was followed by the ideology motivation (for separatists), disgruntlement (retreatists), ingratiation, coercion, and thrills/self-importance (co-opters). Of the total of 115 individuals, 35 had more than one motive. Comparing columns 2 and 4, ideology appeared the same number of times (21) as a primary motive as for one of multiple motivations. For the analysts, this meant that ideology was the predominant motivator. Conversely, thrill and self-importance more frequently appeared in combination with other motives.

Motivations are not easy to explain. What may appear to us to be the primary motivation in a situation can, in fact, mask another reason altogether. For example, a concerned management team could conclude that an employee's primary motive may be based on ideology. In reality, there could be another motivation, or a set of other motivations. The smart employee knows what "hooks" their management and can play to this accordingly.

Based on PERSEREC's research, however, it appears that the motivations delineated above are the primary ones. Money, ideology and disgruntlement/revenge, fairly self-explanatory motivations, are the strongest ones. People leading otherwise normal lives can be challenged by one or more of these motivations. As for the second three—ingratiation, coercion, and thrills/self-importance—let's handle these one at a time. Ingratiation (committing an act to please someone or themselves) is often an equally compelling motivator because alienators want desperately to prove their worth to someone, even if it is to themselves. In this case the alienator's motivation parallels the co-opter discussed earlier. Coercion appears to be occurring less frequently as a motivation. Although it may

Table 6–1 Reasons for Betraying

	% PRIMARY	#	% MULTIPLE	#
MONEY	52.2	60	52.0	78
IDEOLOGY	18.3	21	14.0	21
DISGRUNTLEMENT/REVENGE	14.8	17	14.0	21
INGRATIATION	8.7	10	10.7	16
COERCION	3.5	4	2.7	4
THRILLS/SELF-IMPORTANCE	2.6	3	6.7	10
TOTAL	100.0	115	100.0	150**

N = 115
Missing = 2

** More than the number of individuals because there were 34 people with multiple motivations.

play a more predominant role in government service, coercion (blackmail or extortion) is more difficult to achieve in the private sector. It is more likely that the opportunity for getting thrills and/or the need to demonstrate self-importance will occur in this setting. This motivation incorporates a fascination with danger with seeking personal thrills, flaunting authority, trying to manipulate or outsmart the system (the world of the computer hacker), relishing intrigue, and bolstering the ego.

Discussing the underlying psychological events motivating people to do things is beyond the scope of this book. Nonetheless, it is important to note that employees, at any level, can, and do, turn against their employers. When they do, they can engage in their nefarious activities for a long time without being detected. PERSEREC found that only 29 percent of perpetrators were discovered in their first attempt while another 16 percent went undetected for less than a year. Another 31 percent operated for up to five years, and 24 percent for longer than that. Remember, these were employees operating within a system that has a formal program for detecting such activity. It doesn't take much imagination to speculate how long malefactors could operate, and to what extent, if they had free rein.

Employee theft and sabotage is still the leading source of losses within a company. The San Francisco–based Computer Security Institute estimates that 84 percent of all losses are directly attributable to employees.[25] The San Jose, California, Police Department estimates that Silicon Valley companies lose an average of a million dollars a week, most of the theft being perpetrated by employees, many of whom have an axe to grind with their employers.[26]

DEFENSIVE STRATEGIES—DEMONSTRATING YOUR COLLATERAL VALUE

Having looked at each threat in detail, the question is how do we develop action plans to address these threats and to demonstrate our collateral value? There are a number of strategies. Some are more sophisticated than others, yet the common denominator, as with most effective management approaches, is common sense. The first step requires identifying whether there is a need for protecting proprietary information, processes, and so forth, at your company. There are very few organizations where this is not an appropriate course of action.

Whether you are a resident security manager or a third-party provider, finding ways to protect proprietary information can be fairly easy. For example, post orders, fixed assignments, and scheduled business unit meetings typically integrate physical checks on devices containing proprietary information. Other strategies would include seeking business unit managers out specifically to discuss their particular needs. By sending business managers material obtained from professional journals, business publications, reported research, and so forth, you can help predispose them to the idea of protection. Another awareness strategy is to sponsor a small in-house workshop or to call a meeting to share information that you gather from association meetings and conferences. Regardless of how the need is identified, the object is to define the current state-of-affairs and to develop a baseline for determining priorities and preparing both strategies and resources. Let's look at some of the specific strategies others have found to be successful.

Trade Secret First Aid

Attorney Robert Payne has introduced the concept of *trade secret first aid*, a model designed to assist managers in the development of a proactive strategy to combat the loss of confidential information. In an article for *Management Review* (1994) Payne provides the following anecdote:

> The distressed manager of a company with manufacturing trade secrets has just been given summary notice that a key employee is departing to join a competitor. She fears the departing employee will take sensitive information with him to compete unfairly against the company. She calls upon her legal counsel.
>
> "Was the employee required at the time of hiring to sign a confidentiality agreement?" asks counsel. "No," she answers. "Were any of these sensitive documents labeled 'confidential'?" counsel inquires. She sheepishly replies, "No. Everyone 'understood' that these materials were confidential."
>
> Having a good idea what to expect next, counsel asks to see the portion of the company policy manual dealing with maintaining confidentiality of information. No such luck. "Were there, at least, short memoranda circulated to employees reminding them of their duty to maintain the company's proprietary information as confidential?" Alas, she admits, "Even that 10-minute exercise was not undertaken."
>
> By now, the manager senses the lost opportunities she had to protect her company's valuable information and wonders if all is lost. Counsel reassures her that it is not. However, they now are dealing with a problem of trade secret "first aid." They are forced to focus on what immediate steps can be taken to prevent or mitigate disaster.

These three simple and quick remedies are critical rules of evidence that need to be presented to satisfy even the most sympathetic court; most organizations have yet to incorporate them into the company. Is your corporation one of them? I recently assessed the security program of a major insurance company. In gathering the data, I found that several executives not only had not developed confidentiality agreements for their employees, but also saw no reason to do so. They argued that the insurance industry is so regulated that very little would be classified.

When I asked if they felt that their customer list ought to be protected, one senior executive said with a wave of his hand, "Oh sure, maybe that." I pursued the line of questioning and asked if he thought his company's pricing strategies were confidential. "Yes, of course!" he blustered. "What about your employees' personnel records?" "Well, I guess so," he admitted. "And what of the two new products you will soon be introducing—wouldn't the competition find them interesting now?" He nodded and asked me to stop. The point had been made.[27]

Just how valuable is a customer list? Payne provides us with this insight: "Considerable effort and expense is invested in contacting potential customers and developing a business relationship with them. Cold calls to prospects rarely result in an immediate, successful contact. Continued efforts over time, including market research, often are needed to locate and develop rapport with the real decision maker. Time and money translates to the bottom line. A customer list is not simply a list of Fortune 500 companies."[28] A customer list often contains a number of pieces of valuable information:

- a vetted list of those with a demonstrated interest or need;
- the name of the main contact person, thus allowing a quick and targeted approach;
- the buying history of the customer, including product preferences, cost thresholds, and so forth;
- pricing information, which may affect one's bidding strategy; and
- information about one's suppliers and sources of materials.

Protecting information means all information, even when it concerns initiatives or projects that prove not to work or information about those potential customers who may not turn out to be good prospects.

After all, this information is just as valuable to your competitor as it is to you. Allowing competitors access to confidential material is costly because you give them the ability to bypass the expense associated with developing such materials themselves, thus lowering the overhead involved in competing against you. By dissecting your confidential information, your competitors can zero in on your best customers and redirect their limited resources to other, more fruitful areas.

If you lack a developed program, Payne suggests that you meet with each employee before his or her departure and think, "DRAW"—an acronym for the four main points you should cover in an exit interview to protect trade secrets:

> D—Remind the employee of his or her *duty* to preserve the confidentiality of sensitive information, even after termination of employment. Give specific examples of any critical information that the employee may have.

> R—Obtain the *return* of all company materials.

> A—Request that the employee sign an *agreement/acknowledgment* stating that he or she will honor the company's confidentiality. Even if the employee refuses, you have lost nothing by asking.

> W—Ask *where* the employee is going, *what* the employee will be doing there, and *what* steps the employee will take to avoid using the company's trade secrets in carrying out those tasks.[29]

Even though these suggestions are good, it must be remembered that they are only stopgap measures. They are exactly what Payne says they are—first-aid remedies, and not a cure. Your ability to add value to the corporation comes with the moves you make to introduce or update a formally articulated confidentiality program.

Identifying Potentials for Loss

Tackling the issue of protecting confidential and proprietary information head-on is a true test of your collateral worth. Losses for American businesses escalate each year, yet business executives, for the most part, continue to be blind or ignorant to the true impact of such losses on their company's performance, largely because trying to affix a dollar value is difficult. Studies tend to report findings in aggregate form. Although the numbers as reported are staggering, it is difficult to extrapolate potential exposures and real losses on a company-by-company basis. The result is that it is difficult for executives to identify the real loss.

To be effective decision makers, people need to have information presented to them that they can relate to. As a security specialist, it is your job to describe threats in terms that business managers can understand. For example, telling the company president of a high-tech company that theft of proprietary product costs American business billions of dollars each year is too general. It's an impressive statistic, but most people cannot relate to how it affects them. On the other hand, telling the president that on a specific date his or her competitor suffered a specific loss by a disgruntled employee and that a similar threat exists in the president's company would elicit a much stronger response. Why? Because the executive can readily see the bridge between the two companies.

Just as I discussed in *Business Management Strategies*, the concept of "talking the CEO's language" holds true here. Whether you use a story to illustrate a point or simply rely on talking the business language of the company, the communication between you, the security professional, and the nonsecurity executive must be on the nonsecurity person's level. Remember, bankers relate to balance sheets, retailers to sales, and manufacturers to capacity. To be successful and demonstrate added value, you need to demonstrate that you understand both the business of asset protection and the business they purport to serve. Of the two, the real success rests in an ability to communicate in the language of your senior executives.

Convincing Management to Keep a Secret

Arion Pattakos points out that the CEO, other corporate senior management, and line supervisors must set a positive example regarding the protection of the company's proprietary information if the security program is to meet its objective. As we discussed before, employee ownership and assumption of responsibility for certain aspects of security drives any security program, but especially those aspects of the program associated with proprietary property, because it is oftentimes less than tangible. Pattakos observes, "Security directors responsible for protecting proprietary information can lay the foundations for success by understanding and assisting operating managers in making risk decisions, helping to identify types of corporate proprietary information that are in need of protection, and ensuring that employees take the information program seriously."[30]

To lay the groundwork first you need to develop an awareness of the need for a propriety information protection plan. Corporate executives and department managers should be briefed on the nature of the exposure

and the degree to which such losses can affect the bottom line and, consequently, the financial well-being of every employee. Typically, executives
and their key staff are not conditioned to appreciate the real value of the
company's proprietary information or the security needed to protect it.
Part of the reason is that there is a general lack of attention paid to the
topic by trade journals, business magazines, and the public media. This
lack of attention can be traced back to even the halls of academe. Few
business management schools have incorporated asset protection into
their curriculum as a course of study. Moreover, some risk managers simply view loss and exposure as a cost of doing business. Senior management's lack of security awareness may stem in part from the absence of
security information targeted to the general business audience. Pattakos
supports this idea, reporting that he conducted a survey of business management textbooks and found that most books ignore the topic or fail to
discuss the problem in depth or to point to solutions.[31] When policy makers see the value of information protection they are more likely to approve
and implement necessary security measures.

Pattakos suggests that to achieve these goals there is a critical need
for forming an Intellectual Property Protection Committee (IPPC), which
will provide a forum for senior management's involvement in the planning
process. By chairing this committee you are seen in a higher position,
especially if other senior managers are selected as part of the group. Pattakos disagrees, however, suggesting instead to have a corporate operational
officer with decision-making authority chair the committee. While the
advantages and disadvantages for both sides could be debated, the underlying advice remains the same; namely, developing an IPPC is another
asset protection management tool, and it requires security's active and
acknowledged involvement.

Where Pattakos and I agree is in the composition of the group. The
committee should consist of a core group of senior personnel from the
legal department, public affairs, management information systems, human
resources, and at least one line manager. Others can be added on an ad
hoc basis as issues and concerns are identified; they might include staff
from operations, distribution, facilities management, marketing, procurement, or finance. In short, the IPPC needs to be big enough to do an
effective job, but not so large that it becomes unwieldy.

The purpose of the IPPC is to serve as an overseer to develop policies, to shape corporate positions, to review programs promoting incentives and disincentives, and to chart new directions consistent with the
company's business plan. Equally important, the committee should establish both the criteria and the process for determining the value of corporate information, including its market value and the financial impact on

the company should proprietary information come into the possession of competitors. To stay focused the group should avoid being pulled into the details of the program, such as personnel assignments, managing training programs, and developing implementation criteria. Instead these activities should be handled by the security department or by a subcommittee of the IPPC.

Before leaving the topic, I would like to draw your attention to a final insight offered by Pattakos:

> The security manager is the information security plan custodian—not its owner. The plan truly belongs to the CEO and each department, in as much as the employees have contributed to the molding of the plan. A deeper contribution assures a deeper 'buy in' of the new policy by those employees. When proprietary information protection policies are reasonable and all company employees are made a part of the process, procedures are more likely to be followed, and the security department has a better chance of foiling information pirates.[32]

Creating a Cost-Benefit Ratio

Managing the unknown always leads to overspending and overallocating. We saw this in the 1980s and early 1990s. Corporate executives, operating from a base of fear concerning their own protection or that of their employees, tended to react by building elaborate security systems. Security managers were equally guilty—if not more so. Operating from the great what-if perspective, security decision makers detailed for their senior staffs plans built exclusively on worst-case scenarios. Not wanting to appear cold and callous, especially against the backdrop of downsizing, corporate executives invariably allowed security budgets to become bloated. As the pressure for achieving economic rationality pushed its way into the business plan, senior executives began to take different perspectives toward security spending, much to the chagrin of security directors. The latter saw not only their programs being cut (some cynically characterized the process as a butchering), but also their basic assumptions being challenged.

Quite frankly, much of what these security directors experienced was well deserved. Lacking empirical data or knowledge of security, executives are justified in asking what the cost-benefit ratio is of employing one security plan over another. They need to understand the business rationale behind the allocation of resources. Security of people and assets, while critically important, needs to be measured in the same way that any other requests for expenditures are measured.

Offering a general guide, Rich Owen, manager of data security for Dell Computer, offers the following set of questions to serve as the basis for crafting a proprietary information risk assessment for management:

- How much did the information cost your company?
- How much will it cost to replace the information?
- How much financial benefit will your competition gain if they have access to this information?
- How much hardship would be caused if this information were not readily available to your customer?
- How would the information benefit a third party?

Using risk-based information is a good way to establish threat thresholds that can guide your proposals for resource allocations. It establishes a systematic, reasoned basis for doing some things while opting not to do others. Having these issues documented is particularly helpful in the event of litigation. The courts rarely mandate that one allocation versus another must be applied. Rather, they seek to determine if there was reason applied to the decisions that were made, and, if so, was the reasoning sound. Thus the same management processing that is associated with physical security can also be applied to proprietary information.

Your collateral worth can be significantly enhanced if you can become an active participant in determining such risks. But how do you do it? One way to begin is by offering to calculate the costs you are most familiar with, for example, the expense associated with establishing physical protections, including electronic and manual access control, surveillance devices, barriers, and so forth. Both the courts and underwriters will look first to what physical protections are in place at your company to mitigate the likelihood of a breach of security.

Second, you'll need to figure the costs involved in developing both an awareness of security and an ownership in the security process on the part of employees. This can range from time spent on staff meetings to the costs involved in developing media, electronic and hardcopy. Many firms have produced videotape presentations and integrated them into their employee orientation process. Others have created employee incentive programs for contributing "best ideas" and taking responsibility for challenging strangers in work areas or reporting suspected activities to security.

Third, in keeping with your new vision of asset protection, you should consider having the risk assessors actually develop an in-house formula for calculating the value of the targeted information. John McCumber, writing for *Security Technology and Design,* suggests that such a formula requires a multiple factor analysis consisting of replacement cost (the number of hours required to cover the loss × the cost per hour for the individuals involved), associated opportunity costs (total expenses and revenues lost as a direct result of the loss), and redirected resource allocation costs (the time and resources required of your organization that could have otherwise been spent satisfying existing business requirements).[33]

I would like to offer that these costs need to be reflected in terms of full employee cost. Simply applying staff wage rates (the hourly pay rate) is not enough. Most employees carry an additional 19 percent to 23 percent for associated taxes and benefits. Also there is the cost of overtime, procurement, training, and in some cases even the overhead involved in constructing a parallel facility to minimize the impact on daily activities. There is also the cost associated with lost credibility, lost shareholder confidence, and the time and resources spent on any investigations.

Focusing on the Basics

Demonstrating your added value in protecting confidential and proprietary information is not limited to exotic approaches, and it does not require years of technical expertise. More often your work can begin and end with a concentration on the basics. Because today's world of cyberspace contains the demand for data wizardry, it is easy to get caught up in high-tech approaches or become totally intimidated. For any organization, regardless of size and sophistication, there is always the paramount need to assure that you are covering the basics. But in addressing proprietary information protection you may find that the costs can be much lower than you originally anticipated, and, indeed, the part you play is supplying the basics at a reasonable cost can bring you collateral value.

By returning to the basics I mean the following:

♦ Develop a classification, storage, and retrieval system for confidential information.
♦ Develop and publish the policies associated with employee responsibilities for protection and dissemination of classified information, especially via E-mail and voice mail.
♦ Develop and conduct awareness programs.
♦ Develop personal ownership (responsibility) programs, including both incentives and disincentives.
♦ Help create confidential agreements and implement their use by employees, contractors, and visitors.
♦ Develop procedures governing escorts, access to restricted areas, reproduction of documents, and after-hours security.

♦ Develop and help install and maintain data security software, including anti-virus programs and the use of commercially available firewalls, especially if there is widespread use of the Internet at your company.

♦ Procure and install security devices and barriers.

♦ Deploy minimum security personnel, if appropriate.

♦ Conduct routine, but unscheduled, audits of logs and other audit trails using a system designed to minimize operational impact.

♦ Employ data encryption, especially when data is being transported on LANs, WANs, or to remote or other stand-alone locations.

♦ Protect fax transmissions along the entire network, particularly transmissions between countries.

Managing the Panic

When a loss does occur, especially if it involves particularly sensitive material or if it is the latest in a troubling series of losses, it is easy for senior management to overreact. They want to know how this could have happened to them, why it wasn't anticipated, and who is doing what not only to recover the loss, but also to assure that it won't happen again. Sound familiar? Just as commonly, the source of the loss(es) can be traced back to indifference or the assumption "It won't happen to us," on the part of the same executives. Yet when all of the finger-pointing is over with, what has really been gained? If you have secured new appreciation and support for going forward, then something positive has emerged from the total experience, although the positive outcome may not lessen the sting of the loss.

Panic and outrage may be the natural reaction for executives faced with the likelihood that employees are stealing company secrets. They want to strike out, and in doing so they may propose strategies that, unknown to them, are illegal. The result is that overzealous managers can wind up causing the company more damage than the leakers themselves. "Bosses get paranoid—they want to do everything, illegal or not" to stop a security breach, says Herbert Clough, executive vice president at Paul Chamberlain International, a security and investigating concern. "I tell them, you're a litigation looking for a place to happen."[34]

Executives' confusion over what is allowable and what is not is easy to understand. For example, today eavesdropping equipment is inexpensive and commercially available. Radio Shack is often considered the barometer for what is new and affordable in the world of spy versus spy. Many catalog companies and specialty stores have similar offerings. But just because it may be legal to sell certain items, doesn't mean that it's okay to use them indiscriminately. The courts continue to battle over the issue of privacy, especially when it involves voice mail and E-mail systems.

Few security experts and attorneys would argue with purely defensive measures, such as "sweeping" an installation for suspected bugs. But this doesn't mean that a company has a right to bug its own employees without meeting certain legal standards—and even if the company does meet these standards, it still runs the risk of a likely civil lawsuit. Ironically, as we saw above in our discussion of loose lips, and as Richard Heffernan, an information security specialist observes, "Probably 50 percent to 75 percent of the information being lost got out through inadvertent disclosure."[35] In such cases retribution may be totally inappropriate; education is the truer course of action.

At other times the loss can be the result of a system failure or inadequacy. A major semiconductor company was convinced that an outsider was tapping into its E-mail system. The reason: a message from an outside executive recruiter had found its way into the system. The company's attack plan was to confront the recruiter's boss with the evidence, fire the person in charge of the company's E-mail, and contact a prosecutor about initiating a criminal investigation. Upon investigation it was shown that somebody inside the company had simply picked up the recruiter's message from a public electronic bulletin board and rebroadcast it through the system. More often than not, there's a tremendous amount of emotion when there is evidence of a leak. Hence when suspected threats emerge, relying on the adage, Allow cooler heads to prevail, is vital. This is where your experience as a security specialist can bring immeasurable added value.

Without a systematic or reasoned approach, actual intrusions or losses can turn into public relations disasters. In the early 1990s the Alaska oil company consortium Alyeska Pipeline tried to contain the damage when it was revealed that the company had hired one of the largest security providers and instigative firms to conduct a surveillance operation into the activities of Charles B. Hamel, a prominent oil industry critic. Hamel had been helping a congressional panel investigate the environmental impact of the oil industry in Alaska. Somehow a number of the consortium's internal documents had wound up in Hamel's hands. Among other things, according to affidavits and statements taken from former employees of the security firm, operatives had rifled through Hamel's garbage and electronically monitored his home and business. Even though no laws were violated, the oil industry was severally criticized when the press reported on the activities of the consortium's security provider.

Similar horror stories have occurred with Procter and Gamble and ITT Sheraton. P&G's chairman conceded in a letter to employees that the consumer products company had "made an error in judgment" in encouraging Cincinnati law authorities to search local phone records to help identify who had leaked news to a reporter for a newspaper. Despite a search of 803,000 records, ordered by a local court under a state law prohibiting employees from divulging trade secrets, the alleged leaker wasn't caught. Although P&G's board concluded that the company had "acted in good faith and responsibly," the episode "ended up reflecting quite badly on what is otherwise a socially conscious" organization, according to Robert D. McCrie, an assistant professor for security management at John Jay College of Criminal Justice in New York.[36]

Cooperating with law enforcement officials and obtaining the proper court order, Sheraton Hotels allowed a hidden camera to be mounted in an employee locker room. Even though this action led to a legitimate arrest, the hotel was blistered in the national press, and public confidence in the company was shaken. Does this mean that companies today are handcuffed by public perception from taking legitimate action? There is some degree of truth in this. For the most part, however, it is best to review all of the alternatives before pursuing a traditional approach. Again, based on your experience and access to the professional security network, such situations create an opportunity for you to be involved in areas beyond classic security.

SUPPLEMENTAL VALUE CONTRIBUTIONS

Value added contributions are dynamic. Not all organizations are structured or have business plans that limit a person solely to their core competency. Many security executives have accomplished significant contributions by stepping outside the conventional lines of asset protection and seeking totally unrelated opportunities. I refer to this as *supplemental value* as opposed to *collateral value*. Both are valid efforts, but there is a strong caution associated with supplemental value contributions: *Success outside a core competency is more a reflection of individual ability.* Skill set transference is not easy. Depending on the nature of the work that is being requested, other support functions can require a certain level of experience, technical knowledge, corporate credibility, and so forth. Therefore jumping out of your area of expertise requires careful consideration and planning. Despite the temptation of wanting to be seen as the next corporate hero, supplemental value is not for everyone.

Given the option of pursuing supplemental value, exploring a few examples is worthwhile. In briefly reviewing the following case examples, it is hoped that readers will see that contributions can take many forms.

Corporate Secretary

For more than a decade, John Cosenza has been the corporate security director for Citicorp, the parent of CitiBank. In addition he has also served as the corporation's assistant secretary to the board of directors. In this dual capacity, he has responsibility for the global security program and also assists in the development of matters under consideration by the directors of the company. Cosenza demonstrates value through his ability to understand the big picture and assist in the development of both financial and regulatory reporting requirements. By serving in this dual capacity, Cosenza is uniquely positioned to represent the security interests of the bank at literally its highest level. Moreover, he is familiar with the hot buttons for the most senior managers within Citicorp.

Few other security directors enjoy such an interesting combination of job responsibilities. He is in the singular organizational place to truly have firsthand knowledge of the most pressing business developments and plans under consideration by executive management at Citicorp. His position also allows him to sit on the committees for several national associations and government councils. This, in turn, brings enhanced value to his own organization, since he thereby has additional insight into asset protection issues that have implications for his company.

I first met Cosenza in the mid-1980s when he was serving as chairman of the Executive Committee for the American Banker's Association's Security and Risk Management Division. In this capacity, Cosenza was able to provide the other council members with direction and guidance on a host of emerging security-related topics; most noteworthy was the topic of ATM security in such diversified applications as convenience stores, residential complexes, industrial parks, and campus settings. Thanks to Citicorp's vast interstate banking network and its presence in nearly one hundred countries, coupled with Cosenza's insights obtained from his role as a corporate secretary, our committee was able to set both policies and directions for the security banking community.

Facilities Management

For many security directors taking on additional management responsibility, their duties typically extend into one or more traditional facilities management functions. For example, John Heavey, the corporate security director for John Hancock Insurance Company, has a number of functions related to facilities management, including tenant leasing, mail services, and shipping and receiving. Other security managers have responsibility for library services, food services, and custodial services. All in all, these responsibilities have a synergistic alignment with corporate security insofar as each function is a part of the infrastructure supporting both the corporate complex and field locations. Today, as reported by *Security Magazine* in 1994, more than 67 percent of all security-related decisions are directly or significantly influenced by facility managers. These security directors, who typically report to the head of corporate real estate services, find that their general management skills are tested firsthand.

Other Supplemental Opportunities

Since no two organizations are the same, there is no formula that best determines to whom the security program should report. This can be a frustrating situation for some, but overall it underscores the versatility of asset protection. I am frequently asked what is the most ideal reporting relationship. The simple truth is that there is no one "best" reporting relationship. Depending on the corporate culture, the degree of advocacy for security, and a host of other business considerations, security managers are found reporting to the finance department, legal counsel's office, human resources, administrative services, the office of the president, and so forth.

Security's reporting relationship can be to the advantage of the security executive because it exposes the manager to a multitude of potential new opportunities. Just as we saw with Cosenza and Heavey above, if the personal capability is there, there is the opportunity to expand one's management contribution. Before moving on, though, we must emphasize personal capability. We are all too familiar with the Peter Principle of Competency of operating at a level beyond one's competency. The corporate management road is literally strewn with the discarded bodies of would-be contributory heros.

SUMMARY

The thrust of this chapter has been continuing our discussion of how to demonstrate added value. Having set the stage for the need to posture yourself as a contributory manager, we offered suggestions on how to expand into new opportunities. In doing so we introduced several concepts.

The concept that served as the central theme of this chapter was what I refer to as *collateral value*—the value that can be found in synergistic opportunities. Here we saw the experience of Doug Griffin at Bank of America as he took the role of financial investigations and leveraged it within the internal audit arena. For most of this chapter, however, we looked at the interrelationship between classical security and protecting proprietary, or confidential information. Many organizational experts have begun to define this aspect of security under the umbrella of *intellectual property*—information that allows your company to maintain its market position and contributes directly to bottom-line profitability.

As our discussion of proprietary protection unfolded, we examined the challenges of integrating proprietary protection within traditional asset protection. Guiding our discussion was the concept of dividing intellectual property information into three categories: data security, marketplace property, and confidential information. Having defined proprietary information protection, we examined many of the associated potential threats. These ranged from the most common occurrence, employee complacency or lack of sensitivity to protecting critical information at trade shows, dealing with the press, and countering planned invasions and internal threats from opportunistic or disenfranchised employees.

Recognizing that most sensitive data is lost through employees, we then turned our attention briefly to the four types of employee alienation that challenge managers. As a part of this analysis we visited the research undertaken by both the U.S. Department of Defense and the American Institute for Business Research. Here we found that there are six primary motivations for people stealing proprietary information. Chief among them is financial reward. But this motive is usually directly tied to feelings of disgruntlement, revenge, thrill-seeking, and other psychological reasons.

On the basis of our analysis we developed and reviewed a number of defensive strategies. This is where your collateral value begins to emerge. We examined what the experts had to say regarding protecting trade secrets, engaging the support of senior management, including the development of an overseer committee, and assessing the real level of threat through a cost-benefit approach. Before moving on, we reminded ourselves of the importance of not losing sight of the need to stay focused on the basics. To assist, we identified twelve basic tasks, most of them extracted from the daily responsibilities of classic corporate security. Finally, we explored the concept of *supplemental value*—looking for what is outside of the normal context of classical security. Examples were drawn from corporate security and facilities management. From here we turn our attention to another collateral value, one that is often overlooked even by nonsecurity executives.

7

Competitive Intelligence— The Overlooked Collateral Value

I believe that security declines as security machinery expands.

...E.B. WHITE

As one noted expert in competitive intelligence has observed: "Less than 10 percent of American corporations are sophisticated and competent about gathering information about their competitors. The other 90 percent are downright amateurs."[1] Yet ethically and legally obtaining information about competitors could be one of the most important business strategies your company pursues. Since its inception less than ten years ago, the Society for Competitive Intelligence Protection (SCIP) has seen its membership swell into the thousands as companies across the world are beginning to understand the importance of this activity—from both sides.

On the one hand, protecting information valued by your competitors is critical to maintaining your own market position and profitability. Conversely, discovering what your competitors are up to can be just as advantageous. As previously mentioned, NutraSweet estimates that competitive intelligence provides them a $50 million advantage annually. Other corporate giants share the same respect for this activity.

Leonard Fuld, recognized internationally for his expertise in this area, points out that in industries where a few companies control a large market share, the large firms will know a lot about competitors, and vice versa.

The giants in the telecommunications industry—AT&T, the baby Bells, along with MCI and Sprint—have developed an extensive network and infrastructure to obtain information on each other. Similarly, within the automotive industry the three leading U.S. manufacturers—GM, Ford, and Chrysler—are likely to know as much about their competitor's business as they know about their own. The same can be said for what these automakers know about their major competition from foreign manufacturers such as Toyota, Volvo, and Volkswagen.

Most security professionals are unaware of the value that competitive intelligence (CI) can bring to a corporation's profitability. Many are unaware of the concept, while others believe that it requires skills beyond their expertise. Yet given the investigative nature of gathering intelligence on your company's competitors, there is a significant opportunity for security decision makers to take an active role in this organizational activity, hence to demonstrate considerable collateral value without stepping outside the asset protection arena.

EXPLORING COMPETITIVE INTELLIGENCE

Myths About Competitive Intelligence

There are a number of myths and misunderstandings about competitive intelligence. One belief is that competitive intelligence gathering is illegal, unethical, or immoral. In truth, it is not only legal and ethical but also a smart business practice. Gathering intelligence on competitors can be fairly easy, and, if the intelligence is appropriately pursued, a company need never worry about being charged with engaging in illegal behavior.

The SCIP has developed a code of ethics for its members to assure that their intelligence-gathering activities remain above reproach. Many CI consultants such as Fuld have developed similar guidelines for their employees. Fuld refers to his as the "Ten Commandments of Legal and Ethical Intelligence Gathering."

1. Thou shalt not lie when representing thyself.
2. Thou shalt observe thy company's legal guidelines as set forth by the Legal Department.
3. Thou shalt not tape-record a conversation.

4. Thou shalt not bribe.
5. Thou shalt not plant eavesdropping devices.
6. Thou shalt not deliberately mislead anyone in an interview.
7. Thou shalt neither obtain from nor give to thy competitor any price information.
8. Thou shalt not swap misinformation.
9. Thou shalt not steal a trade secret (or steal employees away in hopes of learning a trade secret).
10. Thou shalt not knowingly press someone for information if it may jeopardize that person's job or reputation.[2]

COMPETITIVE INTELLIGENCE DEFINED

CI, as competitive intelligence is commonly referred to, is the process of collecting data from a wide variety of sources and analyzing it in such a way as to better understand what your competitor is planning, doing, or has completed in their pursuit of a greater share of the available marketplace. As such, gatherers of intelligence are not interested in a competitor's trade secrets; rather, they are more interested in a competitor's marketing, pricing, and so forth since these are the factors that more accurately define the company's direction and position.

Fuld, in his book *The New Competitor Intelligence: The Complete Resource for Finding, Analyzing, and Using Information About Your Competitors*, suggests that it is easier to describe what competitive intelligence is not, than what it is. As he points out, it is not reams of database printouts; it is "analyzed information." By this he means that competitive intelligence gathering is the art of taking information, irrespective of its form, and analyzing it in such a way as to provide targeted information to assist decision makers in developing strategies to maintain their competitive position in the marketplace.[3]

Competitive intelligence is not "business babble" for the 1990s; it is a long-standing activity familiar to business tycoons such as J. T. Morgan, Nathan Rothschild, John D. Rockefeller, and Bill Gates. While these business mavericks may not have referred to their activity as competitive intelligence, their intelligence-gathering skills were adroit enough to allow them to turn the information they gathered into a powerful weapon that gave them a competitive advantage.

Obtaining information for analysis can be done very efficiently and accurately through totally honest and ethical methods. Unlike the romantic pictures of agents like 007 meeting on a fog-shrouded bench in an isolated section of a park or passing notes in a crowded subway, critical information that can give one company a decided advantage over another can generally be found in the public domain. Experts in intelligence gathering suggest that only 5 percent of all the information you need on a competitor is grounded in trade secrets. Often such secrets are the least important information you could use to gain a competitive advantage over the other company. Far more important are tactical and strategic information such as that concerning new products and targeted geographic locations. For example, it would be far more helpful for one manufacturer to know what the other is planning by way of new distribution points, delivery systems and targeted markets. As security director you need to allocate investigative resources to assist in gathering this type of information as opposed to fully dedicating security resources to internal fraud or background reviews.

Why Your Company Needs Competitive Intelligence

The Futures Group, a management consulting firm, surveyed 103 large and midsized U.S. corporations. Only 75 percent of the respondents with more than $1 billion in revenues said they had a formal, organized approach to feed critical information to decision makers. Half the companies that didn't believe the competition was spying on them didn't want intelligence information of any kind. Consequently, obtaining information on these companies is often even easier than it should be.

Does such naïveté put American businesses at risk? Professor Benjamin Gilad, a leading CI expert and associate professor of management at Rutgers University, believes it does. The author of *Business Blindspots* and coauthor of *The Business Intelligence System*, he offers that up until very recently, America has not been in a war for its own survival. Japan, Israel, and France have, and these countries have sophisticated intelligence networks. Consequently, their companies have an intelligence-gathering mind-set more acute than that of their U.S. counterparts. Gilad says, "The Japanese concept is that competitive intelligence is a competency, related to the role of top managers. It is active, not passive, a way of reaching global dominance." As global competition becomes the new theater for business survival, opportunities for developing a comprehensive, but nonbureaucratic, capacity are available to most security directors. Gary Costley of Kellogg Company believes that failure to practice ethical CI is foolish. It may also be corporate suicide.

Underscoring the value of CI, even when it is not necessarily understood to be such, Barbara Ettorre relates the following anecdote involving Gary Costley:

> One morning years ago, as Gary Costley was about to pull into the parking lot of the Kellogg cereal plant where he worked, he glanced to his left. He saw unusual activity at the General Foods' Post cereal plant across the street.
>
> A twin-screw extruding machine was being hoisted by a crane onto the loading dock. A German apparatus, not the usual French-made model.
>
> "I thought, 'Have those guys given up on French machines?' " Costley now recalls. "We were having problems with the French extruders. Maybe we really couldn't make them work, and those guys knew something we didn't."
>
> Costley ran to a nearby store, bought a camera and film and stood across the street snapping pictures. A Post employee came over to him and learned he was from the competition: "Hey, you can't do that."
>
> "I answered, 'I'm standing on a public street taking photos. You shouldn't unload your machines in plain sight,'" Costley says. The information he gathered helped convince Kellogg to switch to the better-made German machines.
>
> Costley cites this as an early example that helped him realize the importance of competitive intelligence. Later, as president of the $4 billion North American division of the Kellogg Co., he became a champion of competitive intelligence and initiated a sophisticated system in his company.[4]

The aim of good business intelligence is to contribute to strategic planning. Simply gathering information for the sake of gathering it, or gathering it but not utilizing it properly misses the true value of CI. When CI is integrated into the mainstream of business planning, your company can achieve more effective allocation of resources. Having security managers enmeshed in the process can catapult them from merely surviving to actually thriving in these unsettled times.

Consider what can happen when the competitive intelligence process is working smoothly. In an article aptly entitled "Running Around in Circles," Oren Harari, professor at the University of San Francisco and a member of the Tom Peters Consulting Group, offers this advice: Companies should give primary attention to whatever it takes "to lead the race" and not get sidetracked by intelligence efforts to spot the next change.

Often, even the most steadfast vigilance is not enough. Covering all the bases is virtually impossible, as we can see in the following examples gleaned from an article on corporate spying:

♦ U.S. tire makers, all bias-ply producers with a sharp eye on one another, failed to anticipate Michelin's next move when it took the market by storm with its radials.

♦ The baby Bells, busy tracking other local phone providers, were bowled over by the AT&T/McCaw Cellular merger, which meant that more and more cellular phone users could bypass baby Bell lines and their allocation fees, which had totalled a cool $14 billion.

♦ AT&T intelligence gatherers had no reason to suspect Williams Co., an oil transport company, until Williams announced its intention to use its pipelines to convey fiber-optic cables, a step that would make the company a major contender in the phone wars.

♦ Coca-Cola and Pepsi, neck in neck for so long, could not have predicted that companies like Snapple that traditionally had just a sliver of the market would grab center stage as health-conscious Americans shifted their preferences in soft drinks away from carbonated, highly sweetened beverages.

♦ Motorola was worried about the possible entry of the Japanese into the lucrative European VCR and television market in which Motorola was thriving. Motorola Europe said Japan was not looking at Europe. The corporation's intelligence unit didn't agree. It sent a Japanese-speaking analyst to Japan to research the capital budgets of Japanese companies, and in turn unearthed information that the Japanese planned to enter the semiconductor market in Europe. Motorola Europe immediately started semiconductor joint ventures and strategic alliances and, according to various accounts, either retained or increased its share in Europe after the Japanese entered that market.

♦ Coors had introduced a wine cooler that failed. It still wanted to penetrate this market, so it assembled a team to study the successful wine coolers of its competitor, Gallo. The team determined the ingredients, priced them, and decided that Gallo (with its own vineyards and label producers) was the low-cost producer. Coors decided not to pursue that market.

♦ Both McDonnell-Douglas and Boeing had indicated that they were considering introducing aircraft powered by a rear propeller fan. McDonnell-Douglas put together an intelligence team that examined Boeing's public documents (annual reports, R&D data, factory capacity) and concluded that Boeing could not make this aircraft at a competitive price or within a reasonable time frame. McDonnell-Douglas proceeded with its plans. Boeing announced it would postpone its development.[5]

Gathering Intelligence

To demonstrate how easy it is to gain information, here is a small sampling of where and how information can be obtained:

Attend a Trade Show

Target the key shows. Don't forget to look at the smaller regional shows because they may hold some of the best information.

Hold a pre-show meeting. The team leader needs to assign specific objectives to each team member. Circulate a checklist of what to look for, including a map of the show floor with key competitors marked.

Debrief during the show. Constantly test your questions and hunches against trade show reality by bringing your team back to a specific booth or hotel room near the show floor where everyone can compare notes.

Go to off-the-floor networking meetings. You might even bump into a rival CEO or VP for marketing and be able to pick up clues to their future plans.

Hold a post-show analysis and meeting. It isn't always necessary to write lengthy reports. Face-to-face meetings can convey the major conclusions from a show.

Conduct a Telephone Interview

Say you were referred. Referrals are door openers.

Ask for a specific person. By knowing the names and titles of knowledgeable sources, you avoid wasting time.

Don't act as though you know everything and don't act tough. Most people love to talk about their areas of expertise and will respond nicely to a disarming interviewer.

There are no dumb questions. Play it smart by saying you have a lot to learn. By stating how little you know about the subject and how you desperately want to learn all you can, you will probably receive more information from the respondent.

Use statistics to bracket data. Give a specific range of numbers for your respondent to work with.

Here is some advice from Leonard Fuld on how to read your competitor's mind:

You don't need a Ph.D. in psychology to predict a company's behavior, but you do need to go beyond the balance sheet to understand that company's management. The following checklist gives you the ability to analyze a competitor's decision makers and predict their next moves.

Style.

♦ Does the manager require consensus to make decisions?
♦ Does the individual tend to make snap decisions, or is he or she methodical, preferring to wait for more information?
♦ How far will the manager allow subordinates to go before stepping in and rendering a decision or countermanding his or her decisions?

Reputation.

♦ Does the person have a reputation for being a "number cruncher," or was he or she taught by those who prefer to examine the big picture?

Orientation.

♦ Does the manager always need to show a profit? Or is market share or some other gain the significant measure?
♦ Does the individual thrive on tension, or will a harsh competitive climate slow the decision maker down?
♦ Is he or she a tinkerer, always seeking to improve a particular product or service, thereby slowing down decisions?

Past Moves.

♦ What is the history of this manager's decisions? Has he or she repeated this pattern many times in the past?" [6]

Other perfectly legitimate, but unsuspecting public sources of information include

Help wanted advertisements. Through their hiring process, companies send a lot of intelligence signals out into the marketplace. To hire employees, a company must disclose a wide range of operating details about its business.

Airplane discussions. As noted earlier, airplanes offer a false sense of privacy. Just the simple act of trying to talk over the sound of a loud engine creates an opportunity for the right set of ears.

Vendor knowledge. Also we've discussed how some suppliers or strategic partners are not bound to confidentiality agreements and are free to serve many companies and talk about their experiences, including their experiences with your company. How simple it would be to invite the supplier of your competitor in to discuss an opportunity and ask if he or she has any similar experiences.

Marketing presentations. Marketing presentations offer timely and relevant source information on new product offerings, whether they occur at a trade show or one-on-one with potential customers.

Press releases. For the savvy intelligence gatherer, a press release oftentimes offers insights not easily obtained elsewhere.

Loose lips. Recalling our previous discussion regarding loose lips, stray talk is all too common, and therefore it is a well-known source for CI specialists. From line staff to CEOs, people like to talk about their businesses with friends, colleagues—even their competitors.

Procurement and leasing. The very process of ordering and buying office equipment or leasing space creates an opportunity for inadvertent or deliberate disclosure. The same holds true when outsourcing or subcontracting occurs, regardless of the degree and the department involved.

Compliance filings. Sometimes companies file too many disclosures, possibly because they believe it is required by governmental entities. Remember, with the Freedom of Information Act, once something is filed with the government, it is out of your control and often available to anyone, especially CI operatives.

These are but a few of the hundreds of examples. Libraries, directories, even nearby residents can be valuable and readily accessible sources.

THE SECURITY SPECIALIST
IN COMPETITIVE INTELLIGENCE

Barbara Ettorre points out the advantages to be gained by employing a security specialist for gathering competitive intelligence:

> CI is a search for clues and evidence that tell an enterprise what its competitors are contemplating or actually doing. CI can be simple—scanning a company's annual report and other public documents. Or, it can be more elaborate—hiring a security specialist to penetrate a competitor's defenses, for instance. The specialist might pose as an ordinary person and ask clever questions at a competitor's booth at a trade show or in the employee cafeteria or local hangout. The specialist might watch raw material shipments, track R&D agreements, or talk with ex-suppliers and ex-customers. He or she might "read" a competitor's new CEO or division president to divine what factors have influenced him or her in past decision-making—factors likely to surface again.[7]

Competitive Intelligence and the Security Investigator: Comparable Characteristics

Making the transition from operating a purely classical security program to participating in or leading the drive for a CI unit is a synergistic process. The characteristics of a CI analyst and a security investigator are remarkably similar. Leonard Fuld has pointed out the affinity between the two when he describes the characteristics of a good CI analyst.[8]

> *Tenacity.* The ability to persist even when there appear to be obstacles in the road to gathering information. Just as a persistent analyst will not give up when confronted with an apparent dead end, the dogged investigator will continue to pursue leads long after most others have written them off as dead ends or will characterize them as "chasing the wild goose egg."

> *Creativity.* The successful analyst spots things like rust on rails and other quirky information that may indeed be the smoke trail left behind by a competitor. A skilled investigator is also in tune with the subtleties of esoteric facts.

> *A good listener.* Listening is universally considered the most critical asset of a good CI analysts. The same can be said for investigators.

It's the astute sleuth who understands that through listening—real listening—facts are evident, even when attempts are made to obstruct the truth.

Persistence. Fuld offers us the image of a rock climber when describing a good CI analyst. Such a person doesn't let go before latching on to some sort of answer or on to another solid lead. In the same way, a security investigator can be described as dogged—as someone who simply will not give up on digging up an answer until the facts clearly indicate otherwise.

Strategist. The CI specialist understands well the value of creating a strategy, a game plan designed to lead to a defined end. Again, the same can be said for a successful investigator. Determining a strategy forces efficiency and minimizes time and resources lost to dead ends.

Experience. CI analysis requires developing networks and understanding the marketplace and its nuances. The same holds true for conducting investigations. The necessary skills and technical knowledge cannot come from college texts or self-taught courses. Developing technical knowledge requires spending time in the field. Once when instructing a group of bank fraud investigators, an attendee asked where the instructor received his MBA. He commented, "From the University of Hard Knocks."

Convincing Management to Adopt Competitive Intelligence

Competitive Intelligence experts almost universally agree that if the highest executive in the organization is not personally committed to CI, the process will fail. Participation must also be corporate-wide. For the process to work, according to Costley, the person in charge of CI needs to report to a fairly high corporate executive. In Costley's case this individual reported directly to him. Others, such as Fuld, would suggest that either the head of strategic planning or the head of business development could serve as the repository of CI information. Regardless of who is chosen, the message needs to be clear: CI activity is critical and deserves attention at the very top of the organization.

AT&T, as a leader in CI, has learned this lesson well, and they learned it some time ago. They have developed a formalized process wherein employees are continuously being tapped for information they may know about the competition. Why? Because they are constantly interacting with the competition. Whether it is an installer, a data processor, or a unit manager, all of these workers travel in the circles of the competition attending meetings, visiting the same customers, reading the same literature—even attending the same professionally sponsored social events. The result is that employees are nothing short of walking libraries—all within reach of AT&T's executives without even going outside the company.

Unfortunately, Fuld notes that some companies, in their haste and shortsightedness, have eliminated or severely curtailed CI activity as a cost-cutting move.[9] For me this seems both incomprehensible and downright stupid. Would a retail company eliminate its sales force? Would bankers cut out loan officers? Would manufacturers eliminate the production head? Why would they cut off the hand that feeds them critical strategic planning data, especially when the results can be directly measured in terms of bottom-line profitability?

The answer, it appears, is that these companies misunderstand the role of CI. Or maybe they have experienced a misapplication of resources and education on the part of CI specialists. Nonetheless, it is clear that security directors face a challenge in promoting CI. The ability to survive, let alone thrive, is in the eye of the beholder. This means that CI must continuously demonstrate its contribution in terms of value added—and this means that CI must do more than help save money.

Ettorre suggests that some organizations' hesitancy to accept CI may also be attributable to a factor comparable to what Costley's described. She suggests that roadblocks can be considerable if the CI function doesn't report to the right individual (for example, someone high enough up). If the CI officer is emersed in a conventional pyramidal organization and reports at or below the appropriate level, business unit heads can tell their staffs to ignore competitive intelligence gathering. The end result is an ineffective program that is probably better off being disbanded rather than continuing to fight a useless war.[10]

The good news, however, is that such outright rejections or failures to support the CI process altogether are diminishing. John Nolan, managing director of the Phoenix Consulting Group, provides us with one example of how to capture senior management's attention and secure their support. Writing for *Security Technology and Design*, he tells of a case involving Lynn Mattice, corporate security director at Whirlpool Corporation. Wanting to underscore the need for a comprehensive intellectual property protection program, which would include preventing losses from CI initiatives, Mattice began by educating himself to the issues and perspectives shared by his senior management. In other words, he set aside the desire to demonstrate how proficient he was in asset protection and began acting on the idea that to be successful he would have to think and talk like a business manager. (Those of you familiar with my previous book and lectures will know how important this step is in determining your ultimate success.)

Mattice's educational process lead to four direct outcomes:

1. a common vocabulary between Mattice and his executive staff,
2. an understanding of trends affecting his company and the effects of these trends on security,
3. the opportunity to be in front of the power curve and not behind it when such impacts were about to be felt, and
4. gaining the confidence and credibility of his senior staff, who would then act on what he had to say.

These lessons also framed his presentation. It wasn't the typical "sky is falling, Chicken Little syndrome." Rather it was thoughtful, fact driven, and reflected a business approach. That, in and of itself, got the executives' attention right away.[11]

Developing an effective CI unit takes time and is not cheap. Fay Brill, a founding member and president of SCIP as of this writing, was manager of competitive intelligence at NutraSweet for nine years. Currently she is CI manager for Miami-based Ryder System Inc. She notes that it takes about three years for a CI unit to begin operating efficiently, and she estimates that the start-up budget at NutraSweet was between $500,000 and $1 million. Let's think in terms of the cereal industry, a highly competitive industry in which name brands still dominate, while everyone else scrambles for the other 10 percent of the market. If the industry typically spends $2 billion to $2.5 billion annually in marketing alone, even a 1 percent improvement on return on marketing dollars spent means $25 million to a company.[12] So operating a competitive intelligence unit in this industry is worth the investment if it can yield such an improvement.

Identifying Bad Data

Another way for security to demonstrate added value, according to Leonard Fuld, is to question how information comes into your organization. As he notes, data may be based on faulty assumptions, third-hand information, unreliable or unknown sources, and so forth. The upshot is that there is a high probability that such information will generate poor decisions, which in turn can cost a company its market. As he observes: "Consider how much information we gobble up without double-checking its origin or validity. Once inside a company, bad data (and the resulting faulty analysis) can corrupt the decision-making process. They can go undetected by computer networks with even the strictest of security procedures. These systems assume that all the data that enter the system are 'good data,' and will trigger an alarm only if this information is in some way changed."[13]

To illustrate, he recalls that a pharmaceutical client of his needed to determine the exact date for a competitor's launch of an over-the-counter version of a prescription drug. Instead of relying on popular press accounts (the bad data), Wall Street research (more bad data), and its own internal resources (even more bad data), Fuld and his client relied on the competitor's import-export data showing movements of bulk chemicals, and on information on the competitor's plant activity. Fuld's client then concentrated its advertising and promotional expenditures in the weeks immediately surrounding the launch date and fought off a loss in market share.

Why is the press, Wall Street, and the company's own resources labeled bad data? As Fuld and other experienced investigators have learned:

1. The press is unreliable,
2. Wall Street researchers can oftentimes be biased, and
3. Internal resources are often self serving.

Together these sources are flawed because they can be inherently self serving. Good data needs to be factually based. Therefore, one needs to draw on such documentation as import-export movements.

Corruption generally begins at the data gathering stage and quietly works its way through a number of organizations until it reaches the top. Analysts, particularly those working for such business trade newspapers as the *Wall Street Journal* or the *Financial Times* are required to generate a column each day. The system of daily reporting is not conducive to researching facts thoroughly. As a result, errors of fact and analysis occur routinely. As one cynical pundit once observed, "The mere allowance for a corrections corner proves that we are human and subject to mistakes. It's part of being a member of the press corps."[14] Yet how many business decisions are made by corporate executives based on data gathered from the public media?

Fuld goes on to make the point that bad data can easily become part of the "establishment's data bank," and as a result those who access it assume it is true. Take, for example, his story of the telecommunications giant that announced two large software engineering contracts, both with Fortune 100 companies and both valued at tens of millions of dollars. Fuld discovered, after calling the awarding companies, that there were no such contracts—nor was it likely there would be. Since the companies did not demand a correction from the newspapers that covered the original announcement, the publications may never have discovered, let alone corrected, the error. The probable end result? A source that is perceived to be reliable is unwittingly compromised. Furthermore anyone subsequently accessing this story or others making business decisions based, in part, on this reporting would be using faulty data.

The next level in the information chain, online databases, is by far the most dangerous. Electronic databases, although a time-saving resource for the information seeker, can also act as catalysts, speeding up and magnifying bad data. Today there are almost nine billion records available online worldwide, with much of the information overlapping and much of it uncorroborated. Once an article appears in a respected business magazine or newspaper, it is likely to be absorbed by scores of databases. Any errors the article contains find their way into dozens of other references.

External data sourcing is only the beginning. Information generated from within an organization is commonly less than accurate. Memos, position papers, and confidential correspondence generally contain the writer's bias, because the writer is trying to make a point, wants something, is defending something, or is presenting a case for opposing someone else's move. Even data that is supposedly based on facts cannot be fully relied on because the data may be tainted by the perspective of the writer.

Even when the data is challenged and found to be flawed, it is not unusual to let the challenge stand without going back and correcting the original document(s). Not knowing the present-day circumstances, subsequent analysts will often look to these documents and make assumptions based on the belief that the original data is a true reflection of the points and/or proofs in existence at the time. But is all internally generated data flawed? Today the joke along executive row goes that many decision makers won't believe something is true until they hear it on CNN. Unfortunately, many times there is more truth in this joke than there is humor.

It's easy not to completely trust what someone from within the company has to say. Because of the bias factor, there is a tendency for the recipient not to trust the source. Fuld tells of how he tests audience bias:

> I once tested this notion with a group of marketers for a petro-chemical company. I handed each member of my audience a single sheet of paper containing three doctored quotations about their competition and asked each participant to rate each one based on its reliability. Unknown to the audience, I kept the quo-

tation on each sheet the same, but switched the attribution from an internal company source to an external trade publication source, or the other way around. In almost every instance where the quotation supposedly came from an internal source, the participant downgraded its reliability and would not act on the data. When the same quotation came from an outside speaker, the reliability factor shot up. I have since tested this notion with other companies and have found virtually the same results.[15]

How do you break this bias factor? Begin by developing practices that can consistently be proven over a course of time. This means that before committing anything to writing, the supporting data needs to be shown to be valid. The source must be known and proven to be consistently reliable. The data also needs to make sense to those in the know. This can be accomplished through a number of forums, but the most straightforward way is to call for a meeting between the mainstream business experts and their technical support team. When combined, their collective knowledge can serve as a powerful barometer for determining if the data is flawed or not.

Fuld offers a simple formula for rating data. Under a 1-2-3 rating code, 1 equals fact and requires the person to offer at least two sources for the information; a 2 requires at least one source and requires further verification; and 3 is given to rumors, with no source attached.[16] Such a rating system disciplines both the person who submits the information and the user. It also helps establish a paper trail that allows anyone to critique its validity. This type of rating system allows the CI investigator/analyst a method for assessing data. A scoring system allows the security department to catagorize one data source over another, thus enabling a truer and more accurate picture to emerge. Through such an approach, you can piece together meaningful information for executive management's consideration and enhance your collateral value.

SUMMARY

There are several excellent texts on how to set up a CI unit and how to both gather information and protect yours at the same time. Throughout this discussion I have relied heavily on the works of Leonard Fuld because I find that his book, *The New Competitor Intelligence,* is among the best of the best. He steps the reader through nearly five hundred pages of how-tos. Just a quick review and the reader quickly understands how to demonstrate added value well within the context of asset protection.

Because there are a number of such texts available, I have avoided creating a how-to discussion. It is to be hoped that our discussion has laid to rest some of the common myths associated with CI, because CI presents one way that a security executive can enhance collateral value. Given the direct economic value that competitive intelligence can bring to an organization, coupled with the synergy it has with traditional security, this is an area that security managers need to explore.

PART TWO SUMMARY

When we began our journey in pursuit of success-oriented management we concentrated on a number of techniques. The same themes were continued in Part II with a focus on the manager. We saw that today's decision maker no longer has a common security background. Even though there are a large number of former law enforcement and military personnel occupying the top security slot in many companies, this profile is changing. Even those with public sector experience are rapidly "coming up to speed" with regard to business management strategies. Borrowing from our discussion in Chapter 4, we are seeing the emergence of the *corporatization of the public servant.*

Today's security managers are just as likely to be employees of an external strategic partner as they are to be resident staff members. They are also just as likely not to have had a formal background in asset protection. The role of security management is changing as well. There is a decided move away from traditional operational management and toward internal consulting and collaboration.

In Chapter 5 we explored the challenges facing external providers as they struggle to establish themselves within the corporate hallways. We saw that there is a need for them to undergo their own paradigm shift, or else fall victim to the hopeless trap of the *commodity syndrome.* Whether one is an external partner or a resident manager, the ability to thrive requires the ability to assume new roles. In Chapters 6 and 7 we explored two such opportunities—participating in proprietary information protection and competitive intelligence gathering. These two potential areas for security professionals serve well to illustrate that value added opportunities can be found within the definitions of asset protection. This is good news because it means that the pursuit of added value does not require that security professionals give upon their core competency. Our journey ends with Part III, Chapter 8. In this last section we explore the positive results that emerge when there is a convergence between leadership and employee empowerment.

Part III
The Collaborative Approach

8

Pursuing Envisioned Leadership

It is one of the most beautiful compensations of this life that no man can sincerely try to help another without helping himself.

... RALPH WALDO EMERSON

Throughout our journey we have stopped along the path to examine a wide array of factors that directly affect the security manager's ability to succeed in today's dynamic times. We have visited with many of the recognized leaders, both past and current, in the world of quality management. We have read anecdotes and explored anecdotes and analogies that have helped to illustrate their points and contributions. We've seen how the pursuit of quality entails both conventional and entrepreneurial strategies. Along the way we have studied what it takes to create an effective quality assurance program and have examined how today's security managers can enhance their program's added value by assuming collateral responsibilities as well as building on their own technical expertise in the area of asset protection.

In this our last chapter, we shift emphasis and explore what happens when managers become *envisioned leaders* and enter into collaborative relationships with employees. By now you have read dozens of examples illustrating that success is more than just surviving. Success in today's uncertain times requires an ability to literally extract different capabilities from yourself and your employees. This, in turn, requires moving away from conventional approaches. As noted consultant Warren Bennis observes, "Today's success is contingent upon being able to move away from being an effective manager. Rather, employees need the guidance and direction provided by a leader." In writing for *Bottom Line*, Bennis points out that managers administer while leaders innovate. Managers also focus on systems and structure, whereas leaders focus on people. While managers rely on control, leaders inspire trust. And finally, while managers have their eye on the bottom line, leaders have their eye on the horizon.[1]

LEADERSHIP DEVELOPMENT AND THE ART OF DISTANCE RUNNING

Over the past twenty years I've enjoyed distance running. Like many people, circumstances have risen along the way that have prevented me from pursuing this sport on an ongoing basis. Injuries, excessive travel, client demand, and inclement weather have all contributed to my on-again, off-again running career. As a result of this stopping and going, stopping and going cycle, I've discovered that there are at least four phases to distance running.

The first is what I call the *grunt* phase. This is because when you first start off running, any distance is hard work. It's accompanied by shortness of breath, aching muscles, and a psychological game that we all play. Namely, you'll pick a distance as our goal (half a mile, a mile, and so forth) and focus your efforts on "just finishing the run." During this phase you don't particularly feel that great about the sport simply because it hurts. In an effort to encourage yourself toward your goal, you find yourself playing a variety of mind games. These include mentally counting to one thousand and back again, reciting the alphabet, listening to music or a radio talk show, or whatever else it takes to distract your mind from the pain that you are experiencing. After a while you find that the pain subsides, the breathing becomes easier, and that you're comfortably able to achieve your goal.

When this occurs, you enter the second phase, which I call *surroundings awareness*. As you run your course, you become aware of your surroundings. For example, as I run through neighborhoods, I discover the different types of landscaping that my neighbors have planted. Or I become aware of the types of automobiles that are parked in their driveways. For example, I recently ran through a section of a nearby neighborhood and discovered that more than 95 percent of the houses on a particular street are all two stories. I've lived in this area for more than fifteen years, but I was never aware of how many houses were more than one story high. In other words, since I'm no longer concentrating on the pain, I am able to expand my awareness and begin to observe things that I would not otherwise notice if I were driving by in my automobile.

The third phase comes when you begin to become very much aware of your physical inner processes. As some runners will tell you, they can actually begin to feel the blood running through their veins or, more commonly, get in tune with their breathing and heartbeat. During this phase, and assuming that one has charted a familiar and safe course, some runners actually experiment with running with their eyes closed for short periods of time. Pain is long gone, and the awareness turns physically inward.

The final phase is what I call *spiritual awareness*. Here running becomes trancelike while your mind explores concepts and issues. You begin to work things through mentally. Many of the ideas for this book have emerged or taken shape during my runs. This final phase is what I enjoy the most about running because it allows me an opportunity to engage in what I call "fun thinking." This is a process of taking an idea and trying to develop it to its full potential.

The art of running has a direct parallel to organizational leadership. Like running, the first phase of leadership development can be very physically taxing. You spend long hours getting to know the fundamentals associated with assigned duties and responsibilities. You're trying to get ahead of the learning curve, and that requires hands-on involvement, long meetings, and a good deal of research. It is that phase of work that some experts characterize as "technical proficiency building." Without it you cannot ultimately become a leader. During the grunt phase little actual leadership is displayed. Time simply will not allow it. You are too busy learning.

The second phase of leadership involves building an organizational awareness that incorporates coming to know end users and their expectations and needs. It also involves understanding the critical organizational players and their hot buttons. In essence, it's the phase in which you become familiar with your surroundings. The security executive becomes familiar with who occupies what position on the organizational pecking order. Turfs are identified, and both advocates and dissenters become known. Leadership begins to emerge, but more in the form of Bennis's definition of a manager.

The third phase can be likened to the runner's inner awareness because it involves coming to know departmental staff members and their capabilities. Each assigned staffer or external partner brings perceptions, biases, strengths, and limitations to the overall operation. During this phase you are still learning as employee characteristics are being defined. However, the learning begins to shift away from strictly inner processes to exploring new potentials for individual employees and the business unit in general. If you are willing to take calculated risks, some level of experimentation is appropriate at this time.

The final phase arrives as a result of the building blocks that you have assembled in the first three phases. Only when you know the technical aspects of your job and can couple that skill set with knowledge of the organization and staff support can you hope to become an envisioned leader. Or as Bennis would likely note, you can put an eye on the horizon because the bottom line has been addressed.

WHAT IS AN ENVISIONED LEADER?

Envisioned leadership involves knowing where you are and where you want to be. It's an ability to look beyond the affairs of today and ask the truly great what-if questions. It entails recognizing that leadership is all about the business of guiding and directing people to achieve their full potential in both their personal lives and in the workplace. The radical times we are experiencing at the close of this century require bold thinking guided by conventional wisdom. Just as it would be inappropriate to cast off traditional organizational values (the profit motive, maintaining market share, expanding products and services, and so forth), it would be just as inappropriate not to seek more effective ways of approaching business management. This means having both the vision and the fortitude to experiment and/or implement new relationships with employees and internal customers.

Envisioned leadership is akin to Peter Senge's notion of *conceptual leadership.* Conceptual leadership is about helping people make sense of what is going on around them. It's the ability to motivate people and make them feel confident about tackling difficult and challenging tasks. Through conceptual leadership you can instill in your employees a sense that they can actually accomplish things that heretofore they may have thought were impossible or out of their reach. Conceptual leaders have the ability to lay things out in clear and precise ways. They have the skill to elevate the quality of thinking and the quality of the discourse between themselves as managers and their staff.[2]

Pursuing the concept of leadership on the lighter side, two noted management consultants provide us with an interesting perspective with their cartoon metaphor of Wile E. Coyote and the Roadrunner.[3] Wile E. Coyote represents an approach that is anchored in traditional thinking, while the Roadrunner characterizes more of the entrepreneurial style. Six characteristics stand out in their metaphor. Let's briefly examine each and how it applies to our leadership model.

Coyotes Are Procedural; Roadrunners Are Experimental

Coyotes are methodical and risk adverse, whereas roadrunners, knowing the procedures, are willing to make exceptions and take risks when necessary. Wile E. Coyote consistently follows the Acme blueprint to the letter. And although Acme's "catch a bird" contraption is always put together properly, it is never effective. We the viewers, always amused at the coyote's hard work and effort, know that until he steps back and looks at the bigger picture he will never catch the roadrunner.

Envisioned leaders know that risk is associated with gain. We are not talking about foolhardy risk for the sake of thrill seeking, nor a desire to try something simply because it has not been tried before. Rather, we are talking about pushing the organizational envelope in pursuit of best practices. Envisioned leaders are not bound by defined limits. They ask the why-not questions and then venture forth, bringing those who dare to come along with them.

Coyotes Are Earnest; Roadrunners Are Passionate

Wile E. Coyote is an excellent example of the traditional professional manager. Conversely we see the passion of the roadrunner in his speed, freedom, agility, and joyful movement. The coyote doesn't believe in magic, so he cannot envision the outrageous possibilities conjured up by the roadrunner (he'll stop and paint a tunnel on the side of a mountain and then actually run through it).

Passion is vital for the envisioned leader. It is the "just do it" spirit and motto that has driven Nike Corporation to the top in its field. Passionate leaders really enjoy leading. Despite his critics, Ronald Reagan was a passionate leader as president of the United States. Even to the most casual observer it was obvious that he loved being president and leading America to a position of undisputed superiority.

Passion drove Bill Gates to lead Microsoft to a level never enjoyed before by any American company. The same passion is what drives turnaround specialists because they ardently believe that sick and failing organizations can be saved. I recall a number of years ago, the number two executive at Montgomery Ward, Ed Lewis, telling his turnaround team not to worry. When asked why, he simply answered: "A $6 billion company simply does not go away. So let's get healthy and get on with it." That's passion.

Coyotes Are Resilient; Roadrunners Are Resourceful

Coyotes display dogged determination. While this trait has its merits, if taken to an extreme it can do little more than to lead the coyote into a cycle of doing the same thing over and over again. Credibility is soon lost when results are not achieved. The roadrunner, on the other hand, balances a sense of experimentalism with a heavy dose of resourcefulness.

Envisioned leaders draw upon the collective intelligence of those around them. They convert the brain power existing in those around them into "brain trusts." Equally important, they allow employees to become involved in the process. To this extent such leaders become the conduits through which individual contributions flow to the organization, creating an energy that yields results and other opportunities.

Coyotes Are Smart; Roadrunners Are Wise

Wile E. Coyote is certainly not stupid. He uses his competencies and skills in a cunning manner. The problem is that his analytical and intellectual skills create a silo effect around his approach, thus limiting the potentialities associated with his latest contraption for catching the bird. The roadrunner relies heavily on his intuition as one of his decision-making tools. In doing so, he is able to perceive any scam that's at hand and reposition himself with an alternative approach. The roadrunner's intuition is more than just a "gut feeling." His awareness of issues and conditions is a type of inner wisdom. Envisioned leaders have the same intuitiveness. Past experiences serve as learning tools. But there is more. Envisioned leaders are constantly looking over the horizon and are in tune with their inner feelings. They see what lies ahead and adjust accordingly. They do not see the world from within the silo.

Coyotes Look Back; Roadrunners Look Ahead

Our consultants point out that after watching nearly an hour of Roadrunner cartoons, they observed that for each time that the roadrunner looked back, the coyote looked back eight times. As they note, the spirit of the roadrunner is about progress, not tradition—about getting ready to lead tomorrow's marketplace, not yesterday's. The coyote overrelies on market research, competitor analysis, and discounted cash flow analysis. The roadrunner sees the value of such business tools but also recognizes their limitations. Envisioned leaders are willing to ask the bold question, "Despite what the evidence might suggest to us, does it really reflect the reality of the situation?" What would our world be like today if we didn't have the bold leadership behind companies such as Xerox, Polaroid, Microsoft, and Apple Computer?

Within the security profession we have seen several examples of such envisioned leadership. We have reviewed the efforts of Mike Foil at Mellon Bank, Mike Farmer at Mobil, Bill Besse at Mary Kay, and a host of suppliers including Denis Brown at Pinkerton, Tom Marano at Argenbright, and Dwight Pederson at American Protective Services. Each of these business executives understands the need to step outside traditional ways of defining asset protection and look forward to new opportunities.

Coyotes Operate from What They Want; Roadrunners Operate from Who They Are

While the coyote focuses on the external reward—catching the bird—the roadrunner is operating on a higher level of thinking. His goal is to demonstrate excellence and speed, mobility and maneuverability. As our metaphorists point out, "The coyote's efforts are a mere inconvenience to the roadrunner—not even an inconvenient blip—as the bird lives these values."[4] It is the roadrunner's joyful speed and flexibility that allow him the ability to "read" the environment and make "impossible" turns while the coyote suffers accordingly.

Envisioned business leaders strive to maximize market share and profitability. But they also recognize that these goals are not the only purpose of being in business. It is equally important to provide an environment that allows people to grow and express themselves positively. The quality-focused organization recognizes the interdependency of both pursuits. Xerox's Paul Allair underscores this point. Speaking before a group of business executives he notes: "Organizations are not simply in business to make a profit. Equally part of their success formula is a commitment to living to certain values for both themselves and their customers. If we do what is right for the customer, our market share and our return on assets will take care of themselves."

LEGENDARY LEADERSHIP

Mike Basch, one of Federal Express's original executives, has developed a model for today's envisioned leader. Trademarked as *Legendary Leadership*, it is a process, developed over the last three decades, for making managers into outstanding leaders. At the core of the methodology is the recognition that workers and managers accept total responsibility for

their organization's success. To underscore the importance of this principle, Basch's first lesson is that every person, team, enterprise, industry,
and culture must add value in greater portion than its cost. The second
lesson is that everyone must accept his or her responsibility as a leader in
adding value. For Basch, the key to true phenomenal success is the
leader's ability to create an environment where people perform at high
levels.[5]

Legendary Leaders are people who are able to transform workers
from saying, "Thank God it's Friday" to saying, "Thank God it's Monday."
The TGIM mind-set dictates that customers are not to be served but
rather become a partner in the buying and selling relationship. Further,
employees no longer perceive themselves as being entitled; instead they
see themselves as responsible for not only their actions but also the success of the company. Finally, owners are no longer the ones who control
an entire system; rather they facilitate a system designed to achieve the
stated goals. Legendary Leaders understand that within the boundaries of
the business world, they must meet the physical, emotional, and intellectual needs of customers, employees, and owners.

This is not to suggest that corporate America is expected to serve as
an individual's caretaker. Legendary Leaders separate personal lives from
professional lives. For that matter, they push hard for employees to accept
greater responsibility, and they rail at the notion of unchecked and runaway employee entitlements. Legendary leaders are envisioned leaders.
They want people to excel, and they know that this is only possible when
individuals step forward and assume personal responsibility at work. For
example, one security manager pointed out that an employee recently
had his wallet stolen from on top of his desk. Despite the fact that the
employee admitted to having left his wallet on top of the desk unattended, the employee felt he was entitled to be reimbursed by the company for the money that was stolen and for the value of his wallet. It is
this type of entitlement mentality that works against creating an organization that can deliver legendary service. Employees do have one entitlement: their employers need to provide an environment in which
employees can develop and contribute in meaningful ways.

As we pointed out several chapters ago, the better the service, the
more invisible it should be to your customers. It is the role of the envi-
sioned-Legendary Leader to make this a reality. This begins by defining
service that identifies customers' needs from the customers' perspectives.
As Basch points out to his readers and seminar attendees, there are two
ways in which a company can become legendary: either by defining customer problems and solving them or by identifying needs the customer is
not even aware of and fulfilling them. Quoting his former boss, Fred

Smith, CEO of Federal Express, Basch stresses, "One function of the CEO is to hear the distant murmur of a need before it becomes the crescendo of a market."[6]

The vision of a legendary organization is that of its people continually soaring to higher levels of service guided by a leader who understands that employees' needs are oftentimes just as important as those of their customers. Basch advises that once you decide to differentiate your organization from the pack, you must create action plans that build an organization of people passionately committed to delivering legendary service.[7]

In one of his recent seminars Basch shared with the audience several examples of what made Federal Express go from being one man's dream to being a company that is a world leader in transportation and overnight delivery. Among his examples of the superior service that established the company's good reputation was a pilot who used his own credit card to fuel an airplane in order to meet his schedule when the company was struggling in its early days. He also shared the story of one of his dispatchers who chartered a private plane to deliver a wedding dress on time. When Mike asked the dispatcher why she had taken this rather dramatic—and costly—alternative, she responded, "You always say that we should make certain that the customer's needs are always met." Taken aback, Basch went on to counsel her that some degree of reasonableness was necessary. Such sage advice didn't go unchallenged for very long, however. Basch concludes this anecdote by pointing out that the bride's father was so impressed by the concern shown by the dispatcher that his company placed one of Federal Express's largest orders and launched them on the road to the financial success that they are today.[8]

Basch's Legendary Leadership model is an exciting lesson in the impact that envisioned leaders can have on an organization and the impact they can have on a company's bottom line. It also helps us to see that leadership is an idea that needs to be nurtured in each employee. At the heart of the Basch's model is *vision*—the invention of the future. This vision consists of:

+ *goals,* which provide direction for people's actions;
+ *gaps,* which define the difference between where you are and where you want to be;
+ *actions,* which close the goals; and
+ *feedback,* which keeps everyone focused.

Basch's approach is to work with managers to transform them into Legendary Leaders by employing methodologies that allow them to define the four basic goals for most organizations: increase revenues, build customer loyalty, create employee passion, and control costs. Once these goals are accomplished, the next tasks are to measure the gaps; map out creative solutions (actions); and provide direct, immediate, and clear feedback to employees. The process starts with a company's desire and commitment to be unique and to be the best.

THE FIVE STAGES OF CORPORATE MORAL DEVELOPMENT

For envisioned leadership to take hold, the company as a whole and its business units must be committed to high ethical principles. It is still possible for there to be unprincipled or unethical operating units, including corporate security, in good organizations. Therefore it's important for the security manager to ask the question, What type of organization am I running? This is especially true for security managers with access to a lot of today's electronic surveillance equipment.

Employee privacy can easily be trod upon. Senior executives, desirous of getting the upper hand, insecure in their own position, or simply out for their own gain have on more than one occasion co-opted a security manager into spying or other unethical behavior. Some security managers have been coerced into engaging in activities that they knew were illegal. Yet for the most part unethical behavior is far less subtle. It involves violating confidences that arise out of sensitive investigations or passing along confidential information to a colleague as part of the good ol' boy network. It may also include taking advantage of special privileges such as access to restricted areas, or converting corporate assets to personal use.

Knowing that other executives are engaging in questionable activity, and not taking action is another type of unethical behavior. Not wanting to become part of the game of "corporate politics," some asset protection managers will turn a blind eye on activities they know to be improper. This particularly can happen with external providers. "After all," they reason, "they're the customer and I'm the provider. Their business is their business, and our business is not to interfere." Such thinking only leads in one direction—down and eventually out.

As Eric Reidenbach and Donald Robin point out, there are five different types of corporate structures:

♦ *The amoral organization.* This is an organization where a high value is placed on winning at any cost. Such an organization violates societal values and laws. A security firm operating as an amoral organization might use hidden CCTV surveillance in violation of company policies regarding rights to privacy. It would justify its actions based on the misguided idea that all is fair so long as they "get their man." Other clandestine activities might include breaking and entering into employee lockers and desks without court orders or, in those places where it is legal to do so, without reasonable cause.

♦ *The legalistic organization.* A legalistic security organization takes pride in subscribing to the strict letter of the law and not the spirit of the law. It might enforce rigid adherence to access control procedures, define escort services only during specified periods of time, or make no allowances for the removal of company property even when it's evident that special circumstances exist and an appropriate audit trail is in evidence.

♦ *The responsive organization.* To be a responsive organization, an organization has to be interested in demonstrating responsibility, socially or otherwise, and be responsive to the needs of others. A security services provider that donates both people and equipment to assist in the recovery process associated with a natural disaster would fit this category. Such work might involve cleanup activity after a hurricane, flood, earthquake, and so forth, or it might entail volunteering staff time for blood drives or other civic events.

♦ *The emergent ethical organization.* This is an organization that recognizes the importance of a social contract existing between business and society. In some cases large-scale product recalls by companies demonstrate an organizations' commitment to balancing profitability with ethical concerns. Within the security industry many companies have participated in writing proposed legislation at the state and federal level calling for the creation of standards for both the service and the product sectors of the profession.

♦ *The ethical organization.* An ethical organization has ethics that are so high that employees are rewarded for walking away from compromising action, and are encouraged to blow the whistle on wrongdoers. New employees are assigned with mentors, who provide moral guidance.[9]

This continuum of ethical behavior provides us the opportunity to ask, Where are we? Sociologists and ethicists suggest that there is no company that can claim it is totally ethical per se. Even though these authors would say that many companies could be classified as emerging ethical companies, they believe that no one has yet to achieve the final step.[10] In the purest sense of the phrase, this is probably true. Yet today many companies have stepped up to this issue and have initiated pro-grams at all levels to instill a strong sense of ethical behavior.

Regardless of where your company is, the challenge for you as an envisioned leader is to move the organization rapidly along the contin-uum toward a total commitment to ethical behavior. I recently had occa-sion to review the security procedures for a major fast-food chain. Among their franchisees it is common to offer free food to mall security officers as a way of enticing them into the restaurant, thus creating the impres-sion that the restaurants have security. One of the restaurants had a pri-mary competitor directly across the street. That other restaurant chain always banned the practice of feeding security officers for free, opting instead to develop a true security program.

When the restaurant offering the free food to officers initially began the program, security and police personnel frequently came by to get their free meals. It didn't take long before it was obvious that they came to believe that they were entitled to the free food, but at the same time they didn't want to be bothered by management's request to assist them with security or respond to customer requests. Since both restau-rants were in a fairly high crime area, it wasn't long before customers began opting for the restaurant with its own security officers, because diners felt safer there. The simple moral here is that if you are going to pursue security, then you should be willing to do it right, especially when it can be shown that long-term results can be measured in direct dollars and cents.

MENTORING—STILL ALIVE AND STILL CRITICAL FOR SUCCESS

Envisioned leaders want to share their experiences and are committed to developing the people who report to them—whether directly or indirectly. One effective tool is mentoring, a practice that has been part of the Ameri-can management scene over the last several decades. Invariably even the most innovative of today's general business management texts spends some time in discussing the how-tos and the whys and wherefores associated with this activity, because mentoring is one of the few tools that allows newcomers an opportunity to be guided by the wisdom of those who have proceeded them. Just as early pioneers required guides to show them the way across this country, today's inexperienced organizational pioneers need their own trailblazers. Just as the elders in many civilizations are sought out for their knowledge and insights, experienced managers are needed to share their wisdom—no matter how big the organization is.

Gordon Shea, author of *Mentoring: Helping Employees Reach Their Full Potential*, points out that there are three types of mentoring acts—situational, informal, and formal.

- ◆ *Situational mentoring* comes into play when a particular event occurs, and an employee needs specific guidance. The intervention can be undertaken by the mentor, knowing that the mentee needs help, or by the mentee, who is seeking specific assistance and counsel from someone who is trusted and experienced in the particular event at hand.
- ◆ *Informal mentoring* is typically voluntary and very personal. Years ago, when I was an assistant professor, one of my mentors was the police chief for a city nearly two thousand miles away. I met this mentor at a professional conference, and through an exchange of mutual ideas it was obvious to me that I could learn a lot from him. Wes Pomeroy continued as my professional mentor while I went on to become a middle manager for a large police department and then rose through the senior management ranks within the private sector. Throughout the relationship Wes was able to provide insights on the business of policing and private security but also guidance in how to succeed in today's organizational climates.
- ◆ *Formal mentoring* programs tend to be very systematic and structured. They are usually initiated by senior management as a way of assisting identified star performers. Such mentoring programs are driven by the organization's needs and are oftentimes defined within a fixed time. It is not uncommon for formal mentoring programs to fail over the longer term because many mentors do not make a true commitment to the relationship.[11]

Shea also points out that despite the many benefits associated with mentoring, mentors need to avoid certain pitfalls, including

- ◆ *Advising.* Giving specific advice as opposed to allowing the mentee to arrive at his or her own decisions.
- ◆ *Criticizing.* Even constructive criticism is value laden and is oftentimes perceived as threatening.
- ◆ *Rescuing.* True growth comes from learning through mistakes. Rescuing gives the individual an out, thereby reducing the total value of the lesson to be learned.
- ◆ *Sponsoring.* Promotions and appointments should be based on merit (earned accomplishments) and not on one higher executive's ability to influence the decision in favor of his protégé. Further, sponsoring

can often get in the way of truly identifying an individual's level of talent and capability.

♦ *Building barriers.* The mere organizational position of a mentor can be intimidating to the mentee. From the mentor's perspective he or she is there to help. From the mentee's perspective the executive's title, physical location (executive row), or peer relationships can be very intimidating.

♦ *Ignoring the why?* As Shea points out, exploring the "reasons why" is at the center of making sense of things. Mentors may be able to accomplish certain things because of their technical skill or political position, but mentees need to learn why certain things need to be done in certain ways.

♦ *Discounting.* People think less of someone else or themselves as an unconscious way of dealing with their negative feelings. A mentor might discount a mentee's interest, ability, or willingness to do something because of the personal relationship that has developed between them. In other words, the mentor may simply discount a mentee's lack of action instead of seeing what is really going on.[12]

Shea cautions about practices to avoid, but he also highlights several practices that should be pursued in the mentoring process, including actively listening to the mentee and providing feedback on the whole message received from the mentee. Active listening allows mentees to maintain ownership of the problem and their decision about how to solve it. It also gives mentees the opportunity to take pride in having solved the problem for themselves. To be effective, feedback must be given on both the facts and the feelings presented by mentees. Since organizational issues involve dealing with facts and feelings, providing feedback that reflects both facts and feelings assures mentees that their message has been heard and that they are able to differentiate between realities and perceptions. This is critical if mentees are to learn problem-solving skills.[13]

Envisioned leaders can be an excellent source for providing information and ideas that will serve mentees well in their decision-making process. They need to understand that as the context of their situation shifts, their mentor is there to help them understand the differences between one issue and another. Mentors can also be very helpful in role-playing situations because they often have insights gained from their own experience and better knowledge of the players involved. Out of this exercise, the mentor can provide one of his most valuable services to the mentee—that of exploring a variety of options to any one decision. Whether it's in the form of brainstorming or casual exploration, the exercise of exploring options can lead mentees to more creative solutions and a broader perspective on the problem at hand.

THE SUPPORT CYCLE

Envisioned leadership requires a certain degree of inherent ability; it also requires know-how gained largely from experience. Part of this experiential learning involves a sensitivity to what I call the *support cycle*. Depending on the particular pressures the overall company is undergoing at any point in time, some business units will draw more attention than others. If it is perceived that one unit can positively contribute to a desired outcome, the organization's resources will be directed that way. Executive management and other department heads will openly and actively show their support for that area of the business. A unit generally loses support when one or more of the following three conditions exist: it is thought not to be carrying its weight, it is viewed as extraneous, or it is viewed as obstructing progress.

The envisioned leader realizes that every business unit cycles through different levels of support and plans accordingly. Sometimes they're on top and can therefore take advantage of a particular situation. Other times the support is waning—even nonexistent. During these low times, leaders should recognize the signs and assume a lower profile. There may be certain things that a leader can do to control events and change the level of support his or her unit receives, to some extent. For the most part, however, such events and circumstances are beyond his or her influence. Therefore, the leader must either opt to stay and ride out the low end of the cycle or leave. The support cycle consists of three phases.

In the first phase there is strong support, and the department head can get almost anything he or she requests. Funding for staffing, equipment, space, and other resources is fairly easy. The reasons for this strong support are extremely varied, ranging from senior managers believing that such support is critical to the company/department's overall success to as mundane a reason as that the manager is a personal favorite of a chief executive officer. Regardless of the reasons, during this phase a leader can achieve significant gains.

Most decision makers fail to understand that the cycle exists. They cannot see the broader picture, so they fail to take advantage of the blessings of the first phase. During the period of bliss and unawareness of the support cycle phenomenon, it is fair to characterize the unit head as a manager, as opposed to a leader. Leaders have vision and see reality as it is. Managers see the here and now and assume that the status quo will continue indefinitely.

The second phase of the support cycle is characterized by periods of confusion. Since the manager has had a recent history of strong support, he or she will initially pass off individual incidents indicating a weakening of support as being an aberration. The manager will excuse the actions, inactions, or comments of others. He or she may rationalize by thinking, "The boss must be having a bad day," or "The boss is really jammed these days with so many other things, he's really not focusing on me." Another comment I frequently hear among unknowing managers in the second phase is: "You know, I don't see much of the boss these days. Oh, there is nothing wrong. As a matter of fact, I kind of like it. There was a time there when it seemed as though I couldn't turn around and not run into him." Sound familiar? If so, you may be in the second phase. The second phase is a natural evolution. Neither a good nor a bad value should be applied to this phase; it is what it is. After all, it is part of the total support cycle. Remember, executives typically focus on what is "hot for the moment."

Another characteristic that makes the second phase dangerous is the silence. You may not readily recognize when you are entering this phase. Yet there are real signs present, if you know what to look for. Indifference and apathy are the two strongest clues. Other signs are more subtle. Here are some indicators you should look for:

◆ *Inadvertent exclusions.* This occurs when meetings regarding issues clearly within the asset protection manager's scope of responsibility are held and you and members of your staff are not included. No one deliberately meant to exclude the manager, they just didn't think to invite you.

◆ *Inadvertent circumvention.* Like the first, events, meetings and activities are planned that clearly should include the manager, but you are not involved. People don't think to include security because they don't associate security with the issue at hand.

◆ *Assumed acceptance.* Here unit heads will make assumptions about your security program or other organizational aspects affecting security without your input.

◆ *Deliberate rejection.* Some people will show the minimum amount of support for you and your program, and therefore it is superficially present, at most. Such people are always found within an organization, irrespective of what phase you are in the support cycle. Tragically, if you are in the last phase and support from others is weak, these restricting supporters have a stronger influence in determining how little, if any support, you ultimately receive.

It is only when decision makers see that they are in the second phase that the realization begins to set in that unfinished projects may flounder or die for lack of support. Then perhaps they can become aware of the cyclical nature of support and see the need to plan for phase 2 in advance.

As people change and/or external events shift, support naturally shifts. As of this writing support for increasing security is generally high among most employees. Americans are uneasy about their overall safety. Workplace violence is on the rise, street safety remains a chief concern, even though crime rates are decreasing. This is because random violence is escalating. There is still a lot of uneasiness regarding the bombings at the World Trade Center, the Oklahoma City Federal Building, and the 1996 Summer Olympics in Atlanta.

Security prevention strategies are now a top priority, yet for many there is still a lingering hope that the recent bombing events are aberrations and that things will return to normal (the way they used to be). If this can occur, they hope, people will not be as worried, and we can put security behind us. This kind of thinking illustrates the characteristic attitude toward support. As we saw in our discussion on motivation, people are moved when they have a need. Once the need has been filled, support diminishes. In time, personal security will take a backseat to something else. It is all part of a cycle.

The second phase occurs when all is running very well and no perceived threat exists. In terms of security, this phase usually coincides with an extended period of time having lapsed since the last serious incident occurred. Executives and employees can't imagine themselves falling victim to a particular incident.

The support cycle can be likened to a wave. It begins building far out, away from the shore. As it is drawn in, it builds in momentum. You can actually witness the various elements at play on the sea or a lake that contribute to the rushing of waves. The wind, the tide, the water's depth all come together to push them forward and build both height and strength. All of this is equal to the first two phases of the support cycle. The wind can be likened to the overall corporate culture and the emphasis it places on security in general. The tide is tantamount to the various forces internal and external to the organization that push and pull on security's resources. The depth is equal to the level of support security receives.

As the wave peaks, it reaches its crest. On a particularly active day, the wave can be spectacular in its size. Nonetheless, it peaks and then it falls. It's at the moment of its peak that we can liken it to entering the second phase of the support cycle. To the casual observer it is exciting to watch a wave crest and break. If you could personify the wave, it would tell you that all is going well as it builds. For that matter, it might remark: "Things can't get better than this!" This despite the fact that it has unknowingly hit its peak and soon will begin to fall away. That is how we know we are entering the second phase. It's the warning sign that says we have become so used to having things go our way, we don't realize that we may well be into our peak.

A wave has only two ways of coming down. It either peaks and crashes mightily, or it peaks and rolls in gently. Either way, it comes to an end. If it is far enough away, it will ride out for some time, only to build in momentum again and repeat itself. If it is close in, it will come ashore, only to be replaced by another. This is like the third phase of the support cycle. It will ride itself out or end and be replaced by another.

Your challenge as a security manager is to discern where you are at in the support cycle/wave action. If you are riding to the crest, seize the moment and build the reserves for the next wave. If you are cresting, see it for what it is and begin to prepare for the next wave, because this high will end sooner than you want or believe. If you are on the backside, begin pulling together those resources necessary to develop a higher, more powerful wave the next time around.

After all, the final phase is characterized by an outright lack of support. Unlike the second phase where support will vary from true support to indifference, the final phase is characterized by outright rejection. When you're in this phase, employees generally have a disdain for security. Executives avoid you or begin serious discussions of either replacing you altogether or—worse yet—eliminating the entire department. In the current climate of cost containment and "reengineering," the decision to do without a formal security program is not at all unusual when there is an outright lack of support to begin with.

It is rare to find an envisioned leader at the helm when an organization enters the third phase. If the leader is gone, it is because he or she has left somewhere between the end of phase 1 and the early stages of phase 2. Often a new leader arrives when the organization is in the hiatus of phase 3. Relationships have fallen to a new low in phase 3, credibility is nil, and change is demanded: when these variables are present, the organization looks for new leadership and the stage is set for the envisioned leader.

Envisioned leaders will readily admit that there was a time when they were a manager and learned/earned their wisdom to transcend to the role of leader. They will tell of how they were once managers and thought they knew best at the time, only to learn that their brilliant insights were not so enlightened as they may have thought. When I think of the envisioned leader, I am always reminded of the an old oak tree. It's real beauty emerges when the wisdom of time and experience shine through its weathered leaves, broken branches, and gnarled trunk.

AVOIDING LEADERSHIP PITFALLS

The envisioned leader is someone who also understands that despite the best efforts of staff members, it is easy for the leader to fall victim to any number of potential traps that result in failure to meet the intended target. Charles Prather and Lisa Gundry, in their book *Blueprints for Innovation,* point out that there are five common pitfalls that can swallow up both time and precious resources.[14] Let's briefly look at each and how it applies to security:

Identifying the Wrong Problem

The security staff for one of the country's largest mass retailers was challenged to reduce the company's losses by at least 50 percent. Over the next three fiscal quarters they concentrated their efforts on what they believed was the root of the problem, escalating shoplifting. Despite identifying several creative strategies that actually reduced shoplifting, much to their disappointment they found that loss continued to rise. It wasn't until they began to look at the company's inventory accounting procedures that they discovered the real cause for the company's escalating loss rate. Because they failed to assess the problem correctly, their innovative shoplifting ideas failed to yield them the results they desired.

Judging Ideas Too Quickly

Security managers are often criticized for being too quick to consider the potential downside of a new idea. This is an understandable tendency given that the nature of asset protection is risk avoidance. Conversely, the nature of innovation is to assume certain degrees of business risk. The envisioned leader is one who exercises patience and keeps an open mind to the possibilities that spring forth from the creative process. This is not to say that the leader ought not voice an objection in the final analysis. But whatever opinion is rendered and whatever level of support is lent to an effort, the decision should be based on facts and ideas that have been given full expression.

The corporate security manager for a large financial services company was asked to reduce his operation as part of a company restructuring program. He asked his staff for ideas. One creative specialist suggested that the department reduce the number of security officers by transferring responsibility for access into work units to individual employees. Several of the other staff members openly laughed at such a ridiculous idea, but the security manager asked the specialist to elaborate.

The employee explained that instead of having a security officer respond to every reported open door or suspicious individual, the responsibility could be shifted to the employees who actually worked in the area. He went on to explain that if security is truly everyone's business, then employees should be willing to assume more individual responsibility and challenge people not known to them. He told the group that he had been thinking about the idea for some time and had been working on an awareness training program for nonsecurity people earlier that day. He said that he had worked up some preliminary numbers and projected that if other operating practices were implemented, the department could reduce the staff well below the numbers requested.

Those who had originally scoffed at the idea continued to do so. The director, on the other hand, found merit in the idea and suggested a trial study. The department selected two of the areas of highest concern, trained the nonsecurity employees accordingly, and implemented the suggested practices. After the first six months, unauthorized access reports declined by more than 78 percent. Needless to say, the program was implemented throughout the corporate complex, and the naysayers apologized accordingly.

Stopping with the First Good Idea

Prather and Gundry caution that the first good idea is *never* the best. That's because more often than not it was the easiest to come up with, so there's little doubt that others have already thought about it.[15] The test for true innovation is to take great ideas generated early on and expand them to their outer limits. This is what is commonly known as "pushing the envelope." In short, it's taking a good idea and exploring ways that it can be reshaped or redefined to achieve even greater efficiency or effectiveness.

As a security consultant I commonly run into security directors who are in a hurry to "get the job done and move on." It's easy for them to seize on a good idea and say: "Well, there's the answer. Let's do it and tackle the next agenda item." Bad strategy. Great ideas only become great after they have been worked through several iterations. Without attacking the nucleus of the original idea, it is far more fruitful to take the great idea and ask how it can be improved during the initial period of consideration.

Invariably it will be revised, and a better end result will emerge. Research and development specialists will readily identify with this. Experience has taught them that the first idea is typically the genesis of something that is far more valuable.

Failing to "Get the Bandits on the Train"

This concept refers to identifying those whose support will be required to make your innovative idea workable. Another way of saying this is to ask, "If you can't beat them, is there a way that you can get them on your team?" Earlier we examined the concepts of advocacy and the support cycle. Both of these ideas help to underscore the need for creating a broad-based ownership for new ideas, especially in areas such as corporate security, which may have historically been seen more as a necessary evil than an organizational benefit.

Obeying Rules That Don't Exist

It's easy to fall into the trap of believing that conditions and requirements exist when in fact they don't. Or maybe we believe that those rules that do exist restrict the possibility that we can pursue alternatives. In either event neither is true. For example, for many large organizations there has historically been a battle within security between what type of workforce configuration is appropriate—proprietary or contract. As many envisioned leaders are discovering, the answer can be a combination of both.

UNDERSTANDING AND IMPLEMENTING EMPLOYEE EMPOWERMENT

Whether one is a critic or a proponent of reengineering, the reality is that in a world of leaner managerial staffs, those that have survived realize that their to-do lists are longer than ever before. Some have assumed more direct reports within their department, while others have assumed greater responsibilities; the net effect is the same—more direct reports. Even though some work can be delegated to subordinates or external providers, ultimate success in management requires a transcendence from delegation to what is now commonly referred to as *employee empowerment*.

Throughout this book the theme of empowerment has been woven through the fabric of many of the concepts. There are those that are critical of empowerment. They contend that individuals can only empower themselves, that they cannot have empowerment bestowed upon them by someone else. When considered from this psychological perspective, I suspect that the concept of empowerment would make for an interesting debate. In the world of business management, however, empowerment has come to mean those activities pursued by management that enable employees to assume a greater role in bringing demonstrated added value to the business plan. Such a practical definition, for me, leaves little room for debate. Empowerment, as we have seen throughout the previous chapters, has proven to be a powerful management tool.

Historically, corporate executives have defined internal relationships and functions in the classical hierarchical structure. This has created a boss-subordinate relationship wherein directives flow downward, and there is little input into the decision-making process flowing upward. For some organizations this model remains relevant, but they are few and far between. The example that comes readily to mind is the military. There are times when this traditional model is appropriate for any organization. Like the military in time of war, when a business is facing a major crisis it needs to shift from whatever model it normally pursues to the traditional staff-line model. During a war (for example, fighting a short-term crisis such as natural disasters, product tampering, and so forth) organizational survival requires adherence to a chain of command so there will be clear uniformity of direction and very focused allocation of resources.

Shifting from an empowered organizational structure to a classical military structure during a crisis can be difficult. Empowerment can be abused or misunderstood. Some managers and employees can fall into the trap of believing that they are fairly autonomous. Under normal conditions there is a higher degree of tolerance, and such misperceptions can be dealt with on a case by case basis. With true empowerment, however, employees recognize that there is always one final decision maker. If the concept is properly implemented and followed, everyone understands this, and during times of crisis they will yield to the decision maker, offering no resistance. Here's a quick example to illustrate the point.

A few years ago there was a serious fire in a Boston high-rise. The building was largely a single-tenant property, serving as the world headquarters for a Fortune 100 company. When the fire broke out, the fire annunciation system was affected, and internal communications was severely compromised. The security department had recently undergone a number of management changes, and shift commanders were empowered to make critical decisions regarding their shift operations. When the fire broke out and the magnitude of the event was apparent, the director stepped in and began making command decisions and directing resources accordingly. Even though the fire broke out during a shift change, what could have been a communications and command decision-making nightmare turned out to be an opportunity for security to demonstrate its true added value.

Understanding well what empowerment really means, the shift commanders deferred to the security director and shifted from an empowered management style to a classic military model immediately. They recognized that empowerment incorporates an ability to rapidly shift from "normal operating conditions" to "emergency operating conditions" and assume a chain of command mind-set. The end result was the successful evacuation of more than five thousand people, suppression of the fire with minimal property loss, and a rapid return to business as usual.

Empowerment is more than simply handing the reins off to one or more employees. Rather, like other carefully constructed management processes, empowerment requires planned execution over a period of time. This is particularly important when dealing with longer tenured employees. Over time it is natural for a traditionally defined subordinate staff to have some degree of suspicion regarding management and their motives.

When cast against the turbulent times of outsourcing and downsizing, any radical change in the business approach can be very threatening to even the most loyal employee. As one cynical security manager remarked at a recent seminar on management practices, "I will tell you what empowerment is. It's management's new way of coaxing unsuspecting employees onto a high wire and then watching to see if they can make the crossing or fall off." Sadly, for many there is more fact than fiction to this perspective. In such cases, I would contend that their victimization is more the result of misguided, unintended, or deliberately planned misleading under the guise of empowerment. True empowerment requires an open mind and a clear understanding of what is being agreed to prior to employees making a commitment to a new way of doing things.

For empowerment to succeed, employees must have trust in their leader. The manager should have a proven track record with respect to positive encouragements—even when dealing with employees who have made well-intentioned mistakes. The characteristics of an environment in which empowerment is resident would include trust, respect, support, risk taking, and innovation. Interestingly enough, I would propose that if someone were asked to characterize an environment in which best practices were evident, the same list would emerge. That is because those who pursue best practices understand the necessity for empowering employees to be able to stand on their own and contribute in positive ways.

Empowerment, particularly in its early stages, can be a scary proposition for both the manager and the employees because it requires both a change in attitude and a willingness to accept outcomes that are not necessarily clearly defined at the beginning. As we noted above, as a way of doing business, empowerment would not work well under battle conditions, wherein the leader is expected to give orders, and the soldier's role is to execute them. Yet many of today's American businesses operate in a similar vein. Senior managers have come to believe that they have earned the right to give orders and expect most employees to carry them out without asking a lot of questions. Despite a plethora of management texts espousing the new and enlightened principles of modern management, the reality remains that for most employees their input is either not sought out or is not given full consideration.

Empowerment, if properly implemented and maintained, need not threaten the management decision-making process. On the contrary, as Florence Stone and Randi Sachs have pointed out, "High value managers have learned how sharing their power gives them the time to work on high-visibility projects, to identify and pursue opportunities for their operation or company as a whole, and consequently to increase their worth in the eyes of senior management and, ultimately, it can lead to advancement."[16]

To accomplish successful empowerment, the concept has to be built into the workings of the organizational structure as well as into individuals. To accomplish this requires doing an assessment on three levels:

Level One: Individual Mind-set.

- ♦ Do individuals believe that they can be a source for creativity and innovation?
- ♦ Do they listen to themselves?
- ♦ Do they seek out new ways instead of being content to simply talk about them?
- ♦ Do they believe in what can be?

Level Two: Personal and InterGroup Relationships.

- ♦ Are people willing to act in responsible, self-managing, and accountable arrangements with one another?
- ♦ Have people learned the skills of collaboration, trust, shared problem solving, and conflict resolution?
- ♦ Have people demonstrated that they know how to create a learning team?
- ♦ Is there evidence that informal links between groups have been developed and that cooperation across groups within the organization is occurring?

Level Three: Organizational Policies and Structures.

- ◆ Have policies and procedures been written that support and encourage individuals and team empowerment?
- ◆ Is the vision clear and accepted by everyone?
- ◆ Have mechanisms been put into place that allow employees to have input into these policies?
- ◆ Is job security and fair treatment readily apparent?

These three levels cut across the organization. Developing the proper mind-set, establishing intergroup relationships, and developing a company-wide commitment take time. Trust building is an earned process, but once it is in place results flow quickly and commonly exceed expectations. People want to contribute and can do so in many meaningful ways once given the opportunity.

SUMMARY

With this chapter we bring our journey to an end. We began by seeking to define ways to enhance value and achieve success through examining specific strategies. Our journey lead us through a forest of challenges and opportunities for individual asset protection managers. Beginning with an examination of programs and individual management responsibilities, it is only fitting to conclude with a review of the interrelationship between the manager—turned leader—and his or her staff.

In Chapter 8 we began by comparing what it takes to become a distance runner with what it takes to be a leader. We saw that there were some interesting parallels in the development process for both. This allowed us to set the stage for introducing what I call the *envisioned leader.* This is the person who goes beyond the bounds of simply managing, emerging from a long learning process like a runner matures through training. The end result is an experienced person who is capable of seeing how things are and envisioning how they should be.

We saw the differences between managers with conventional perceptions and approaches and leaders with an entrepreneurial vision. Having fun with the analogy of the coyote and the roadrunner, we explored how perceptions vary, and what the underlying drives are that lead one further than the other. Our discussion also passed through the concept of the *Legendary Leader.* Here we saw that Legendary Leaders have the vision and commitment to lead their staff to new levels of service excellence.

Our journey also carried us through the ups and downs associated with mentoring. We found that when pursued correctly, mentoring is still an effective leadership tool. From here we examined several of the barriers that can get in the way of innovation. We discovered that even enlightened employees can become victims of their own assumptions and limited perceptions. In turn, these limitations can cause them to miss the mark and not achieve results despite their best efforts. It is the role of the envisioned leader to see these pitfalls and steer his staff around them.

To serve as helmsmen, security managers need to recognize the often subtle signs of the cycle of support. They need to read the actions of others in order to monitor where they, as individual managers are, and where their department is in the minds of those they serve. Knowing the true level of support is critical to winning approval for continuing and new programs. Just as we saw that a wave rises and falls—some gently, others with a crash—security directors need to be able to read the signs to determine what phase their wave is in and anticipate how it will crest.

Together, these discussions set the stage for the final element of our journey—employee empowerment. Despite the presence of a great number of articles and books on the subject, this concept is still largely misunderstood and misapplied. Yet it is essential to success in today's world of business management. When properly pursued, empowerment has been demonstrated to be one of management's most powerful tools. Positive results flow when people are given the opportunity to take responsibility at work.

Epilogue:
Success in Today's
Corporate World

> The quest for success is a journey, sometimes difficult, sometimes easy,
> occasionally brief, but often long, a journey of effort, frustration and joy.
>
> …TOM MORRIS

The pursuit of quality is a mixed blessing. Since the first businesses were founded, owners have wanted to maximize profits and demonstrate that their products and services are driven by quality. These aims are an inherent part of business. Over the course of time owners have been penalized for breaches in ethics, violations of laws, and transgressions of social codes. The same can be said for government and religious leaders. Yet these are the exceptions. Most owners and managers have an intrinsic desire to deliver the best they can. I strongly believe this.

I also believe that American managers in particular are constantly looking for the "quick fix." It's part of our cultural psyche. Despite all of the evidence to the contrary, we continue to measure success and progress in incremental bits. We look at quarterly earnings as if they were lasting indicators. Business executives have long believed that there really is one best approach, one best formula that can assure high profits, happy employees, and satisfied customers. Unfortunately, such pursuits are about as fruitful as following a rainbow in hopes of finding the leprechaun's treasured pot of gold. Quick management fixes are opium for desperate managers addicted to the belief that success is but a step away.

Success requires hard work and a grounded sense of teamwork. It requires vision and the guts to step away from the pack and pursue strategies that are different. In my previous book I began with a poem that defines what it takes to succeed. In this book I would like to end with Professor Tom Morris's Seven C's of Success:

1. We need a clear *conception* of what we want, a vivid vision, a goal or set of goals powerfully imagined.
2. We need a strong *confidence* that we can attain our goals.
3. We need a focused *concentration* on what it takes to reach our goal.
4. We need a stubborn *consistency* in pursuing our vision, a determined persistence in thought and action.
5. We need an emotional *commitment* to the importance of what we're doing, and to the people with whom we're doing it.
6. We need a good *character* to guide us and keep us on a proper course.
7. We need a *capacity* to enjoy the process along the way.[1]

As both a practitioner and a consultant, I have thought long and hard about what it takes for a security professional to succeed in a business world that is both chaotic and ordered. Arriving at my ideas and discovering those of others has been an enjoyable experience for me. It has also helped me better understand the world in which we live and work. I hope you have found some of the same. My purpose in writing this book was to create a dialogue among professionals and students of asset protection. In exploring the thoughts contained herein, it is my hope that you have found some new insights and reinforced a few old ones.

We have seen the security profession explode from a second-class career alternative to a $50 billion industry in the span of twenty years. As American companies continue to redefine themselves, the role of security will only gain in importance. Built deep within our culture is a warrior mentality. We live to compete. It is woven into the very fiber of ourselves. Competition is healthy, but it is also easily abused. When mixed with greed and self-interest, it puts a company and its employees at risk. That's where security's role is defined.

Today many lament the demise of corporate security. I am sorry, but I don't see this happening. Security is certainly changing and will continue to do so. For many the changes it mean seeking careers with third-party providers. For others they mean pursuing new definitions of security that complement the information age. Some will perish; some will survive. It is my hope that this book will help some of you thrive!

End Notes

Chapter 1

1. These maxims provided by George Murphy, Virtual Security, 1996.
2. Richard Buskirk, *The Handbook of Management Tactics* (Boston: Cahners Books, 1976), p. 28
3. Florence Stone and Randi Sachs, *The High-Value Manager* (New York: AMACOM, 1995), p. 37.
4. *Ibid.,* p. 38.
5. *Ibid.*

Chapter 2

1. Luther Gulick and L. Urwick, eds., *Papers on the Science of Administration* (New York: Institute of Public Administration, 1937).
2. Debra L. Morehouse, *Total Quality Management: A Supervisor's Handbook* (Shawnee Mission, Kansas: National Press Publications, 1992).
3. *Ibid.,* p. 32.
4. *Ibid.,* p. 34.
5. *Ibid.,* p. 40.
6. *Ibid.,* p. 48.
7. Jim Harris, *Getting Employees to Fall in Love with Your Company,* (New York: AMACOM, 1996).

Chapter 3

1. Genevieve Capowski, "The Force Value," *Management Review,* May 1995.
2. *Ibid.*
3. *Ibid.*
4. Brian R. Hollstein, "Internal Security and the Corporate Customer," *Security Management,* June 1995, p. 61.

5. Capowski, *Management Review*, p. 34.
6. *Ibid.*, p. 38.
7. S. E. Toth, "How We Slashed Response Time," *Management Review*, February 1993, p. 51.
8. Oren Harari, "The Lab Test: A Tale of Quality," *Management Review*, February 1993, p. 55.
9. *Ibid.*
10. *Ibid.*, p. 58.
11. Price Pritchett, *Service Excellence* (Dallas: Pritchett & Associates, 1991) p. 11.
12. *Ibid.*, p. 15.
13. *Ibid.*, p. 21.
14. Price Pritchett, *The Employee Handbook of New Work Habits for a Radically Changing World* (Dallas: Pritchett & Associates, 1994).
15. Alex Vaughn, "Security Management Survival Skills (Ten of Them)," *Security Management Bulletin*, April 1996, p. 4.

Chapter 4

1. Jeremy Tarcher, *The New Paradigm in Business* (New York: Putnam, 1993).
2. Ron Fischer and Mary Rabaut, "A How-To Guide: Working with a Consultant," *Management Review*, February 1992, pp. 52-55.

Chapter 5

1. Dennis Dalton, *Security Management: Business Strategies for Success* (Boston, MA: Butterworth–Heinemann, 1995).

Chapter 6

1. Catherine Romano, "To Protect and Defend," *Management Review*, May, 1996, p. 25.
2. *Ibid.*
3. John O'Leary, "Combining Classic Security and MIS," *Security Management*, July 1995, pp. 143-147.
4. *Ibid.*
5. *Ibid.*
6. *Ibid.*
7. Leonard M. Fuld, "Competitor Intelligence, Can You Plug the Leaks?" *Security Management*, August 1989, p. 85.
8. Leonard M. Fuld, *The New Competitor Intelligence* (New York: John Wiley & Sons, 1995), p. 82.

9. Timothy J. Walsh and Richard J. Healy, *Protection of Assets Management Manual* (Santa Monica, CA: The Merritt Company, 1984).

10. Mark Radcliffe, "Multimedia Alert," *New Worlds To Conquer*, Supplement to Los Angeles *Daily Journal* and the San Francisco *Daily Journal*, April 27, 1995, p. 12.

11. Patrick Keough, "Talking Trash," *Security Management Magazine*, February 1995.

12. Lawrence Ingrassia, "How Secret G.E. Recipe for Making Diamonds May Have Been Stolen," *Wall Street Journal*, February 28, 1990.

13. John Whalen, "You're Not Paranoid: They Really Are Watching You," *Wired*, March 1995, p. 76.

14. Mike Moreno, "Chip Robbers Hit Fremont," *San Jose Mercury News*, June 1, 1995.

15. *Ibid.*, p. 4.

16. Henri Bérubé, "Bungled Burglary? Don't Be So Sure," *Security Management Magazine*, November, 1995, p. 26.

17. Jay Peterzell, "When 'Friends' Become Moles," *Time*, May 28, 1990, p. 50.

18. *Ibid.*

19. Tony Mauro, "Cellular Spies," *USA Today*, April 20-22, 1990.

20. *Ibid.*

21. *Ibid.*

22. Lawrence Ingrassia, "How Secret G.E. Recipe For Making Diamonds May Have Been Stolen," *Wall Street Journal*, February 28, 1990.

23. S. Wood and M. F. Wiskoff, *Americans Who Spied Against Their Country Since World War II* (Washington, D.C.: U.S. Government Printing Office, 1982).

24. American Institute for Business Research and National Security Institute, *Protecting Corporate America's Secrets in the Global Economy* (Framingham, MA: American Institute for Business Research, 1992).

25. Computer Crime Survey, Computer Security Institute, San Francisco, CA, 1994.

26. Mike Moreno, "Chip Robbers Hit Fremont," *San Jose Mercury News*, June 1, 1995.

27. Robert W. Payne, "Trade Secret First Aid," *Management Review*, March 1993, pp. 33-34.

28. *Ibid.*

29. *Ibid.*

30. Arion N. Pattakos, "Convincing Management to Keep a Secret," *Security Management*, November 1995, pp. 35-39.

31. *Ibid.*
32. *Ibid.*
33. John McCumber, "Developing and Implementing Security Policy for Corporate Information," *Security Technology and Design*, December 1995, p. 24.
34. Michael Allen, "Security Experts Advise Firms to Avoid Panic, Excess Zeal in Probing Data Leaks," *Wall Street Journal*, September 20, 1991.
35. *Ibid.*
36. *Ibid.*

Chapter 7

1. Barbara Ettorre, "Managing Competitive Intelligence," *Management Review*, October 1995.
2. Leonard M. Fuld, *The New Competitor Intelligence* (New York: John Wiley & Sons, 1995), p. 34.
3. *Ibid.*, p. 23.
4. Ettorre, "Managing Competitive Intelligence."
5. Anne Skagen, Editor, "To Spy or Not to Spy," *Executive Management Forum*, April 1995.
6. Fuld, *The New Competitor Intelligence*, p. 408.
7. Ettorre, "Managing Competitive Intelligence."
8. Fuld, *The New Competitor Intelligence*.
9. *Ibid.*
10. Ettorre, "Managing Competitive Intelligence."
11. John Nolan III, "What Does Our Competition Know About Us?" *Security Technology & Design*, March 1996.
12. Fay Brill, "I Spy, You Spy," *Industry Week*, October 3, 1994.
13. Fuld, *The New Competitor Intelligence*.
14. *Ibid.*
15. Leonard M. Fuld, "Competitor Intelligence, Can You Plug the Leaks?" *Security Management*, August 1989.
16. *Ibid.*

Chapter 8

1. Warren Bennis, "Lessons in Leadership from Superconsultant Warren Bennis," *Bottom Line*, July 1, 1996.
2. Peter Senge, "The Art and Practice of the Learning Organization," *The New Paradigm in Business*, M. Ray and A. Rinzler, eds. (New York: Putnam, 1993), p. 126.
3. Oren Harari and Chip R. Bell, "Is Wile E. Coyote in Your Office?" *Management Review*, May 1995, pp. 57-61.
4. *Ibid.*
5. Mike Basch, *Legendary Leadership*, 1996.
6. *Ibid.*
7. *Ibid.*
8. *Ibid.*
9. Linda Starke, "The Five Stages of Corporate Moral Development," *The New Paradigm in Business*, M. Ray and A. Rinzler, eds. (New York: Putnam, 1993), p. 203.
10. *Ibid.*, p. 204.
11. Gordon F. Shea, *Mentoring: Helping Employees Reach Their Full Potential* (New York: AMA Membership Publications Division, 1994).
12. *Ibid.*
13. *Ibid.*
14. Charles Prather and Lisa Gundry, *Blueprints for Innovation: How Creative Processes Can Make You and Your Company More Competitive.* (New York: AMA Membership Publications Division, 1995).
15. *Ibid.*
16. Florence Stone and Randi Sachs, *The High-Value Manager* (New York: AMACOM, 1995).

Epilogue

1. Tom Morris, *True Success: A New Philosophy of Excellence* (New York: G.P. Putnam's Sons, 1994), p. 286.

Bibliography

Albrecht, K. *The Northbound Train: Finding the Purpose, Setting the Direction, Shaping the Destiny of Your Organization.* New York: AMACOM, 1994.

Allen, M. "Security Experts Advise Firms to Avoid Panic, Excess Zeal in Probing Data Leaks." *Wall Street Journal,* September 20, 1991.

Bechtell, M. L. *The Management Compass: Steering the Corporation Using Hoshin Planning.* New York: AMA Membership Publications Division, 1995.

Bennis, W. "Lessons in Leadership from Superconsultant Warren Bennis," *Bottom-Line,* July 1, 1996.

Berry, T. H. *Managing the Total Quality Transformation.* New York: McGraw-Hill, 1991.

Bérubé, Henri. "Bungled Burglary? Don't Be so Sure." *Security Management Magazine,* November, 1995, 26.

Bridges, W. *Transitions.* New York: Addison-Wesley Publishing Company, 1980.

Brill, F. "I Spy, You Spy." *Industry Week,* October 3, 1994.

Buskirk, R. *The Handbook of Management Tactics.* Boston, Mass.: Cahners Books, 1976.

Capowski, G. "The Force Value." *Management Review,* May 1995, 34.

Champy, J. *Reengineering Management: The Mandate for New Leadership.* New York: HarperBusiness, 1995.

Crosby, P. B. *Quality Without Tears: The Art of Hassle-Free Management.* New York: Penguin, 1984.

———. *Quality Is Free.* New York: Penguin, 1979.

Dalton, D. *Security Management: Business Strategies for Success.* Boston, Mass. Butterworth–Heinemann, 1995.

Daugherty, D. A. *The New OSHA: Blueprints for Effective Training and Written Programs.* New York: AMA Membership Publications Division, 1996.

Davidow, W. H., and M. S. Malone, *The Virtual Corporation: Structuring and Revitalizing the Corporation for the 21st Century.* New York: HarperBusiness, 1992.

Drucker, P. F. *Managing for the Future: The 1990s and Beyond.* New York: Penguin, 1992.

Ettorre, B. "Managing Competitive Intelligence." *Management Review,* October 1995.

Fischer, R., and M. Rabaut, "A How-to Guide: Working with a Consultant," *Management Review,* February 1992, 52–55.

Fuld, L. M. *The New Competitor Intelligence: The Complete Resource for Finding, Analyzing, and Using Information About Your Competitors.* New York: John Wiley and Sons, 1995.

————. "Competitor Intelligence, Can You Plug the Leaks?" *Security Management,* August 1989, 85.

Gates, B. *The Road Ahead.* New York: Penguin, 1995.

Gulick, L., and L. Urwick, *Papers on the Science of Administration.* New York: Institute of Public Administration, 1937.

Haavind, R. *The Road to the Baldrige Award: Quest for Total Quality.* Stoneham, Mass. Butterworth-Heinemann, 1992.

Harari, O. "The Lab Test: A Tale of Quality." *Management Review,* February 1993, 55.

Harari, O., and C. R. Bell, "Is Wile E. Coyote in Your Office?" *Management Review,* May 1995, 57–61.

Harris, J. *Getting Employees to Fall in Love with Your Company.* New York: AMACOM, 1996.

Hollstein, B. R. "Internal Security and the Corporate Customer." *Security Management,* June 1995, 61.

Horton, T. R. *The CEO Paradox: The Privilege and Accountability of Leadership.* New York: AMACOM, 1992.

Ingrassia, L. "How Secret G.E. Recipe for Making Diamonds May Have Been Stolen." *Wall Street Journal,* February 28, 1990.

Johnson, M., and L. A. Allard, eds. *Global Management 1996.* New York: Sterling Publications Limited, 1995.

Kahaner, L. *Competitive Intelligence: From Black Ops to Boardrooms—How Businesses Gather, Analyze and Use Information to Succeed in the Global Market Place.* New York: Simon and Schuster, 1996.

Keough, P. "Talking Trash," *Security Management Magazine,* February, 1995.

Kushel, G. *Reaching the Peak Performance Zone: How to Motivate Yourself and Others to Excel.* New York: AMACOM, 1994.

Marshall, E. M. *Transforming the Way We Work: The Power of the Collaborative Workplace.* New York: AMACOM, 1995.

Martin, W. B. *Managing Quality Customer Service.* Los Altos, Calif. Crisp Publications, 1989.

————. *Quality Customer Service.* 2nd ed., Los Altos, Calif. Crisp Publications, 1989.

Mattimore, B. W. *99% Inspiration: Tips, Tales and Techniques for Liberating Your Business Creativity.* New York: AMACOM, 1994.

Mauro, T. "Cellular Spies." *USA Today,* April 20–22, 1990.

McCumber, J. "Developing and Implanting Security Policy for Corporate Information," *Security Technology and Design*, December, 1995, 34.

Moore, J. F. *Death of Competition: Leadership and Strategies in the Age of Business Ecosystems.* New York: HarperCollins, 1996.

Morehouse, D. *Total Quality Management: A Supervisor's Handbook.* Shawnee Mission, Kan.: National Press Publications, 1992.

Moreno, M. "Chip Robbers Hit Fremont." *San Jose Mercury News,* June 1, 1995.

Morris, T. *True Success: A New Philosophy of Excellence.* New York: G. P. Putnam's Sons, 1994.

Moyers, B. *A World of Ideas.* New York: Doubleday, 1989.

Noer, D. M. *Healing the Wounds: Overcoming the Trauma of Layoffs and Revitalizing Downsized Organizations.* San Francisco: Jossey-Bass, 1993.

Nolan III, J. "What Does Our Competition Know About Us?" *Security Technology and Design*, March 1996.

O'Leary, J. "Combining Classic Security and MIS." *Security Management,* July 1995, 143–147.

Pattakos, A. N. "Convincing Management to Keep a Secret." *Security Management,* November 1995, 35–39.

Payne, R. W. "Trade Secret First Aide." *Management Review,* March 1993, 33–34.

Peters, T. *The Pursuit of WOW!: Every Person's Guide to Topsy-Turvy Times.* New York: Vintage Books, 1994.

Peterzell, J. "When 'Friends' Become Moles." *Time,* May 28, 1990, 50.

Pirsig, R. M. *Zen and the Art of Motorcycle Maintenance.* New York: Bantam Books, 1974.

Prather, C. W., and L. K. Gundry, *Blueprints for Innovation: How Creative Processes Can Make You and Your Company More Competitive.* New York: AMA Membership Publications Division, 1995.

Pritchett, P. *Service Excellence!* Dallas: Pritchett and Associates, 1991.

————. *The Employee Handbook of New Work Habits for a Radically Changing World.* Dallas: Pritchett & Associates, 1994.

Pritchett, P., and R. Pound, *The Stress of Organizational Change.* Dallas: Pritchett and Associates, 1995.

Protecting Corporate America's Secrets in the Global Economy. Framingham, Mass. American Institute for Business Research, 1992.

Radcliff, M. "Multimedia Alert," New Worlds To Conquer (Los Angeles: *Daily Journal,* 1995), 12.

Romano, C. "To Protect and Defend." *Management Review,* May, 1996, 25.

Sashkin, M. and M. G. Sashkin, *The New Teamwork: Developing and Using Cross-Function Teams.* New York: AMA Membership Publications Division, 1994.

Scott, C. F., ed. *How to Qualify for ISO 9000.* Watertown, Mass. American Management Association, 1993.

Senge, P. "The Art and Practice of the Learning Organization." *The New Paradigm in Business.* New York: Putnam, 1993, 126.

————. *The Fifth Discipline.* New York: Currency Doubleday, 1990.

Shea, G. F. *Mentoring: Helping Employees Reach Their Full Potential.* New York: AMA Membership Publications Division, 1994.

Skagen, A., ed. "To Spy or Not to Spy," *Executive Management Forum,* April 1995.

Starke, L. "The Five Stages of Corporate Moral Development," *The New Paradigm in Business,* New York: Putnam, 1993, 203.

Stone, F. M., and R. T. Sachs, *The High-Value Manager: Developing the Core Competencies Your Organization Demands.* New York: AMACOM, 1995.

Thomas, P. R., L. J. Gallace, and K. R. Martin, *Quality Alone Is Not Enough.* New York: AMA Membership Publications Division, 1992.

Tomasko, R. M. *Rethinking the Corporation: The Architecture of Change.* New York: AMACOM, 1993.

Toth, S. E. "How We Slashed Response Time, Management Review, February, 1993, 51.

Vaughn, A. "Security Management Survival Skills," *Security Management Bulletin,* April, 1996, 4.

Walsh, T. J., and R. J. Healy, *Protection of Asset Management Manual.* Santa Monica, Calif. The Merritt Company, 1984.

Whalen, John. "You're Not Paranoid: They Really Are Watching You." *Wired,* March, 1995, 76.

Wood, S., and M. F. Wiskoff, *Americans Who Spied Against Their Country Since World War II.* Washington D.C.: U.S. Government Printing Office, 1982.

Index

168s/336s accounts, 156

A
Abraham, Jay, xv
  unique selling propositions, xv
Acceptance, personal, 194–195
Access control units (ACUs), 130–131
Accountability
  accepting, 11–12
  administrative, 119
  for quality assurance, 42–43
Account management, 126–127
Action plans, 66, 197–198
Adaptability, 22, 112
Added value, 23–30
  establishing your, 165–211
  for external providers, 24–25
  managing for, 163
  for resident security departments,
    25–30
Adversarial organizations, 78
Advising, vs. mentoring, 243
Advocacy, 132
Allair, Paul, 237
Alternatives, pursuing, 53
Alyeska Pipeline, 207
American Commercial Security Services,
    48
American Institute for Business Research,
    195
American Management Association, 81
American Protective Services (APS),
    40–41, 93
America Online, 8–9, 78
Amoral organizations, 240–241

Applied Materials, Inc., 120
Appraisal costs, 44
Argenbright, 36
Arko Executive Services, 64
Armstrong, Dave, 64
Asset protection
  redefining, xxiv–xxv
  security manager vs. customer defini-
    tion of, 87–88
Assumed acceptance phase, 246
Assumptions, challenging, 47, 53
AT&T, 81–82, 85, 217, 222–223
Award programs, employee, 52–53
Awareness training, 28, 198

B
Baldrige process. See Malcolm Baldrige
    process
Barriers, removing, 38
Basch, Michael, 161
  Legendary Leadership process,
    237–240
Bates, Norman, 178
Benchmarking, 28. See also best practices
  best practices and, 55
  efficiency and, 51
Bennis, Warren, 232, 234
Bérubé, Henri, 189–190
Besse, Bill, 237
Best practices, 21, 45–60. See also quality
  as common practices, 46
  and effective service delivery, 49–50
  and efficient service delivery, 50–51
  four-step process in, 55–56
  fundamentals of, 45

Best practices *continued*
    and getting the job done, 46–49
    measuring, 45–46
    resident security department and, 28
    security applications in, 59–60
    and senior management, 54
    tips for pursuing, 51–58
Bias, testing, 226–227
Blueprints for Innovation (Prather, Gun-
    dry), 249–251
Boeing, 217–218
Brain problem syndrome, 64–65
Brill, Fay, 224
Brown, Denis, xxiii, 89
Bureaucratic
    organizations, 78
    procedures, 84–85
Burns, William J., 105
Business management skills, 127–128
Business relationships, 24. *See also*
    relationships
Business Strategies for Success (Dalton), xv,
    53
Buskirk, Richard, 10–11
Buyer-seller relationships, 125, 142

C
Capacity, success and, 258
Capital expenditures, creative financing
    for, 40
Career development, 64
Caring, xiii–xiv
Cellular phones, 190–192
Certification, 153
Change
    best practices and, 54–55
    and employees, 253–254
Character, 258
Charity fine programs, 63
Citicorp, 209
Clough, Herbert, 206
Collateral capabilities, xxi–xxiii
Collateral value, 165–211. *See also* added
    value
    basics of, 205–206
    competitive intelligence as, 212–228
    defensive strategies for demonstrating,
        197–208
    defining your, 168–170

    in protecting proprietary information,
        170–180
    supplemental value contributions and,
        208–210
Comdex, 186–187
Commitment, 16
    to best practices, 58
    to quality, 41–42
    success and, 258
Commodities
    security services as, xii–xiii
    support services as, 137–138
Commodity syndrome, 54, 137–164
    and demand-side cost control,
        143–147
    opposition to, 142–143
    strategies for breaking, 157–163
    and supply-side cost control, 147–156
Communications, 25–26
    protecting internal, 175–177
Compensation packages, 152–154
Competence, 11
    and individual ability, 208–210
Competition
    eliminating internal, 37–38
    internal, 146
Competitive intelligence, 212–228
    characteristics for, 221–222
    definition of, 214–220
    determining useful, 216–218
    ethics of, 213–214
    gathering, 218–220
    identifying bad data from, 224–227
    importance of, 215–218
    security specialists in, 221–227
    selling management on, 222–223
    texts on setting up, 227–228
Competitors, acquiring intelligence about,
    212–228
Complaints, handling, 99
Compliance filings, 220
Concentration, 258
Conception, 258
Conceptual leadership, 234
Confidence, success and, 258
Confidential information, 175–180
    classification of, 179–180, 185–186
    internal communications, 176–177
    litigation, 178

personnel records, 175–176
reports/work products, 179–180
research and development, 177–178
supplier agreements, 178–179
Confidentiality
agreements, 179
internal security departments and, 27
Conflict, 17–18
Consistency, 16, 258
success and, 258
Console operators, 154
Consolidation, 167
Consultants
false assumptions about security pricing by, 147–157
generalist managers and, 133–134
selecting, 134–135
Contact, establishing point of, 94
Contingency plans, 51
Continuity, 80–81
Continuous quality improvement. *See also* quality
developing strategy for, 34
external providers and, 25
internal providers and, 30
vs. warranties, 39–40
Contracts, as confidential information, 178–179
Co-optation, 193–194
Coors, 217
Core competencies. *See also* collateral value
security as, 24
and supplemental value contributions, 208–210
Corporate culture, 49–50
and computer security *vs.* traditional security, 171–173
and moral development, 240–242
and public security background, 112–115
quality as, 53
Corporate espionage, 189–190, 195–197. *See also* competitive intelligence
Corporate head/field offices, 115
Corporate structures, 240–241
Correctional management, 116–117
Cosenza, John, 209
Cost-benefit ratios, creating, 203–205

Cost containment, 28
Cost control, 28, 143–156
demand-side, 143–147
supply-side, 147–156
Costley, Gary, 215–216, 222
Costs
and best practices, 56
reducing by reducing demand, 156–157
reducing operating, 167
Coverage, organizational, 20–21
Creativity, 221
Credibility
cost of lost, 205
establishing, 8–9
leaders and, 173
loss of by nonsecurity security managers, 133
unique selling propositions and, 160
Crisis management, 29
Criticism, *vs.* mentoring, 243
Crosby, Philip, 44
Customer lists, 199–200
Customers
defining your, 79–82
definition of, xxiv–xxv
definition of timeliness of, 82
expectations/needs of, 5
feedback from, 56, 96–98
focus of, 67
identifying your primary, 160
internal, 45, 80, 144–147
knowing your, 4–5
loyalty of/to, xiii, 76, 85–87
managing relationships with, 90–92
needs of, 86
similarities among, 80–81
tailoring security programs to, 20–21
Customer satisfaction
measurability of, 46
mistakes in pursuing, 98–100
moving beyond, 76–100
perception and, 84–85
pursuing, 84–85
and security, 29–30
service excellence strategies for, 88–92
vs. loyalty of, xx–xxi, 76
Customer-supplier gap, 77, 87–88

D
Data analysis strategy, 66
Data security, 174
Dauzat, John, 189
Delegation, 32. *See also* empowerment
  upward, 114–115
Deliberate rejection phase, 246–247
Dell Computer, 204
Deming, W. Edwards, 33–43
Department of Defense Personnel Security
  Research and Education Center
  (PERSEREC), 195–197
Detext guard watch tours, 37–38
Discarded items, and confidentiality,
  184–186
Discounts, employee, 62
Disney Corporation, 61–62
DMV (Department of Motor Vehicles)
  syndrome, 78
Document destruction, 178
Downsizing, 3
DRAW, 200
Due diligence investigations, 27

E
Eclectic managers, 105–136. *See also* man-
  agers
  definition of, 117
Efficiency, 50–51
Eglert, John, 156
Electronic systems, protecting, 174
Electronic threats, 190–192
ELVIS (Executive Level Vicious Infighting
  Syndrome), xviii
E-mail, 207
Emergent ethical organizations, 241
Employee assistance programs (EAPs),
  123
Employees
  accepting responsibility for security,
    19–20
  assuming ownership, 35, 57
  awareness training, 28, 119–120
  compensation packages, 152–154
  competitive intelligence and, 222–223
  customer-focused, 95
  in decision-making process, 61
  developing/maintaining loyalty of,
    52–53

disclosure of proprietary information
  by, 181–187, 192–195
disenfranchised, 192–195
empowering, 13–14, 251–255
enrichment programs, 62–66
exit interviews, 200
insecurity of, 4, 253–254
needs of, xix–xx
protecting, 122
respecting rights of, 9–10
security's credibility and cooperation
  of, 8–9
sense of entitlement of, xx
as thinking doers, 81–82
Empowerment, 13–14
  assessment of, 254–255
  best practices and, 58
  definition of, 252
  implementing employee, 251–255
Entitlement, employee, xx, 145, 238
Envisioned leadership, 231–256
Escalator packages, 153–154
Essential services, 137
Ethical organizations, 241–242
Ethics
  of competitive intelligence, 213–214
  five stages of corporate moral develop-
    ment and, 240–242
Ettorre, Barbara, 216, 221
Executive infighting, xviii
Executives. *See* managers
Expectations
  of continuity, 80–81
  of customers, 5, 84–85
  and customer-supplier gap, 87–88
  identifying customer, 55–56
  of management, 49–50
  as realities, 57–58
  soliciting, 66
  unrealistic customer, 98–99
Experience/expertise, 26, 58
  and competitive intelligence, 222
  as proprietary information, 174
External failure costs, 44

F
Facilities management, 209–210
Facsimile transmissions, 191–192
Fagiano, David, 81

Failure
    importance of, 63
    mentoring and, 243
    translating into learning opportuni-
        ties, 64–65
Farmer, Mike, 6, 237
Feedback, 66
    and best practices, 56
    customer, 56, 96–98
    mechanisms for, 96–98
    mentoring and, 244
    and vision, 239–240
Feigenbaum, Armand, 43–44
Fischer, Ron, 134–135
Flexibility, 22
    for external providers, 25, 129
    and third-party providers, 129
Foil, Mike, xxiii, 130–131, 237
Forgiveness notes, 63
Formal mentoring programs, 243
Franklin, Paul, xv, 14–23, 158, 160
Fredericks, Joan, xx
Fuld, Leonard, 175, 176, 213–214, 219,
    221–222, 224–227
    The New Competitor Intelligence, 214,
        227–228
Functionalism, 32
Funding, presentations for, 7–8
Futures Group, The, 215

G
Garbage/trash, and confidentiality, 185–186
Gates, Bill, 235
    The Road Ahead, 3
Geiger, Robert, 79–80
Geographic bundling, 148–150
*Getting Employees to Fall in Love with Your
    Company* (Harris), 60–66
Gilad, Benjamin, 215
Global competition, 215–218
Goals, and vision, 239–240
Government reporting requirements,
    170–171
Greed, 145
Griffin, Doug, 168–170
Grunt phase, 232
Guaspari, John, 76, 77–79
Gulick, Luther, 31–32
Gundry, Lisa, 249–251

H
Hamel, Charles B., 207
Handbook of Management Tactics, The
    (Buskirk), 10–11
"happy dentistry," 158–159
Harari, Oren, 37, 83, 84–85, 216–217
Harris, Jim, 60–66
Health care industry, 116
Health care prevention programs, 39, 41
Heavey, John, 209–210
Heffernan, Richard, 207
Heitman Retail Properties, 60, 106
Helpfulness, 91
Help wanted advertisements, 220
Hewlett-Packard, xvi
Hierarchical structures, 114–115
    vs. empowered structures, 252–253
Hierarchical systems, 114–115
Hierarchy of horrors, 161
High-tech facilities, 162–163
    losses in, 188–190
High Value Manager, The (Stone, Sachs), 13
Hiring
    and customer orientation, 95
    and niche markets, 162–163
Hollstein, Brian, 81
Hospital greeters, 59
Human resources departments, coordinat-
    ing with, 123

I
Image preservation, organizational, 27–28
Inadvertent circumvention phase, 246
Inadvertent exclusions phase, 246
Incidents, and "someone on the way," 12–13
Indifference, 145
Individual ability, 208–210
Informal mentoring, 243
Inspections, 35
Integration, roadblocks to, 171–173
Intellectual property. *See* proprietary
    information
Intellectual Property Protection Commit-
    tees (IPPCs), 202–203
Internal failure costs, 44
International Bank Security Association,
    xii
International Security Management Asso-
    ciation, xii

Internet, 65
Intuition, and leadership, 236
Investigations
    and best practices, 46–47
    due diligence, 27
    measuring performance on, 56–57
    proactive, 6
    prosecutorial threshold for, 47
    responsibility for, 122–123
Invoicing, 24
Ishikawa, Karu, 44–45
ITT Sheraton, 208

J
Janitorial staff, 19
Job descriptions, security manager,
    106–110
John Hancock Insurance Company,
    209–210
Judgment, premature, 249–250
Juran, Joseph M., 43

K
Kaiser Permanente, xvi
Knowledge base, 26

L
Labor pools, 65
Leadership
    compared with distance running,
        232–234
    conceptual, 234
    and credibility, 173
    definition of, 36
    definition of envisioned, 234–237
    legendary, 237–240
    mentoring and, 242–245
    pitfalls in, 249–251
    promoting, 36–37
    pursuing envisioned, 231–256
    shared, 14
    and support cycles, 245–249
    and trust, 253
LeBeau, Michael, 191
Lee, John, 32
Legal issues
    confidentiality of litigations, 178
    documentation and, 204
    establishing attorney relationship, 179

and panic management, 206–208
    walking away from contracts, 157
Legalistic organizations, 241
Legendary Leader (Basch), 161
Legendary Leadership process, 237–240
Leveraging, 25, 52
    networks, 62
    unique selling propositions and, 160
Lewis, Ed, 235
Liaisons, external, 120
Libraries, professional, 64
Limits, setting, 99
Listening
    and competitive intelligence,
        221–222
    to customers, 91
    encouraging interactive, 38
    mentoring and, 244
Los Angeles Police Department, 78
Losses, improper use of time as, 50–51
Loss prevention programs, 123
Loyalty. *See also* customer satisfaction
    definition of, 85
    developing/maintaining customer,
        85–87
    developing/maintaining employee,
        52–53, 192–195
    satisfaction and, xiii, xx–xxi

M
Magennis, Joe, xi–xiv
Malcolm Baldrige process, 67
Malls, retail, 115
    as niche market, 162
    teen control in, 60
Management
    charter for, 34–40
    Murphy's maxims for, 4–13
Management theory, 32
Managers. *See also* leadership
    biases of, 112
    collateral capabilities and, xxi–xxiiii
    and commitment to best practices, 54
    expanding responsibilities of, xxi–
        xxiii, 105–136
    meeting with customer managers, 99
    migration/turnover of, 39, 40–41
    and panic management over losses,
        206–208

and proprietary information, 201–203
as security managers, 129–135
supporting, 10–11
transforming into Legendary Leaders,
239–240
understanding concerns/needs of, 27,
83–84
vs. leaders, 232–256
Managers, security
backgrounds of, xxiii, 105–106,
110–115
as business managers, 110
commitment of, 118
contract providers as, 124–129
credibility and, 8–9
eclectic, 105–136
emerging role of, 106–110
expanding roles of, xxi–xxiii
managing for added value, 163
mobility of, 40–41
nonsecurity, 129–135
organizational role of, 131
as problem solver or problem creator,
17–18
pros and cons of resident, 123–124
pros and cons of third-party, 128–129
from public sector backgrounds,
110–115
reporting lines of, 87
resident, 117–124
responsibilities of resident, 120–123
sample job descriptions for, 107–110
support of sponsors by, 10–11
Managing, xviii–xix
Marano, Tom, xxiii, 36, 126–127, 139,
237
Marketing presentations, 220
Market niches, 149
developing, 161–163
Marketplace proprietary property,
174–175
Marriott International, 81
Mary Kay, 60
Maslow, Abraham, 6
Mattice, Lynn, 223–224
McCrie, Robert D., 208
McCumber, John, 204–205
McDonnell-Douglas, 217–218
McKiernan, Jim, 5–6

Media
as bad competitive intelligence data,
225–227
dealing with the, 127–128
discarded, 184–186
and proprietary information, 187–188
Medical emergency response, 60
Meisel, Allen, 79
Mentoring, 242–245
pitfalls in, 243–244
Mentoring (Shea), 243–244
Merrin, Mary Beth, 81
Mobil Oil, 5–6
Money containers, self-sealing, 59
Montgomery Ward, 12
Moral development, corporate, 240–242
Moreno, Mark, 189
Morris, Tom, 258
Motivation, 16–17
gain as, 18–19
pain as, 18
for stealing assets, 195–197
toward goal of quality, 33–34
Motorola, 217
Mottos, 61–62
Multimedia companies, 183–184
Murphy, George, xviii
maxims of, 4–13

N
National contracts, 148–150
Networks, xi–xii
leveraging, 62
professional associations and, 26
New Competitor Intelligence, The (Fuld),
214
New Paradigm in Business, The (Tarcher),
114
Nolan, John, 223–224
Nonconformance cost model, 44
Nordstrom Department Store, 63

O
Oki Semiconductor, 188–189
O'Leary, John, 171–172
Online databases, 226
Operating expenses, budgeting, 40
Operational feedback, 97. *See also* feed-
back

Opportunities, taking advantage of, 6
Organizational anomie, 194
Outsourcing, 137. *See also* commodity
    syndrome
Owen, Rich, 204
Ownership, employees assuming, 35, 57

P
Panic management, 206–208
Papers on the Science of Administration,
    31–32
Passion, leadership and, 235
Pattakos, Arion, 201–203
Paul Chamberlain International, 206
Payne, Robert, 198–200
Pederson, Dwight, 237
Perception
    and added value, 165–166
    and customer satisfaction, 84–85
    as reality, xii
Performance
    customer-focused measures of, 96
    objectives, measurable, 56–57
    reviews, 39, 40
Personal identification numbers (PINs),
    191
Personnel records, 175–176
Peter Principle, 210
Peters, Tom, 67
Peterzell, Jay, 190
Pfizer, Inc., 79
Phoenix Consulting Group, 223–224
Physical invasions, 188–190
Pinkerton, 58, 89
Pinkerton, Alan, 105
Planning, 21
    getting involved in, 17–19
Policies
    corporate security, 121
    vs. procedures, 20–21
Positioning, organizational, 19–20
Potter, Tony, 41
Prather, Charles, 249–251
Preferred vendors, 125
Premises liability, 40, 178
Presentations
    level for, 19–20
    simplicity in, 7–8
    timing for, 16–17

Press releases, 220
Prevention costs, 44
Pricing
    competitive, 59
    false assumptions regarding security's,
        147–157
    and quality of service, 140–143
    strategies, 24
Priorities, establishing, 5–6
Pritchett, Price, 88–92
Privacy issues, 9–10
    E-mail, 207
    employees, 240–241
    telecommunications and, 190–192
    written communications and, 11
Proactive orientation, 5–6, 29
    and trade secret first aid, 198–200
Problems, identifying correctly, 249
Procedures
    challenging basic operating, 48–49
    vs. policies, 20–21
Processes, charting/mapping current,
    82–83
Process mastery, 77–78
Procter and Gamble, 208
Professional associations, 173
    networking and, 26–27
Professionalism, 80
Profits
    assumptions about security industry,
        147–155
    erosion of in guard operations, 137–138
    focusing on near-term, 38, 40
    reasonable for security industry,
        155–157
Promises, 100
Property development, 115
Proprietary information/property
    confidential information, 175–180
    customer lists, 199–200
    and data security, 174
    determining value of, 202–203,
        204–205
    electronic threats to, 190–192
    identifying loss potentials for, 200–201
    managers and, 201–203
    marketplace, 174–175
    operationalizing, 174–180
    physical attacks on, 188–190

protecting, 122
threat analysis for, 180–195
working with computer security and,
171–173
Prosecutorial thresholds, 47
*Protecting Corporate America's Secrets in
the Global Economy,* 195–197
Provider-client relationships, 126–127
Public domain information, 215
Public law enforcement
liaisons with, 120
/private security alliances, 116–117
value system of, 131–132
Public relations. *See also* media
losses and, 207–208
vs. customer orientation, 96
Purpose
developing long-term, 38
organizational sense of, 77–79

Q
Quality
best practices and, 45–60
caring and, 33
case studies in misguided programs for,
68–74
as corporate culture, 53
Crosby's view of, 44
customer-driven approach to, 92–98
customer perception of, 77
Deming's view of, 33–43
elements of true QA programs, 66
emergent nature of, 32–33
failure as part of, 68
failure of programs for, 92–93
Feigenbaum's view of, 43–44
Harris's techniques for, 60–66
Ishikawa's view of, 44–45
judging by price, 140–143
Juran's view of, 43
measuring, 68
obstacles to, 42–43
programs, elements of true, 66–68
pursuing, 31–75
seven deadly sins against, 38–42
vs. cost, 35–36
Quality circles, 44–45
Quick fixes, 42, 257
Quotas, 37–38

R
Rabaut, Mary, 134–135
Radcliff, Mark, 183–184
Reagan, Ronald, 235
Reality, expectations as, 57–58
Receptionists, 154
Records retention, 178
Reengineering, 3
history of, 31–32
Regulatory agencies, 120
Reidenbach, Eric, 240–241
Relationships
business, 24
buyer-seller, 125, 142
customer, managing, 89–92
customer, reasons to build, 88–89
preferred vendor, 125
strategic partnering, 125–126
with suppliers, 35–36
Reporting lines, 87, 210
competitive intelligence and,
223–224
Reports, confidentiality of, 179–180
Rescuing, *vs.* mentoring, 243
Research/analysis capabilities, 26
Research and development, protecting
information from, 177–178
Resources
allocation of, 146–147
allocation of staff, 29
creating reserve, 65
utilization of, 29
Resource specialists, 55
Response
developing strategy for rapid, 82–84
and "someone on the way," 12–13
timeliness of, 26
Responsibility
for leadership, 238–239
without power, 11–12
Responsive organizations, 241
Retaliation, employee, 193–194
Retreatism, 193–194
Retreats, 15
Risk
and gain, 235
transferring, 25, 129
Ritz Carlton Hotels, 61
Robin, Donald, 240–241

Romano, Catherine, 170–171
Royal Canadian Mounted Police (RCMP),
    49

S
Sachs, Randi, 254
    The High Value Manager, 13–14
Salary study, 151–155
Salter, James, xx
Satisfaction surveys, client, 97–98
Security
    employee responsibility for, 19–20
    physical, standards for, 121–122
Security management, 3–30
    compared to fly-fishing, 14–23
    contract providers as, 124–129
    models of, 117–135
    Murphy's maxims for, 3–13
    nonsecurity manager of, 129–135
    resident manager of, 117–124
*Security Management: Business Strategies
    for Success* (Dalton), xv, 53
Security Management Magazine, 185–186
Security programs
    adaptability/flexibility in, 22
    adjusting, 21–22
    customer satisfaction and, 29–30
    determining point at which to create,
        118–120
    getting attention for, 22–23
    promoting, 20–21
Security services
    best practices in, 59–60
    budgets, 121
    as commodity, xii–xiii, 54, 138–164
    and competitive intelligence gathering,
        221–227
    and computer security professionals,
        170–173
    as cost center, 145–146
    and cost control, 147–156
    creating cost-benefit ratio for, 203–205
    as customer, 67
    defining, 105–106
    developing support for, 6
    funding proposals for, 7–8
    history of, 105–106
    integrating into business plan,
        165–166

    measurability of, 56–57
    measuring effectiveness of, 49–50
    with medical emergency response, 60
    national contracts, 148–150
    niche marketing of, 149
    pricing assumptions about, 147–157
    proactive *vs.* reactive, 5–6
    and profits, 137–139, 150–157
    rapid response strategy for, 82–84
    selecting on price *vs.* quality, 138–139
    seven deadly sins against quality and,
        40–42
    standards and, 45–46
    support for, 247–248
    as support function, 106
Security services, external
    added value for, 24–25
    changing roles in service markets,
        115–117
    client/contractor relationships of,
        125–127
    as security manager, 124–129
Security services/departments, internal
    added value for, 25–30
Seifert, George, 167
Self-actualization, 6
Self-confidence, 14
Self-knowledge, 114
Senge, Peter, 234
Separatism, 193–194
Service delivery systems, 94
Service Excellence (Pritchett), 88–92
Service excellence strategies, 88–92
Service markets, security, 115–117
Shea, Gordon, 243–244
Silo thinking, 81
Situational mentoring, 243
Smith, Fred, 238–239
Society for Competitive Intelligence Pro-
    tection (SCIP), 212, 213
Sole providers, xiii. *See also* customers
Specialization, 51
    and niche marketing, 161–163
Spiritual awareness, 233–234
Sponsoring, *vs.* mentoring, 243–244
Staffing
    allocating resources for, 47–48
    challenging assumptions about, 47
Standards, 45–46

Status meetings, customer, 97
Stone, Florence, 254
    The High Value Manager, 13–14
Stone, W. Clement, 89
Strategic alliances, 25
Strategic oversight groups, 93
Strategic partners, xiii, 125–126. *See also*
    customers
    risk transfer and, 25
    security managers and department
        managers as, xvi–xvii
Strategic planning, 216–217
Strength, playing to, 160–161
Success
    Seven C's of, 258
    spheres of organizational, 11
Supervisors, 154
Supplier agreements, 178–179
Suppliers
    developing relationships with, 35–36
    information leaks by, 183–184
    interfacing with, 120
Support
    cycles, xxi, 245–249
    external, 133–134
    groups, 52
Support services, 137–138. *See also* com-
    modity syndrome
Surroundings awareness, 232–233
Synergies, 167
Systems management, 120

T
Taguchi, Genichi, 50–51
Taguchi Loss Function, 50–51
Tarcher, Jeremy, 114
Target hardening, 160
Targeting, organizational, 21–22
Teams, on-line, 65
Technical proficiency building, 233
Technology
    disruptive, 166–167
    over-reliance on, 42
    using appropriate, 48
Technology Theft Prevention Foundation
    (TTPF), 189
Telecommunications
    competitive intelligence and, 213
    privacy and, 190–192

Telephone answering, 98
Telephone interviews, competitive intelli-
    gence and, 218–219
Temperament, organizational, 17–19
The Road Ahead (Gates), 3
Threat analysis, 180–195
Threat thresholds, establishing, 204
Tilley, Fred, 173
Timing, organizational, 16–17
Total quality management processes,
    Harari and, 37–38
Toth, S. E., 82–84
Toth Productivity Institute, 82–84
TQRDCE program, 68–71
Trade secret first aid, 198–200
Trade shows
    competitive intelligence and, 218
    and confidentiality, 186–187
Training, 36–37, 66
    customer-focused, 95–96
    shared programs, 168–169
Trust
    earning, 29
    and leadership, 253
    success and, 11

U
Unique selling propositions, xv–xxiii, 141
    and Basch's hierarchy of horrors, 161
    definition of, xv
    developing, 158–160
Urwick, L., 31–32

V
Value, hidden, 39
Value-added opportunities, 23–30
    for external providers, 24–25
    managing for, 163
    for resident security departments,
        25–30
Value-creating organizations, 79
Value force concept, 76, 77–79
Value matrix, 77–79
Values. *See also* corporate culture
    articulating service, 93
    co-optation of, 193–194
    of police, 131–132
Vendors, as consultants, 133–134
Vertical markets, developing, 161–163

Vested interests, 28, 131–132, 143
Virtual organizations, 124–125
Virtual support systems, xvi
Vision, and leadership, 236–237, 239–240

W
Wackenhut Corporation, 116
Wall Street Journal, 186
Walsh, Bill, 167
Warranties, 39–40, 41
Well-intentioned organizations, 78
Whalen, John, 187–188

Witco Chemical Company, xx
Woodell, Mary, xviii
Workplace violence, 4, 144–145, 247
Work products, confidentiality of,
179–180

X
Xerox Corporation, 81

Z
Zero-defects, 44
Zuckerman, Marilyn, 81–82

Other Books from Butterworth-Heinemann

Encyclopedia of Security Management: Techniques and Terminology
Edited by John J. Fay
1993   450pp   0-7506-9660-5   pb $59.95

Handbook of Loss Prevention and Crime Prevention, Third Edition
Edited by Lawrence J. Fennelly
1995   640pp   0-7506-9703-2   hc $84.95

Security Consulting, Second Edition by Charles A. Sennewald
1995   192pp   0-7506-9643-5   pb $34.95

Security Management: Business Strategies for Success
by Dennis R. Dalton
1995   326pp   0-7506-9492-0   hc $34.95

The Ultimate Security Survey by James L. Schaub and Ken D. Biery, Jr.
1994   256pp   0-7506-9577-3   pb (with 3.5" disk) $124.95

Workplace Violence by Sandra L. Heskett
1996   210pp   0-7506-9671-0   hc $34.95

Detailed information on these and all other BH-Security titles may be found in the BH-Security catalog(Item #800). To request a copy, call 1-800-366-2665. You can also visit our web site at: http://www.bh.com

These books are available from all good bookstores or in case of difficulty call: 1-800-366-2665 in the U.S. or +44-1865-310366 in Europe.

E-Mail Mailing List
An e-mail mailing list giving information on latest releases, special promotions/offers and other news relating to BH-Security titles is available. To subscribe, send an e-mail message to majordomo@world.std.com. Include in message body (not in subject line) subscribe bh-security